STRINGS & CURTAINS

FAMILY AND PERSONAL MEMOIRS

RINGS & CURTAINS

FAMILY AND PERSONAL MEMOIRS

JACK LE WHITE & PETER FORD

QUARTET BOOKS

To Charlotte, Miles
and Dominique

First published by Quartet Books Limited 1992
A member of the Namara Group
27/29 Goodge Street
London W1P 1FD

British Library Cataloguing in Publication Data
White, Jack Le
  Rings and Curtains: Family and Personal
  Memoirs of Albert Whiteley
  I. Title   II. Ford, Peter
  920

ISBN 0 7043 7010 7

Phototypeset by Intype, London

Printed and bound in Great Britain by
BPCC Hazells Ltd
Member of BPCC Ltd

Acknowledgements

First and foremost we must express our grateful thanks to Harold Whiteley, who over the years preserved so much of the Whiteley family memorabilia. The survival of this material helped in a fundamental way to make the writing of the book possible.

George Speaight read and commented on the book in an early draft and offered warm encouragement. Michael Pointon then kindly scanned the final text with a critical eye to check our navigation of the hazardous waters of showbusiness history; he has made some useful suggestions and saved us from several embarrassing errors. Any mistakes that remain are all our own. John Fisher generously made his personal collection of Whiteley family photographs available and allowed us to choose freely from among them for the illustration section. Les Curtis of Chilton Colour Laboratory, Sudbury, gave expert advice on various difficult photographs; he and his colleagues produced wonderful results from faded prints that we thought beyond retrieval. Val Napier discovered the review of the Whiteleys in Melbourne in 1907. To all these we are grateful. We are also indebted to Armour Foods (UK) LTD and to the *Radio Times*.

Finally, a very special honorary word of thanks goes to Jimmy Garrod, late of the Artists Associated agency, whose interest in the last phase of one old pro's active career helped to make it so rewarding and enjoyable.

Contents

Foreword

by Roy Hudd

I've always loved circus and circus folk. They always have to do it for real. By that I mean that for them, unlike us talkers and singers, there is no coasting through a perform-ance, no 'marking' it, no not giving one hundred per cent. If they don't do it 'for real', then they get hurt, or someone in their family does, for, as Jack's gloriously detailed parade will reveal, most circus acts are family affairs. The story of Jack's family is like a huge jigsaw, and when you get to the end and see the picture whole, it will make you stand back and say, 'Wow, what a family!'

Of course, in a way the whole of showbusiness is a family in which everyone apparently knows everyone else. Yet think of almost any name, big or small, from the past, and half the time it seems Jack is actually related to them! From the earliest days of 'Lord' George Sanger's Circus to *The Liver Birds* in the television age, Jack's family – Matthewses, Gregorys and Whiteleys – have been involved, and he's got stories about them all: the man who invented the leotard, Egoes the Armless Wonder, Fred Karno, Dr Walford Bodie, Pearl White, Ted Ray and Max Wall.

But the book isn't in any way a boring old name-dropping one. Jack's best stories are about people you've never heard of, the 'wines and spirits' of circus and variety, those very folk who always had to do it 'for real'. And the book is even more than a terrific collection of showbusiness anecdotes. It gives, like the very best books about entertainment, a sharp insight into our social history. It is a behind-the-glamour saga, to make you laugh, cry and shiver, of a true show-business family. A family who worked, lived and loved – 'for real'.

1

Child of the Showbusiness

I was born into a speciality act, as we used to call it. This is an act where the performers specialize in their own particular talent. Maybe it's juggling, acrobatics or conjuring, or maybe it's a musical turn, or performing dogs or pigeons. Years ago there used to be many such acts on the music halls, supporting the top-of-the-bill names like Florrie Forde or Dan Leno. It all made for variety, and so the term 'variety' came to be used to describe this type of entertainment. It's hard to realize today how much variety there used to be in the old palaces of varieties and, later, on the Moss and Stoll circuits in London and the provinces.

My own family was certainly varied in its talents. The Whiteleys – the main family act was known as the Five Whiteleys, though at other times it was called the Henry Whiteley Trio or the Henry Whiteley Four, according to how many were available or old enough to perform – were trapeze artists, tumblers and acrobats. We had to learn to clown – in French and German as well as in English – and to play several musical instruments. There were seven of us. My eldest brother, Henry, was born in 1899. Ben, Harold and Paul, and my sister Leonora, then following at fairly regular intervals. Another sister, Lydia, died when she was only a baby. I was the last but one, arriving on 4 January

1912; and last of all came Raymond, who followed me into the world three years later.

A little detail like the arrival of a new baby was never allowed to hold up the act's engagements up and down the country. As soon as possible, Mother rejoined the troupe and the newcomer was placed in a foster home, and stayed there until old enough to commence training. And so it came about that I was lodged, an infant only a few months old, with the Fraynes, in the small town of Eastwood in Nottinghamshire. By the time baby Raymond caught up with me, I was well established in the Frayne household at 14 Scargill Street. The roomy stone-built house stood quite close to where the novelist D. H. Lawrence had lived when he was young.

My foster parents, Mama and Papa Frayne, had four grown-up children of their own, Dick, Wilfrid, Cyril and Alma. I never thought of them as anything else except my very own older brothers and sisters. Papa Frayne was a bricklayer, but I only remember him spending his time sitting in the corner next to the fire which burned in the big old-fashioned grate. On either side of the fire were hobs, and the grate's iron bars were always being black-leaded by Mama Frayne, who was a very good cook. I particularly looked forward to high tea on a Sunday, when it would be salmon with salad and lots of home-made cakes. Alma was usually the one put in charge of me. If I was naughty, as I'm sorry to say I often was, I got sent to bed without any supper. Then, after a very short while, the door would always open and in would come Alma with a tray of cakes and lemonade.

The Frayne family were wonderfully good to me. I never had any sense of deprivation. Apart from providing creature comforts, they supplied me with so much warmth and love. I count myself fortunate. It's not every child who's lucky enough to acquire two families. The Frayne boys worked down the mine, and I'll always carry in my mind a picture of a much-used tin bath and three funny young men, black one minute, white the next.

Suddenly the curtains started to be drawn and the gaslight

with its incandescent gas mantles turned down. I began to hear a word I'd never heard before – 'Zeppelin'. The toy soldiers I played with turned into the real thing. First of the Frayne boys to join up was Cyril, followed by Dick, then by Wilfrid. Whenever one of the boys came home on leave, I'd try on his tunic and helmet and pick up the P14 rifle (a weapon I became more familiar with and heartily loathed in 1940).

Another clear memory is of waiting to go on a Sunday-school picnic. It must have been about the time of my sixth birthday, and it was a Catholic Sunday-school outing, the Fraynes being Catholic. I stood outside the house, clutching my mug, plate and spoon and waiting for the horse-drawn dray to come by and collect me. The memory was brought back to me years later when I heard a piece of patter being delivered by the comedian Vivian Foster, who was always billed as 'The Vicar of Mirth'. He said, supposedly reading out the church notices: 'Our Sunday-school treat will be held next Saturday. I shall be there, and I would like to see the little boys dressed in blue, and the dear little girls dressed in white, and they will be conveyed to the field in a coal cart.'

It was Alma who took me to church. I remember the smell of incense distinctly, but not a word of the Latin service. By then, had I been Catholic, I'd have been taking lessons in the catechism in preparation for confirmation, but my parents were 'of another persuasion', being Protestant. The Fraynes respected the fact, and often told me how I'd return one day to my real mother, who was not Mama Frayne but Mama Whiteley. Visits from my real family didn't occur often, and then only when the act was working in the area. My father used to correspond with the Fraynes and send them the money for fostering.

One day merged into the next. I began to believe and hope that, whoever Mama Whiteley was, she had forgotten all about me. Imagine my surprise one morning when Alma walked into the classroom at school. She had a few words with the teacher, and I was called out and told to go home. There, Mama Frayne scrubbed me till I glowed and put me in my Sunday best. I had been sent for. My parents were playing that week at Stoke-on-Trent, and I was to travel there at once with my brother Ben, who'd come to fetch me.

The great reunion was here at last, and I felt nothing except a sense of adventure and excitement. Tears would flow later, when feelings of homesickness overtook me. Eastwood, after all, was the only world I remembered knowing. A lodger with the Fraynes, 'Uncle' Owen, was forever telling me about some wonderful place called Derby, but Britain was far bigger and had more places in it than I could have imagined.

When we arrived that afternoon at Stoke-on-Trent, Ben took me straight to the family's lodgings. (To call them 'digs' was vulgar; you should say 'accommodation' or 'rooms'.) There I was met by my mother and my father, and two more elder brothers, Harold and Paul, and my sister Leonora. The eldest son, Henry, known as Harry, was away serving in the army, though he was barely eighteen and had never been robust. He was prone to severe attacks of bronchitis, but when my parents tried to get him a deferment, the medical officer said to them, 'If you didn't want him to be a soldier, you shouldn't have looked after him so well.' Harry passed A1, and found himself in the trenches a few weeks later.

Mother was a small lady, just five feet tall but a very strong personality. It soon became clear that her word was law. She could sometimes become quite excitable, though she had been very strictly brought up. Intensely religious, she read a Bible text daily and knelt in prayer every night before retiring. She wore her hair 'ear-phone' style, with buns at the side of the head, and was always neatly dressed. The first impression I had of Father was of his very erect bearing, his blue eyes, a fine head of dark hair and a black moustache with waxed ends. I must admit he inspired a feeling of awe, though he said little.

Family reunion over, I met the landlady, my 'auntie' for the week. I was shown all the bric-à-brac – the ornaments, the aspidistras. These, I was told, I must on no account touch, since they all belonged to 'auntie'. We had the use of

4

a sitting room, with piano, and two bedrooms. There was no bathroom, but that was nothing uncommon, and the outside earth closet was also a usual arrangement.

The first family routine I experienced was afternoon tea, a light meal of bread and jam with a small cake or a biscuit. It was considered unwise to perform acrobatics or tumbling on a full stomach. As soon as tea was out of the way, I was shown the two bedrooms. One accommodated my three brothers, Ben, Harold and Paul. The other, my parents' room, had a big double bed, but by now I was beginning to worry over where I was expected to spend the night. There was no sign of another bed anywhere. Unbeknown to me was the fact that the family always travelled with two large theatrical baskets. If it proved impossible to secure accommodation with three bedrooms, the baskets could be converted into beds for the two youngest members (in this case, Leonora and myself) by laying mattresses on top of the lids. Ahead of me were many occasions when I'd settle for the night on top of a basket bed.

That evening, the performing members of the family departed for the theatre and the three youngest were left 'at home'. Our supper was laid out for us, with a cup of milk each to which Mother had added a dash of water. This had nothing to do with frugality, but sprang from the belief that milk was bad for youngsters unless diluted. The landlady was told to see we were in bed by 8.30, and so I found myself placed in the charge of Leonora and Paul, who insisted that I, as the youngest, ought to go to bed first.

It was only when I lay on my basket bed that I was over-come by the lonely feelings of being amid a new family who were strangers to me. The tears welled up at last as I longed for Mama Frayne and Alma and baby Raymond. Leonora came to comfort me. She showed me her cigarette-card photos of film stars, including Eddie Polo and Pearl White. I'd seen both of them at the Empire, Eastwood, in the 'to be continued' cliff-hanging serials. The comforting worked. I was already an out-and-out film fan. The penny matinées at the Empire had been one of the highlights of my life. The cinema's manager, Mr Stubbs, used to walk up and down

5

the aisles with a stick to rap on the backs of seats whenever there was too much noise or our behaviour was getting out of hand.

Comedies were my favourite items. I'd seen many of those who followed in the wake of John Bunny, the first film comic of international renown. They all dazzled me – Snub Pollard, Larry Semon, Ford Sterling, the cross-eyed Ben Turpin, Harold Lloyd, Fatty Arbuckle, Harry Langdon and Buster Keaton; not to forget the one and only Charlie Chaplin. When he made *Shoulder Arms*, the kids in the school playground took to singing the little ditty going round the music halls at the time:

> For the moon shines bright on Charlie Chaplin.
> His shoes are cracking for want of blacking.
> And his little baggy trousers want mendin'
> Before they send him to the Dardanelles.

I also liked the cowboys, such as Tom Mix, and remember the first screen Tarzan, Elmo Lincoln, so it was a real delight to find my brother and sister sharing my enthusiasm. Whenever we played games after that, it was always films, films, films – hero, heroine and villain. If there was a revolving piano stool handy, we'd have it transformed in no time into the cockpit of an old biplane.

Paul and Leonora also told me about London, and said it was the biggest city in England. I wouldn't have it that this could be so. Loyal to the last, I insisted that Eastwood was bigger. As I finally dropped off to sleep, though, there was a grudging feeling inside me that they could perhaps be right.

So there I was, well and truly committed to a life of rings and curtains. My brothers and sister were already skilled in basic techniques and on the way to being acrobatic and musical entertainers. Each could play piano and violin to a level in line with age and experience. Where my parents gained their original musical knowledge I have no idea, but it was they who taught us, or, anyway, who took us through

6

the most difficult early stages – how to read treble, bass and tempo.

The domestic routine was strictly observed. A light breakfast at eight o'clock sharp, a good lunch at one o'clock prompt, the light tea already mentioned and, right at the end of the day, a large supper. Supper was the meal performers looked forward to most. They could relax over it, and discuss the act and how the audience reaction had been.

After breakfast, the young ones were usually packed off to school, but as I'd arrived mid-week I did not go to school straight away. Instead I went with Ben and Harold to a cinema as the family were playing ciné-variety that week. That morning I went on to my first stage, saw my first dressing room with the stage make-up laid out ready: sticks of five and nine, carmine, powder and cornflour, not to mention the home-made removing cream. (Here's a useful recipe: place lard in a basin and pour boiling water over it. When it's cold, dig in a fork and pour off the water, in this way also getting rid of the salt. Beat to a fine cream. Add a little scent.)

By the time Father caught us up, Ben and Harold had changed into practice clothes and tumbling pumps. (We never bought our pumps from a theatrical supplier. They were made by Father, who showed us in turn how to make our own – a task the whole family became proficient in.) Once the tumbling mat was down, Ben had a rope, the lunge, tied around his waist. The object of the lunge was to allow the ends to be held for safety to let the wearer practise a whole set of movements that went by names like flip-flap, fore-spring, head-spring, upstart or back and forward somersault. Many of these tricks, I gathered, needed to be performed while playing the violin, though the rule was that you practised with a paper violin and bow until you had the confidence to use the real thing.

When the time came for a break, Ben and Harold went down into the auditorium to amuse themselves by walking up and down the aisles on their hands. I'd dearly have liked to join them, but Father started off my training with the first thing all acrobats have to learn – a simple roll-over. My head tucked between my knees, I did a forward roll and came back up to a standing position. How to fall without hurting yourself was another of the very first lessons to be mastered.

One evening I was taken backstage before the first house. The dressing room had a washing line strung all the way across; stage clothes must always look fresh and well laundered. Mother was in full make-up, and I felt puzzled by pieces of tissue paper covering each ear. Father had bought her a pair of fine diamond earrings and she was anxious not to get greasepaint on them. She showed me the dry rouge in her make-up box and the rabbit's foot she used to apply it – items quite extinct in dressing rooms today. (Here's another useful recipe, for making your own eye black: invert a teaspoon over a candle flame till it smokes black, then add a little olive oil. The product's as good as any mascara.) I watched curiously as one of my brothers put on a funny-looking elastic belt, not knowing yet (though I soon would) that there were sound reasons for a male acrobat to wear a jock-strap. Father also made these appliances himself. With money so short all the time, anything that could be home-made was home-made.

In those days we were hardly coining our fortune, but at least the bookings came through fairly regularly. Father had his own method of looking for bookings. As my brother Harold remembered, and wrote in his Foreword to the published edition of Father's memoirs (H. A. A. Whiteley, *Memoirs of Circus, Variety, etc., As I Knew It*, limited edition, Society for Theatre Research, 1981), he would sit on the floor and write

> twenty-five or fifty business letters to agents and managements; he often asked one of us children to take the letters and throw them up in the air; we often found that the letters that came down with the address up would answer or send contracts.

Towards the end of each week, Father would receive a list of lettings from the stage manager at the theatre where the act was booked in next. He'd write off at once to the landlady he picked to ask her to get in some groceries. If the journey was short, and we might arrive towards lunch, he'd ask her to cook us a joint of beef with roast potatoes and veg and rice pudding to follow. If the journey was a lengthy one, Mother would get our current landlady to cook us a joint on the Saturday. It would then be produced as we travelled next day in a reserved compartment. As the train rattled along, Father carved the meat into slices to be placed inside fresh bread rolls.

This style of dining was rather out of the ordinary for the time. We'd get funny looks from passengers in the corridor, the English being in those days very conservative about eating in public. You could spot them furtively nibbling sandwiches as if thoroughly ashamed to be caught at it. It was all very unlike the general style I encountered a few years later on the Continent. There *baguettes* some two feet long would be broken into pieces and passed with gusto about the compartment with *paté de foie* or *fromage* fillings.

Through travelling on a Sunday, I discovered that even a railway compartment can become an acceptable setting for family life. At our destination, the theatre baggage man would be standing by, ready to take Father's instructions on which pieces of luggage contained costumes and equipment needed at the theatre and which were to be delivered to our accommodation. The many family acts on the circuits were accustomed to travel with everything they needed – sheets, blankets, towels. They'd even take their pots and pans abroad, for the British tradition of theatrical lettings was unknown on the Continent, where it was hotels, *pension* or self-catering. Mother always had her sewing machine with her. It was an essential piece of equipment. You never knew when a costume would need an emergency repair. She also always travelled with many large and heavy baskets and continental trunks that, although she was only slight, she could rope together expertly herself.

Whenever a vacant week came up, it was always to Father's chagrin. It meant we had to stay put in our lodgings for a further week. But, an arrangement being made, as like

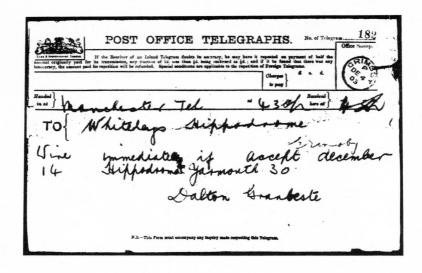

An agent's telegram of 4 December 1904 offers the Whiteleys, then at Grimsby, a date for the end of the month at Yarmouth

as not a telegram would arrive on the Monday morning and ask, 'CAN YOU OPEN TONIGHT?' at wherever it might be. Out would come the proverbial *Bradshaw*, the ABC of all train times. Father was an expert at deciphering its intricacies. So long as the journey was possible, he'd send a sixpenny telegram of acceptance (an expense of 2.5p in today's money). Meanwhile our landlady had to be paid in full for the week we'd booked, and stood to do well if she managed to pick up another letting. But we were left with two lots of lodgings to pay for and precious little profit by the end of the week. Half a loaf is better than no loaf was always my Father's motto. He never turned down an engagement if there was a chance of getting us there on time.

I must admit that my parents went on being rather remote figures to me at first. In retrospect I see that Mother's own tough upbringing gave her a hardness that discouraged emotion, but this quality was essential to our survival in the life we led. She was a good mother, and Father was kindly. Organizing a large family, with all the work and travelling,

10

didn't leave either of them with much spare time to give their children individual attention. It was left to the older ones to take care of me, and of course they were hardly delighted with the chore, especially since I was not the easiest child and had a habit of getting into scrapes. After a while, they accepted me, and I grew to be very close to my brothers and sisters. My brother Ben in particular became like a second father to me. Once, when I fell out of a tree and broke my arm, it was Ben who took me to hospital. To Harold fell the task of making me practise the piano once Mother had taught me the basics. I'm sorry to say he got very little thanks and the occasional kick on the shins.

So long as the school we attended in a town was close enough, we'd make a dash to the theatre at lunchtime (no such things as school dinners in those days) to have a short practice. With afternoon school over, it was more piano or violin lessons right up to when the rest of the family departed for the theatre. After that, the younger ones were free to play till bedtime. In summer, we might be given a bottle of lemonade and some sandwiches and allowed to go to the local park for an hour or so. It really seems to me that children off on their own in those days didn't face the dangers that seem so common now. I never remember hearing of child molestation or murders.

But what of mischief and pranks? We got up to those, of course. We were always acting out the parts of our film heroes. Any tree that was climbable would be sure to be climbed. Leonora was quite a tomboy in that direction, and I was as bad. Many were the pairs of trousers I ripped. Then I'd have to wheedle some dear old kind-hearted landlady into undertaking a repair. Once I successfully camouflaged fresh white cotton thread by putting blacking on the stitching.

Paul and Leonora were first-rate teachers, and they could hardly have found a more attentive pupil than they did in me. Whenever we stayed in a country town with fine houses and gardens, we'd knock at a likely door and ask to buy some garden flowers for the few coppers we had between us. We wanted to give something to our mother, we explained, and I don't think we were ever refused. Nor did anyone ever take our money, though we were quite prepared to pay. It would never have entered our heads to steal or do any damage, but we saw nothing wrong in repeating our routine at the next house round the corner. The result was that there'd be the biggest, freshest, most beautiful bouquet you could imagine for presentation to Mother that evening as the act took its curtain call.

In the June of 1918, I finally got to see the wonderful London I'd heard so much about. By this time I'd set eyes on a number of sizeable towns, but London was something else. At the underground stations I took joy-rides up and down the escalators – those wonderful moving staircases I'd been told about. I was thrilled to pieces. The tube trains astonished me. Then there was Selfridges! They could have fitted the whole of Eastwood inside that mighty emporium. A child's eyes always see everything larger than life.

Father had an engagement at the Shoreditch Empire, and so we stayed with Grandma Whiteley, who had a large house at 8 Wynne Road, Brixton. Brixton was known for its showbusiness families. I was born there. So was baby Raymond – in the middle of a Zeppelin raid. Not many streets away, the bombers came close to depriving England of one of its greatest comic drolls when a Zeppelin bombed the house belonging to Mr and Mrs Jack Lorimer. The Lorimers were noted entertainers – he was known as 'The Hielan' Laddie' – and one of their sons was Max Wall. Max survived in the wreckage, but his little brother Bunty died. I'm sorry to say that 8 Wynne Road was blown to smithereens during the blitz in the Second World War.

Once I was in London I began to meet a never-ending stream of relations. Besides Grandma Whiteley, there was Mother's mother, Grandma Mellors, the widow of Arthur Gregory, né Mellors. There was an Uncle Ben and an Uncle Rudolph, an Aunt Madalena, an Aunt Leonora and even an Aunt 'Ernie'. There was Uncle Dan and his wife Aunt Lydia who lived in Forest Gate and whose front door displayed a printed card reading 'Dan Gregory – the Royal Clown'. Various cousins included an Alfred, a Nella, a Rita and two

Jacks. And last, but by no means least, there was our great-grandmother, Lauretta Matthews, then aged eighty-four. She had been christened Caroline Lauretta, but always went by her middle name, and lived in one of a terrace of houses bought by her late husband, W. F. Matthews, and named after her: Lauretta Villas, Third Avenue, in the East London borough of Walthamstow.

Great-grandmother Matthews was a wonderful old lady. Like many of her generation, she wrote a fine hand, and throughout her old age kept up a correspondence with all her extensive family. She told me with her own lips how it was she, not the American actress Adah Isaacs Menken, who was the first woman to play the title role in *Mazeppa*, the spectacular equestrian melodrama – or hippodramatic spectacle, as such entertainments were often called – based on Byron's poem. We sat entranced as she told us the story of Mazeppa, a prince of Tartary captured by the Poles, who fell in love with the daughter of a Polish nobleman. When the nobleman caught them together, he had the youth roped to the back of a wild horse that was then turned loose. For three days and nights the horse galloped away with Mazeppa, plunging through torrents and crossing mountains. Mazeppa was finally rescued by a roving band of Cossacks, and promptly led them in an attack on the nobleman before reclaiming his true love.

The story offered many pretexts for equestrian trick riding, and while Mazeppa was originally a man's role, it came to be considered more attractive, not to say rather scandalous, to have the part played by a provocatively clad female. Menken was known as 'The Naked Lady' for her playing of the role; not that she played it naked. She played it in tights, or fleshings, which was thought almost as bad. Great-grandmother must have done too.

A vacant week followed the Shoreditch Empire engagement, and so we stayed on in London, and it was there that a letter marked 'O.H.M.S.' caught up with Father – his attestation for military service. He was then aged forty-six, and liable to be drafted unless doing war work of national importance. All my hopes of seeing more of the sights of

London came to an abrupt halt as Father faced the urgent task of putting a Whiteley Trio act together for Mother, Ben and Harold to carry on with in his absence. The act opened at the Palace, Northampton, and played the next week at the Marina, Lowestoft. It was at Lowestoft that Father managed to catch up with us. He had been declared fit after his medical and told to expect the official call-up papers shortly. Meanwhile Ben, limbering up in the way of tumblers, had thrown a handstand to the accompaniment of an ominously loud crack. He managed to finish out the week at Lowestoft, but on Sunday visited the hospital. They confirmed a broken finger that needed putting in splints (no longer heard of in medical circles today). It was Father therefore who after all headed the trio the following week, back in London at the Mile End Empire.

Father's call-up papers arrived all too soon, on 25 August. He put in for a three-month deferment to make the trio stronger while Ben's finger was recovering. This was granted and in due course, on 9 September, we arrived at Greenock where my brother Paul, though only eleven, was worked into the act. He was well able to take part by then. It was policy to include the younger ones in those places where it was permitted, and Scotland was generally more lenient than England when it came to children performing in public.

The aspect of Greenock I most enjoyed was its being the home of the Tate & Lyle sugar refinery. Whenever a dray loaded with sacks of sugar passed by in the street, you could usually grab a handful where some sacking was torn. (Interestingly enough, the comedian Harry Tate, then called Robert Macdonald Hutchison, had worked in the refinery when it was Henry Tate & Co., and took his stage name from his former employer when he became professional.) The Empire Theatre at Greenock had netting fitted across its gallery, and wire netting to protect the footlights. Certain Scottish audiences enjoyed a fearsome reputation. It wasn't just a joke that led to Glasgow being called the graveyard of English comics. Happily for us, audiences north of the Border showed a keen appreciation of speciality and family acts, but it was always acknowledged that northern audiences were hard to please. 'Pick and shovel next week,' we'd say whenever we headed north.

Father's deferment was due to run out on 10 November, but he took the precaution of putting in for another three months' grace. For the week starting 4 November, we played at Coatbridge, close to Glasgow, and on the following Sunday, the 11th, were crossing the Forth Bridge by train on our way to Dunfermline. It was about eleven in the morning. All at once, as we looked down at the submarines and battleships on the water, we heard shots being fired. Then we saw sailors waving their arms and shouting. When the train slowed, we heard the excited words, 'It's all over, all over!' It was the news of the Armistice, and what expressions of relief must have filled our faces as we gazed at Father. That Sword of Damocles, his call-up, no longer dangled above his head, and the only thing to grieve him was that the second fee to the lawyer who got him his deferment had been paid unnecessarily. In Dunfermline that week, the Whiteleys played to capacity audiences. For the first time in years, people felt they could go out and enjoy a show in peace.

The next week found us at the naval port of Invergordon, where the upheavals of sudden peacetime had made it impossible to book accommodation in advance. Wherever we tried to find rooms, the answer was, 'Sorry, full up!' We suggested to the theatre manager that we doss down in the dressing room, but he told us this was forbidden by the licensing laws. At last, as a desperate measure, we tried the Sailors' Rest. They could spare us no more than a single room for the whole family, so we lived in the theatre by day and returned to the Sailors' Rest to sleep at night.

At Invergordon, we saw American sailors for the first time. You could tell them from the British jack tars by their distinctive doughboy hats, which they'd snatch off their heads whenever they needed to dodge one of their shore patrols. We got talking to a group of them in the park one afternoon, told them how our family was just then playing at the theatre, and launched into a demonstration of the act.

15

By then even I was a fair sort of acrobat. As a reward, they handed us bags of chewing gum and all the loose change they could find in their pockets. Later the chewing gum was, to our sorrow, confiscated by Mother. In her view, it couldn't be good for the jaws to keep working away non-stop. In after years I came to agree with her as I found that to see men or women forever chewing was one of the most irritating things imaginable.

Christmas was approaching. Mother began to keep an eye open for something cheap, and whenever she spied a likely item would say, 'Ah, that'll do for so-and-so,' and put it away in the bottom of the basket. Many of the presents for our family Christmases were hand-made. Ben and Harold had a fine dolls' house that could be dismantled for travelling. It was constructed from tea chests, bought for a few coppers from the grocers, Thomas Lipton. On one occasion Father made a whole circus.

My first Christmas with the family was spent by the sea, at Fleetwood on the Lancashire coast. It relieved me to discover that Father Christmas would manage to find me wherever I was. Sleeping on the basket bed, I woke just before dawn on Christmas morning, wriggled my toes out from under the covers and felt for my stocking to make sure he really had called. Then I did my best to hold back the little bit of patience I possessed to wait for morning proper, when I could show everyone what Santa had brought me. The grown-up celebration had been held on Christmas Eve after the show, as was usual. Christmas Day itself then became the children's day.

A traditional feature of Christmas dinner was Mother's collection of small cloth flags, gathered from all corners of the world during her travels. These she would use to decorate the pudding. After dinner we played games, including lotto and the board game Grand National. We also played snap-dragon. Raisins were put into a frying pan with a drop of methylated spirits and then lit with a match. As soon as the lights were out, each player had to dip for raisins in the blue flames. No one got burnt, for it wasn't a dangerous game so long as properly supervised. It only took a puff to blow out any fire that jumped on to your fingers.

The last ritual of the day, before we were packed off to bed, came as everyone gathered around the Christmas tree – a tree decorated with glass ornaments Mother had bought pre-war on tours in Germany. Apart from the decorations, the tree held a small quantity of presents, each bearing a number. The numbers were put into a hat and we each drew for our last present. Then, with Christmas Day over, the troupe went back to work to keep Boxing Day audiences entertained.

Much was made of birthdays too. I have the happiest recollections of dressing-room parties held after a matinée when every other act on the bill joined in the celebration. Yet, by 'normal' standards, our lives were most irregular. Schooling was always interrupted. We could never join in school activities or become friends with other children. When it came to examinations, either we'd be a week late or else thrown in at the deep end without time for preparation or revision. On the other hand, the disadvantages we suffered in some areas were offset by gains in others. Geography was always a strong point, as you might expect from the amount of travelling we did. Meeting and travelling with so many continentals, we also developed an ear for languages. Both our parents were excellent linguists from their years of working with continental circuses.

We never wanted for friends. We met up with them all the time, finding them on the same bill as ourselves or running across them on station platforms, such as Crewe or Newcastle. 'What are your dates, then? When do we next play the same theatre together?' were the immediate questions we'd ask. It was always a happy week to look forward to when there were old friends playing on the bill.

The war over, my brother Harry returned, but there was no question of him rejoining the act. He was badly shell-shocked. His nervous system was never to recover completely from the harm it suffered in the trenches. He had set out to the war with his violin in his luggage, and on 14 May 1917 Rifleman H. E. Whiteley had appeared on the bill of

17

the Knut Konsert Kompany to play a violin solo, 'Chanson Polonaise'. When he got to the front he still had his violin with him. During the push against the Hindenburg line, he'd put the instrument in the cook's wagon for safety. As he moved away, the wagon received a direct hit. The loss of his precious instrument was an added trauma. On another occasion, when he was in the trenches, an officer had ordered him to go into no man's land to retrieve a four-pound tin of jam. He'd refused, and the officer had said, 'You're putting yourself in a sticky position. I'll have you court-martialled.' He got out of the 'jam' when the officer was posted without the offence being entered in the records. It made an amusing story to tell afterwards, but couldn't have been so funny at the time.

With the help of his army grant and our great-aunt Leonora Matthews, a teacher at the Royal Academy of Music, Harry managed to pass his academic violin exami-nations, and I have no doubt that he might have become a concert violinist if his health had allowed. In fact he became music master at Uppingham College in Leicestershire, took up the cello, wrote studies for children and got to be closely involved in the Scout movement. Later on he married a schoolteacher and they started a private school together, at Stamford in Lincolnshire. Harry was lost to the show-business tradition, but the disciplines of his early years helped to see him through life.

The variety tradition was still very much alive at the time when I began to travel with the family. Father's generation, though, had seen it at its peak. When he was a young man, twenty acts a night were quite the norm on a bill. When my day came round, the number of acts on the average bill had slipped to eight, with performances twice-nightly. Ciné-variety, too, was all the vogue. Before the development of cinema, every town and many a village could boast its own theatre. As the silent films came in, many theatres converted into cinemas. Managers realized they only needed a ciné sheet and projector to cut staffing and reduce overheads. But as soon as the novelty of the two-reelers, the staple products of the new industry, began to wear thin, proprietors found they also needed some live variety slots to keep on attracting audiences.

In this way, ciné-variety was born out of an attempt to offer the public the best of both worlds. A typical ciné-variety programme started with the *Pathé News*, then showed a two-reel comedy, and after that the live acts performed. The acts might consist, for instance, of a dancing troupe followed by a juggler, then by an acrobatic group like the Henry Whiteley Trio. Small cinemas with limited funds sometimes hired just one act for an evening and got them to do two spots before the main film had its showing.

Whenever the family played ciné-variety, I'd keep my fingers crossed that it would give us a chance to catch up on the next episode of the current movie serial, featuring, as like as not, my special favourites, Pearl White or Eddie Polo, or that other serial queen, Ruth Roland. Wherever we played, we always set out to chat up the projectionist. Then, very likely, he'd pass on to us bits of film left over from splicing broken reels. These we'd project on to a wall or a sheet with the help of a battery light. We also got to see the films of the dramatic actors of the day, including William Farnum or the great H. B. Warner, who later in the 1920s played the part of Christ in *The King of Kings* (always shown in an atmosphere of due reverence – a choir in attendance and no smoking!) We were never, on the other hand, allowed to watch a film unless our parents saw it first and approved it. At that time, censorship was strict enough in the adult area, never mind children's entertainment. It was a contrast to the way things are now. In my opinion, youngsters get to see too much too soon these days.

Eddie Polo came, as we did, from a circus family. He'd worked in a vaudeville act, 'The Three Polos', before going into movies. He always played the dashing hero, rescuing the lady in the nick of time in circumstances that called for an impressive display of acrobatics, though romance itself was kept to a minimum. What we wanted was action. Imagine the thrill we had when, in 1919, Eddie Polo made a personal appearance at the Seymour Palace, Glasgow, where we were also on the bill. During his visit to Glasgow,

Mr Polo dived into the Clyde to rescue a young lady. (I don't doubt with hindsight that this was a publicity stunt.) Several years further on, I also met my heroine Pearl White, whom I remembered seeing in *The Exploits of Elaine* and *The White Moll*, not to mention *The Perils of Pauline*. She was similarly famous for carrying out all her own stunts.

In the halcyon days of music hall, every town and many large-sized villages were accessible by rail. We paid, as all regular artists did, a nominal annual subscription to the MHARA (the Music Hall Artistes' Railway Association), and for that obtained the concession of a one-third reduction on all normal fares and baggage and cloakroom charges. For seven passengers, you were given a reserved compartment. Every Monday morning, the local railway representatives of the LMS, LNER, GWR or SR would visit the theatre, asking where acts were going to be the following week and competing for their custom. We relied very much on the railways to keep to our dates.

On one occasion, in September 1919, we had played a week in Dunfermline and were due to go on to Paisley the following week, when a railway strike prevented it. A rail strike was a rare phenomenon in those days, and this one lost us our week in Paisley and made difficulties for our next booking at Forfar. In the end, we hired a horse and dray to take us on from Dunfermline by road. The man who drove us to Forfar had arranged a date with his girlfriend back at Dunfermline the same night. Sad to say, he urged the horse along so fast that the unfortunate beast dropped dead in the shafts.

Bunk beds let into the wall, one above the other, were one of the features of Scots life we most enjoyed. In an instant you had a play theatre, complete with proscenium arch and curtains. Several times, when the family was away performing, we laid on a show for the landlady and her husband and anyone else who happened to be about. Once, when the act was early on the bill, the family arrived home before we expected them. As the audience beat a hasty retreat, the cast made a dive for their beds, drew the curtains and contrived to be asleep while wriggling into night clothes under the covers. Mother, as usual, asked the landlady if we'd been good. Of course, she reported we had.

We also travelled into Wales from time to time. Our dates were mainly in the south, in the mining areas. Morning matinées were an institution in the mining communities. This was to give the men coming off the night shift a chance to catch the show. They'd arrive straight from the pit and, there being no pit-head baths in those days, the audience filled the auditorium with a sea of coal-black faces. In one village, we played a miners' hall whose resident orchestra consisted of five musicians – piano, drums, violin, trumpet and bass. Their lady pianist went into a complete tizzy when she saw our scores. 'Do I play the tacets?' she inquired nervously, oblivious of the fact that 'tacet' only means so many bars' pause. It was clear she could never cope with our arrangements, which were admittedly on the complex side, and Leonora, then aged nine or ten, went into the pit to play piano for the act.

Once, at the Temperance Hall, Merthyr Tydfyl, we shared a bill with Alexander Zass, the Russian strong-man, who went by the name of 'Samson'. He was famous for his ability to carry a horse. The horse would stand on a couple of pedestals, allowing Samson to duck underneath its belly and drape it over his shoulders. Then he'd straighten up to carry the animal off-stage, so bringing his act to an end in a roar of applause. On the same bill was Wal Langtry, a well-known comedian. Wal offended civic pride by cracking a joke about the Merthyr trams being like snails on wheels. The corporation served him with a notice. Either he cut the joke or else he consider his engagement terminated.

Wherever we travelled, north or south, east or west, we always needed a billet to call 'home' for the week in question. It was the custom for landladies – or landlords, for that matter – to keep a visitors' book for guests to sign and write comments. There was a recognized code among artists to indicate whether or not their stay had been happy. For example, if we wrote, 'To Mrs X, from the Whiteley family. Theatre very comfy. Hope you have a happy week,' the capital H at the beginning of 'hope' would tip off the next

21

guests to arrive that happiness was not on the whole to be anticipated.

I wonder how many of those books have survived. Many of them dated back into the previous century and would be of great interest to collectors and theatre historians today. During the First World War, for instance, a police regulation laid down that you must also record where you played the previous week, together with your date of arrival and departure, your permanent address and whether or not you were a British subject.

The great majority of theatrical landladies or landlords were worthy of the highest praise. It was the ones who fell short of the ideal who stuck most strongly in the mind. Not that the profession itself lacked its bad pennies – most of them the victims of an incorrigible addiction to the bottle. These were the guests who'd arrange for a one o'clock dinner and not show up till after closing time. In Dunbar, on the other hand, we ran into a landlady who was an out-and-out alcoholic. She was incapable of cooking a meal. It was a question of 'burnt sacrifice' if cooked at all. The house was in chaos.

The last straw came on the Tuesday night. We found ourselves locked out and had to wait an eternity until she lurched home from the pub. When we did get in eventually, we had to go to bed without any supper. How, you ask, did such a woman continue to attract guests? Simple. Among local landladies, she dropped the stage manager the biggest tips. She also knew that if an artist walked out on her, she'd still be paid her rent. The state of the accommodation had no bearing on the matter – a letter of acceptance stood as a contract in a court of law.

There could be as many as eight of us travelling in the family act. It might therefore be thought that landladies would be apprehensive about our arrival. Not a bit of it. We were often told that we were far less bother than the 'twos' and 'threes'. We were so very disciplined, you see. We always cleared away the pots and plates and took them down to the kitchen. We made our own beds. In other words, we showed consideration for the hardworking landlady, who had to be up first thing to light the stove and the fires – real coal fires in those days.

Standards of cooking varied. Some landladies could cook almost to Cordon Bleu level, but others spoiled good food. They didn't mean to, but did it out of ignorance while being too proud to admit they were unaccustomed to cooking anything out of the ordinary. Our tastes, under the influence of Mother's and Father's journeys, were quite sophisticated for those days. Many landladies' families subsisted on bought pies or fish and chips. Fish and chips was a cheap meal when a large bag of chips could be bought for a penny.

There was one time when we decided on macaroni for lunch and gave the landlady two pounds of macaroni to cook. It should have been ample for our large family, but arrived at the table in a very small tureen. 'Did you cook all I gave you?' Mother asked, and the woman replied, 'Oh, yes, but it do shrink a lot.' That night, after the show, we dashed home to get there before Mother and Father. We liked to have supper ready on the table for their return. The landlady was out, but her teenage son was home. We asked him to fetch our fish supper from the oven. He took out a pie dish but said at once, 'Oh, this isn't your fish.' Just then his mother came back. 'Mum,' he told her, 'I was getting the Whiteleys' supper out of the oven, only I took out this macaroni pudding by mistake.' The box on the ears the poor lad received sent him across the kitchen.

Another time rabbit was on the menu. When Mother cooked a rabbit, she usually did it the French way – in vinegar and basted with lard. To save complications on this occasion, it was decided to ask the landlady to stick to preparing rabbit stew, humble and unadorned. The stew duly arrived in a large tureen. As Father lifted the cover, our faces turned ashen. The rabbit, though skinned, was cooked whole and sat bolt upright on an island surrounded by a dozen soggy dumplings.

As if it wasn't hard enough to get an engagement in the first place, there was always the hazard of a theatre manager doing a bunk with the week's takings. It happened to us once during the last week of a pantomime season at the

Empire, West Hartlepool. It was no laughing matter to realize your wages had done a disappearing act and the ghost wasn't going to walk, as we used to say. 'Has the ghost walked yet?' was a way of asking if it was pay day. The expression had its origins in the story of a production of *Hamlet* in which payments to the cast were proving unreliable. One evening, at the point where Hamlet speaks the lines, 'I will watch tonight, perchance 'twill walk again,' the actor playing the ghost announced in a loud stage whisper from the wings, 'Not unless he gets paid, he won't!'

To this might be added a story of two old Shakespearian actor laddies. They shared a room and they'd been 'resting' for some time. One day the elder of the two came in and said, 'I'm sorry, dear boy, but you'll be on your own for Christmas. I'm booked for a season up north, playing the ghost in *Hamlet*.' Having received his friend's congratulations, along with a borrowed pound for the fare, he departed. It was a dreadful winter, with much ice and snow. Christmas came. The second actor sat alone in his room, partaking of a frugal repast and thinking with envy of his colleague in a cosy saloon bar and, he had no doubt, amid convivial company. Just then a knock sounded at the door. He had to struggle to open it against the biting gale, and once he got it open, there stood his old friend in a most bedraggled state. Icicles hung from his nose and fingers. 'What happened? Didn't the ghost walk?' he asked him. 'Yes,' replied the other in sepulchral tones. 'All the bloody way from Carlisle.'

The theatrical profession has always had its precarious side. There is also the story of the man who did an act with performing pigeons. He received a telegram: 'URGENT CAN YOU OPEN TONIGHT AT THE EMPIRE BIRMINGHAM?', but all he could reply was: 'REGRET HAVE EATEN THE ACT.' Many a true word is spoken in jest.

Before we leave this part of my story of rings and curtains, I would like to offer you a glimpse of how things were backstage, for that whole world is often something of a mystery to the uninitiated. The first member of the backstage staff to say good morning to the variety artists as they arrive at the theatre on a Monday morning is the stage-door manager – or perhaps he only gives you a grunt if you failed to tip him the last time you were here. He's the one in charge of the mail, and he places any letters that come on the 'A – B – C' board. The first move of the new arrivals is to find the dressing-room list. The stage manager (the SM) should have put this up by now, though if you are top or bottom of the bill you don't need to look. There is an unwritten law: top of the bill – Room No. 1; bottom of the bill – Room No. 2; middle of the bill – Room No. 3; but where the rest may be is anyone's guess. Some smaller theatres don't have more than four dressing rooms, in any case, and small cinemas running ciné-variety only provide two.

Backstage, the stage manager is in full command. He is the one responsible for the smooth running of the show. Under his control come the electrician, known as 'Sparks' or 'Juicer'; the fireman, ever hot on the trail of crafty smokers in that highly combustible setting; the stage hands, the 'lime', or lighting, boys (always called boys regardless of age) and the flymen. This, counting in the manager with his front-of-house and box-office staff and cleaning ladies, is the average administrative strength needed for running a theatre. The 'No. 1's', as the biggest theatres are known, may also have a stage director over the head of the stage manager, as well as providing a call boy, a dresser and an assistant manager.

As we arrive on stage, we find it full of men fixing up their apparatus and ladies bringing their wardrobe out of trunks and baskets and getting down to the ironing. As all of this goes on, the SM will be putting up the running order and times allocated to each of the acts. Then he comes round to establish what stage you require – full stage, half stage or front cloth – and whether you can 'open in one or close in one'. In other words, he wants to know whether you can begin or end your act on less than full stage, so enabling props and instruments to be brought on or taken off without interrupting the continuity of performance.

Next we must find the electrician to give him the lighting plot and the individual lighting plots to pass to the lime boys. Our lighting plot will read something like: 'Open FU/

at cue drop to BOWF/ when violin-bow between knees PF on faces/ DBO after waving flag/ FU after crash/ flickers for tumbling/ then FU till end of act.' To translate: full lighting to begin with; on cue, drop to blackout and white focus; at violin-bow between knees, focus on faces; dead blackout after waving flag; full lighting after crash; during tumbling, use the flickers (a wheel with open slits spun in front of limelights – a precursor to the strobe lighting of a later age's disco effects); and finally full lighting through to the end.

It is already 11 a.m. Time for band call. The call isn't taken in any sort of rotation, but goes according to whoever can get their band parts down first, starting from the left. The musical director (the MD) takes the band books and hands them out to his musicians. For the variety performer, the drummer can be the most important of the musicians, especially in obtaining the comedy effects. His cue sheet is likely to contain such items as, 'when gent scratches head with bow – SP', that is, sandpaper; 'bow pulled over nose – siren'; 'ratchet for chair biz'; 'glockenspiel for funny walk'; 'for slow bend three beats BD [big drum], roll and cymbal'. All praise is due to those pit orchestras when one remembers that for eight very different acts they have to play music of every kind, ranging from operatic arias to jazz numbers; and that the only time they have available in which to get their contribution together is a run-through on a Monday morning with all the actions on stage being mimed.

It goes without saying that there are occasions when you can't recognize your own music and are put to the ultimate test of carrying on regardless. From an audience's point of view, of course, an act is either good or bad, and their judgement has nothing to do with the fact that it may be working with an incompetent backstage staff and a pit orchestra that would be better off down a coalmine. This, thank heavens, happens in only a minority of cases. As a general rule, the SM is in his corner, the flymen are in the flys and, as the signal is given, the MD begins to conduct the overture. A warning light to the flys is succeeded by a red light – 'sudden death'! The curtain rises and the show

26

runs like clockwork. The variety stages on which we work are a mass of holes. These have been drilled by the acts themselves, using a brace and bit, to take the turnbuckle and eye bolts that secure the stage hooks and guy lines for wire and trapeze acts, and other types of apparatus. When an artist pays a return visit to a theatre, maybe a year later, he knows he will be able to find and re-use his old holes.

Our own travels continued. I began to realize that the life I'd been born into was something out of the normal run, and that my family wasn't really an ordinary family. Gradually I formed a picture of how out of the ordinary they tended to be, as far back as anyone could trace them. There were the Whiteleys on my father's side, and the Matthewses and the Gregorys on my mother's. My parents' marriage had been an alliance of showbusiness clans whose histories were legend. Over the years I managed to piece together a lot about my heritage. Some of it was written down and some of it I was told.

2

A Theatre and Circus Life

Mother's grandfather, William Matthews, the son of Joseph Matthews, was born on 6 June 1830 at 6 King David Fort on the Ratcliffe Highway in the East End of London. He was christened at the church of St George in the East. When he was eleven, he started work as a plaiter in the local rope works. Plaiters were the young lads who ran from side to side of the shed, plaiting the ropes in the same technique used by ladies to plait their hair. For this William was paid a weekly salary of 2s. 10d. (about 14p today). He was not too happy in his work, and who could blame him? He wanted to do something very different with his life. Early one morning, as he told it in some memories written down in his notebooks, he heard a great commotion outside the house. Looking out of the window, he saw 'crowds of people and lots of excitement'.

> They were putting up a big wooden building. It was a portable Theatre. I'd heard about them but never seen one before. I marvelled at all the coloured posters. I wondered if I could get a job there, and I did, selling programmes. From that time on, I knew what I wanted to do. It was to be a Theatre and Circus life for me.

The next time a travelling circus showed up in the neighbourhood, William went straight away to search out the
boss's caravan. The owner was no less a person than Mr John
Clarke, famous as one of the first generation of proprietors to
take tenting or open-field shows on the road after the pur-
pose-built amphitheatres, like Astley's in Westminster
Bridge Road, made circus a popular form of entertainment
at the end of the eighteenth century. Said Mr Clarke:

'So you want to be a circus artiste, do you? Well, what
do you think your mother will say about it?'
'Oh please, sir, will you ask her?'
I could not believe it when he agreed to see her. My
mother was a very good judge of character. She realized
that Mr Clarke was a reliable man who would be a strict
but fair master, so she agreed to my apprenticeship.
And what an apprenticeship! I wondered what I had let
myself in for. I did all the dirty jobs: mucking out the
stables, boot and shoe cleaning, spreading sawdust,
grooming! This I did not mind as I got on with all the
animals, but how I longed to get into the ring as a performer and show them what I could do. Oh yes, someone
was in for a surprise!
One morning I had been raking the ring and helping to
put up the low tightrope as another apprentice was ready
to practise under Mr Clarke's eagle eye. Well, the apprentice was not doing very well, and I was grinning at the
poor lad's attempts, when Mr Clarke said, 'What are you
grinning about? If it's so easy, now's your chance.' So I
got on the rope and, to his surprise, went through a
routine of tricks I'd seen the other acts perform. What
he didn't know was that I'd been practising in the early
mornings and some of the performers, seeing how
ambitious I was, helped me on the quiet!

William's début in public was at Pope's Hall, Shadwell.
His second appearance took place at a newly built establishment known as the Yorkshire Fraternizing Theatre. There,
while he was performing his rope-walking cat act, the stage

hands pulled too hard on the rope. To save himself, he grabbed hold of the chandelier, which accompanied him in his descent. Despite this fiasco, it was the launch of a remarkable career. William became a good all-rounder – rider, tumbler and vaulter, as well as actor and pantomimist. In those days, dramatic presentations were an integral part of a circus programme.

After a while, William was tempted away to join Fraser's Circus, though his new employer doesn't seem to have had Mr Clarke's solid dependability. On one occasion, as William was about to commence his Indian riding act, he noticed some policemen coming towards the ring. 'If the police ask questions, say it's my horse!' Mr Fraser told him. But before William could say a word, the police were trying to pull him off the horse's back. As a result, the animal bolted.

We leaped over hedges and ditches, with the police in pursuit. Luckily some farm hands opened a gate to prevent an accident, and we stopped. I was taken to Ilford police station and put into a cell for the night, together with the horse! The next morning Mr Fraser came and paid a fine and we were let out. But I never found out what it was all about.

William, still wearing his Indian costume, then walked with Mr Fraser to Poplar. There he was kindly loaned a suit of clothes by a Mr Wattie Hillyard, who went by the stage name of Witty Watty Walton and later in his own career was known for his playing in *Charley's Aunt*. In the more immediate future he'd become a brother-in-law, for he and William were to marry a pair of sisters.

William met his future partner, Lauretta, at this time, in 1851, at the fair at Poplar. Her father, Mr Tanner, was proprietor of a portable theatre, and Lauretta worked in his booth of drama and mechanical dolls – a fit-up that we may imagine as being not unlike Mrs Jarley's waxworks in Charles Dickens's *Old Curiosity Shop*. As a fearless tightrope walker, she'd once walked a tightrope above the Clifton Suspension Bridge, Bristol, and, at the Great Exhibition in

Hyde Park, she played the part of Jack Shepherd in a drama booth among the attractions entertaining the visitors who thronged to see the wonders of the age assembled in Mr Paxton's Crystal Palace. She was, said William admiringly, 'a fine actress and tightrope dancer', and they were married at St Martin-in-the-Fields. She was destined to make William the proud father of twenty-one children – nineteen girls, two boys.

Accompanied by his new bride, William set out to rejoin John Clarke, whose troupe was at the Pavilion, Blackpool. William was billed as a clown, but 'also did French Vaulting, first over ten horses, then over forty soldiers with fixed bayonets'. Lauretta, too, came into her own, performing a rope dance and acting Columbine in pantomime as well as the title roles in versions of *Mazeppa* and *Joan of Arc*. By now William had grown into an impetuous young man, and I'm sorry to say he soon fell out with Mr Clarke, the proprietor in return reproaching him with the fact that he'd taught him all he knew. Off he went again, this time to join a new venture, Boone's Circus. Here he found himself not only breaking in Mr Boone's horses for him, but also teaching and training his three children. 'I soon realized,' William confessed, 'I had made a mistake and left a good master.'

With only 3s. (15p) in his pocket, William decided that he'd walk from Oxford to Gloucester, find Mr Clarke, swallow his pride and beg to be taken back. Behind him he left his wife and their first born, my grandmother, little Laurina. That night he was pursued by highway robbers, and managed to escape them, but then had to part with one of his precious shillings to a farmer to be allowed to sleep in his barn. Next morning he walked the remaining thirty miles to Gloucester, and arrived to what wasn't a very gentle reception. 'You are a vagabond!' Mr Clarke shouted. 'Why have you run away from your wife and child?'

William shamefacedly explained that he must get some money before he could send for them, gritted his teeth and, with 'blisters as big as half-crowns' from the thirty-mile walk, gave fifteen performances. Even after that Mr Clarke refused him any advance, though he did write a letter to authorize the conveying of Lauretta and Laurina from Oxford. 'It never rains but it pours,' commented William, for on the journey Lauretta managed to lose her balancing pole. They were then granted a day's grace to rest before having to do another fifteen shows for Mr Clarke.

The circus travelled on from Gloucester to Winchester, and in no time William found himself in another pickle. He was walking at the rear of the wagons with some fellow acrobats – 'a Mr Plunket, a Mr Walker, and a Frenchman, Monsieur Pledge' – when they came to a village along the route where there was an inn called the Coach and Horses. Adjoining the inn was a smithy. And on the roof of the inn there happened to be some birds. Monsieur Pledge, who was carrying a gun, began to fire away at the birds, doubtless to satisfy the continental urge to shoot and eat anything that flies. The smith, his assistant and several villagers emerged in a state of high indignation and set off in pursuit of our heroes, who meanwhile took to the open fields. They managed to lose their pursuers, but also lost themselves in the process.

They wandered into another village, yet could see no sign of the circus. What was more, Lauretta was carrying the money and the friends hadn't a penny between them. Acting on inspiration, William set up a cry of 'Fire!' and, as soon as they'd drawn a crowd, they launched into an impromptu display of acrobatics and tumbling. Passing the hat yielded a reward of 1s. 3d. (about 6p), enough to buy them a meal of bread and cheese before continuing. By nightfall they'd got as far as Blackwater, near Camberley, where they asked a policeman if he'd seen a circus thereabouts. No, he told them, but he added that everyone was over at the village hall. 'Something's going on there, so perhaps they'd like some acrobats,' he suggested.

So we all went to the hall and found the man in charge. We asked him if he would like some acrobats. He replied, 'No, we don't need acrobats, but would any of you like to box the local champion?' We were desperate, so we all had a go. Mr Plunket and Mr Walker managed two rounds

32

each; Monsieur Pledge was knocked out in the first; I went last and managed three rounds, though I finished with two black eyes and a bloody nose. They were a good crowd though, and collected 10s. for us.

Eventually they did catch up with the circus, and with Mr Clarke, 'who was not very pleased with us, to say the least'. For some time after the boxing incident, they needed to use extra make-up to hide the bruises. It seems, though, that there was little hope of Mr Clarke and William ever getting along harmoniously. William rejoined Fraser's Circus for a short time and, having saved a few pounds, just as briefly became the owner of a wagon. The wagon he sold at Henley-on-Thames, and went north once more to catch up with Boone's Circus at Liverpool. Mr Boone had evidently got a little further with establishing himself in the circus world by then. This time the association lasted three years and the circus played at all the Lancashire and Yorkshire fairs.

To accommodate William's growing family, Mr Boone bought him a wagon – the price to be repaid on easy weekly terms – and loaned him a horse. Yet business continued to be hard. At Boone's suggestion, William fixed up a side-line on the fairgrounds: the 'Mould', as it was called, though it was 'better known as the Mountebank'. This was a tent that had, at the front, a large apron platform on which Lauretta would do her rope dance as William beat away at the big drum. A selection of 'free gifts' – watches, tea services, ladies' gowns – would be handed out to the audience, which, as William confessed, always contained 'plants'. A few more acts would be offered, and then they would 'do the nob', as taking up a collection was termed. They'd play a fair for three days, and on the last day 'give away' two fine clocks; except that the lucky recipients soon found they needed to cough up two bob (10p) to the clowns to obtain the weights, lacking which the clocks were useless. The Mould was wound up before long, following a stern police warning, and William rejoined the circus proper.

At Ilkeston Fair at nine o'clock one evening, one of the violent set-tos occurred that were a regular hazard in the

33

lives of travelling showmen. Even as William was asking Boone whether they'd finished for the day, a dozen or so ruffians moved in with menaces to demand the day's takings.

This started a free-for-all. As I was in my clown make-up I was a good mark for the roughs and they started hurling bricks and stones. Mr Boone was badly hurt, and Mrs Boone had a nasty cut on the face. We managed to pull down the show, however, and start it on the way to Mansfield.

There was another fight along the road, where the roughs lay in wait for the circus convoy, but William, having gone on ahead, missed out on this bit of the excitement.

Not long after this, Boone's Circus played at the Birming-ham Onion Fair, held in the Horse Market. They played the fair on the Thursday, Friday and Saturday, and on the Saturday, the busiest day, Lauretta performed her tightrope act some sixteen times. The circus then remained encamped in the market area, which was protected by high walls and locked gates. Early on Sunday morning, Lauretta started to complain that she felt unwell. Certainly she 'looked very poorly', thought William, so he summoned one of the ladies from a neighbouring caravan.

She bit my head off and said, 'You should know what's wrong by now. You'd better get a doctor as quick as you can.' So I got over the wall, and, at the first doctor's sign on a door I found, I knocked and knocked until finally the doctor answered. Poor chap, I had got him out of bed but he came with me. Then, when we got to the Market he said, 'How can I help your wife when we are locked out?' I said, 'Don't worry, doctor, this is where you become an acrobat.' So I got him on my shoulder and soon had him sitting on top of the wall. He was on the stout side and it made me think of Humpty Dumpty. Of course it was easy for me to take a running jump and catch the top of the wall, then I lowered him down the other side and took him to my caravan. Half an hour later

34

as I paced up and down he came out and said, 'You have another little daughter.' I said, 'What do I owe you, doctor?' He said, 'Half a sovereign,' which I gave him. Then he had a good laugh, handed me back half a crown, and said, 'I must get this put into the Birmingham paper.'

On Monday morning, the rest of the circus train had departed for Redditch. Only William's wagon remained in the market. The market police told him he must shift it out of the way, but he couldn't find a public house that would let him park in its yard.

Then my dear wife said, 'Try and get me to Redditch.' I managed to buy a cheap horse at the Birmingham market, but I soon discovered he was broken-winded, so I had to go very slowly. It took me hours to cover the fourteen miles. At Redditch I quickly took the poor creature out of harness, got into my clown's costume and into the ring.

When William went to the field to feed his horse next morning, he found it leaning against a tree and knew its days were numbered. He sold it to a butcher for 10s. (50p), then needed to hire another animal to continue his journeyings. At Banbury, a Mr Charlie Richard lent William £5, on the promise that this would be repaid at Sheffield Fair when they met there later in the season. William invested the cash in another horse, but his run of bad luck with horses continued. Now this beast too fell sick. It got the gripes so badly that it could no longer draw the wagon uphill. A gentleman took pity on their plight and allowed the horse to stay in his stables. Here a groom tried to feed it some corn, though it wouldn't eat, and William hired two donkeys to draw the wagon clear before departing to perform at the circus. A day or so later, he returned to try to feed the horse again, but found that one dead as well.

This, as he recollected it, was his unluckiest time, but Mr Boone lent him another horse to see him through to the end of the season. Even so, when Mr Charlie Richard called round at Sheffield to claim his £5, William couldn't pay the debt. Instead he sold him his best-trained dog. Mr Richard made a generous gesture in paying him £3 above the fiver, saying he had a need for a good dog to perform in his theatre and music-hall act.

By this stage, William had a good bit of experience in the training of animals, and he claimed that dog training was nothing difficult. At one time or another he'd broken in talking pigs and talking ponies besides performing horses and monkeys and, he said, 'most animals'. The secret was patience, in William's opinion: 'Animals have more sense than they're given credit for, and are well aware of applause.'

Later on at Liverpool, however, Mr Richard tracked William down again to complain that the dog wouldn't perform.

He said, 'You've given me the wrong dog.' So I put on my clown costume and took the dog into the ring, and he performed perfectly. Evidently the dog had found the theatre different to a Circus ring. So I built a makeshift stage, and got him to work for Mr Richard. He was very pleased and gave me another £3, and the dog went away happily with his new master.

The famous circus of the brothers John and George Sanger was also at Sheffield just then; and, if truth be told, it put Boone's circus in the shade. In fact it almost put it out of business, and many of Boone's acts were laid off. William had to admit that the Sangers 'had much the better show'. When he ran into his brother-in-law Wattie Hillyard, Wattie told him 'in strictest confidence' that John Sanger would be travelling ahead to Liverpool to book the ground for winter. William at once tipped off Mr Boone, who set off speedily for Liverpool to get in his booking first, not realizing that recent legislation required a circus proprietor to hold a licence. The Sangers arrived, their licence in perfect order, but generously proposed that Boone might like to amalgamate forces. The offer was accepted. A wooden building was erected. Charges for admission were a penny and twopence, and the combined strengths of the circuses mustered an impressive troupe of twenty horses. The link-up with the

Sangers was important to William, for it opened a whole new phase in his career.

In his classic account of a showman's life, *Seventy Years a Showman* (1910), 'Lord' George Sanger records how it was after his summer tour of 1854 that he took a piece of ground in Bannister Street, Liverpool. The whole idea was to make winter pay instead of letting it lie a fallow season. Sanger 'built a large show, with boarded sides and a canvas top . . . Here we had a semi-dramatic-cum-circus sort of entertainment that exactly suited the neighbourhood.' The circus itself became only a small part of the show, though there were two hours' practice each morning to keep the acts in trim.

> What we mostly did was acting on the gaff principle, and there was nothing we were afraid to tackle in the dramatic line, from Shakespeare downwards. For twenty-three weeks we gave three performances a night with a change of piece each evening, always to full houses.

Mr Sanger was a smart operator, and what he called his 'cross-bred affair in Bannister Street' went down well with the public. One of his best and most popular actors, he added, was 'Bill Matthews'.

> He was a good rider, tumbler, vaulter, and clown; in fact an excellent all-round performer. His wife, too, was a splendid little woman. She was our leading lady, and very clever; she was otherwise remarkable, too, for she had twenty-one children . . . The family have since been well known as the Matthews Family, the Sisters Matthews especially being great favourites at the theatres and circuses, both at home and abroad.
>
> Bill Matthews made a big hit this winter, which was the terrible one of the Crimean War, by his impersonation of Paddy Kelly, an Irishman who had distinguished himself as a soldier at the Alma, news of which battle, fought on September 20th, had thrilled the nation. Well, Matthews did a riding act, 'Paddy Kelly, the hero of the

37

Russian War', and in his uniform, slashing at the enemy with a sword and plentiful dabs from a sponge of rose-pink, excited the audience to a frenzy.

William's recollection was that 'Mr Sanger, for reasons of his own' changed the name of Kelly to 'Sergeant Davies', but the production was a huge success. The paying crowds it attracted enabled Mr Sanger to buy his first band wagon. Unfortunately, one of the plays previously included, a concoction entitled *The Blue Devil*, had to be removed from the repertoire.

I was to play the title role, and my make-up, complete with horns, was horrific. For the play a hole was dug in the middle of the ring and a passage dug leading out of the circus. A big tub was put over the hole and, near the ring doors, a cottage piece was erected. (In the story, you see, the Blue Devil is chased and jumps into the tub. A lid is put on the tub, a rifle fired through a hole into it, and, the next thing, the Devil appears on the roof of the cottage.) Well, one night as I was making my way out of the tunnel an old lady was going past on her way to get her beer 'supper'. Suddenly, to her horror, she came face to face with the Devil himself, straight out of the bowels of the earth! And not even the more conventional red Devil, but a blue Devil! No wonder the poor soul screamed and fainted dead to the world! A doctor was sent for, and she recovered. Mr Sanger gave her a brandy and 5s. 6d. We were lucky she didn't die of heart failure.

The disaster of *The Blue Devil* was followed up with a production of *The Mistletoe Bough*, that fine old melodrama in which a young bride, Lady Agnes, chooses to play hide and seek at her wedding party and disappears; and it is then many years before the explanation of the tragedy is gruesomely discovered.

She finds her way into an attic in which there is an old-fashioned linen chest. She climbs into it, and the lid crashes down and locks her in. Sanger's wife played this part. One night we were playing to a capacity audience, and we were so busy seeing the people out at the end of the performance that we completely forgot Lady Agnes was still in the chest. She was certainly no lady when we let her out. Nor did she call us gentlemen.

At about this time, William took on, with Sanger's backing, an apprentice of his own, a clever young contortionist called Herbert Juder. Herbert had worked in the theatre but now sought to acquire some measure of circus technique. William was also teaching the Sanger children, and one day he overheard Mr Boone say, in conversation with his wife, that he'd take Herbert Juder away unless William stopped teaching the young Sangers. So William handed Boone his notice and accepted an exclusive contract from Sanger, and the future began to look more secure. The following summer, the Sanger outfit, with its fine new band wagon and a big show, toured Scotland. After Lauretta's tightrope act, William would introduce the Queen Pony with his little daughter Laurina as a prelude to the bareback rider, Miss Caroline. William himself then went out to get dressed in a smock, hat and many waistcoats and to pick up a big stick. A spot of introductory patter between the ringmaster and one of the clowns then went like this:

RINGMASTER (to Clown): There is the horse. You can take him home and rub him down.
CLOWN: I will ride him to church on Sunday.
RINGMASTER: No, you will ride him here first.

As the clown began to ride around the ring, William appeared, stumbled over the ring fence in the part of a drunken yokel, and tried to stop the rider. The ringmaster and the clown then had to try to get him back into his seat at the ringside while the audience shouted in the clown's favour. So good was William's drunk impersonation that one night a real policeman joined in with trying to chuck him out.

I had to whisper to him, 'It's all an act!' He went back to his place very red in the face. In the end, still pretending to be drunk, I managed to get on to the horse, and then, taking off all the waistcoats, performed a fine riding act.

The next winter they over-wintered for three months at South Shields, where Sanger put up his first 'permanent building' circus. As the time approached for William's bene-fit night, he looked about for some special attractions. He 'drove four cats in harness round the ring, did fifteen somer-saults on the slack rope, performed an acrobatic act with my daughter Harriet and Johnny Walton, and gave away six big pigs. Truly a fine benefit!'

Meanwhile he'd been harbouring ambitions to start up a circus of his own. He invested in several horses, which he broke in, and that summer set out with a 'sand pit', as it was called – an open-air circus with wooden sides. The enterprise was a family business. The troupe all consisted of Matthewses or Waltons. They opened at Durham, but disas-ter struck in the shape of a fire that destroyed the timber wallings. All that remained of William's slender savings went into buying new timber and getting the show back on the road, but still they failed to drum up sufficient business. In the end, William sold out his share to his brother-in-law, Witty Watty Walton, and retained only one of the horses. On to the animal's back he loaded pack, tightrope and bal-ancing poles and set out to walk to Newcastle to find his former employer. He'd come to realize that, for the time being, his own fortune depended on Mr Sanger.

Sanger bought the horse and put William on a three-year contract, for which security William, his wife and children were duly thankful. He'd rejoined Sanger in time to accompany another tour of Scotland, and bore out my later experience of Scottish audiences by remarking how they were 'always appreciative of clever and skilful performers'. Between Forres and Inverness there was a toll bridge for horses and wagons, and

fifty yards on there was another toll gate. I forget what

the charge was for elephants – but it was getting very expensive. One of the locals said he could take us over the river by way of a ford. But once again I was unlucky. Halfway across we found ourselves in deep water; we must have moved away from the ford. I really thought our time had come. But fortunately Mr Sanger threw us a lifeline and one of the big horses pulled us to safety. I shall never forget his kindness. So we had to go via the toll gates in the end, and as some repayment, I paid for the whole show to go through.

In Edinburgh, William found his riding act in great demand, especially among the students. It was an adaptation of the 'Paddy Kelly' drama, the name of General Havelock being substituted for the hero this time, and Lauretta playing the heroine, Jessie Brown. At the height of a spectacular battle:

Havelock and his horse were both shot down, but Havelock still managed to brandish his sword and hold up the Union Jack. Then twenty sailors arrived with a board to carry off the horse, also Jessie Brown with her brace of pistols, and finally the Scottish pipers entered to loud cheers. All good patriotic stuff!

The lions proved troublesome in Scotland for some reason, and one morning, as William and his troupe went to start their practice, they had a nasty moment. They came face to face with the great beasts loose in the ring.

Laurina managed to get behind the stable door. Then the trainer, Mr Crockett, came in and, with the help of the Sangers, managed to get the lions back into their cages . . . which reminds me of another time when we were to put on a pantomime called *Young Scotland*. The fairy scene was performed by young local children, but as one of the fairies was passing near the lions' cage she was caught by a lion and held in its mouth. Quickly old Mr Griffiths took the other children out. I took off my heavy buckled belt and beat the lion as hard as I could. Mr Crockett got the hot irons that were used to make blue fire and thrust them into the cage. Eventually the lion let the child go, fortunately not hurt although very frightened.

Other benefit nights followed, and on one occasion the problem of finding an extra novelty was solved when William succeeded in persuading the famous Scottish clown, Billy Seal, to emerge from retirement at a hotel he owned in Newcastle and appear for a fee of £10 plus expenses. The fee was a good investment, William reported, but a later benefit at Exeter was more of a challenge. The people of that city weren't responding well to the show and Sanger himself was pessimistic about his chances. But, said William,

> *Nil desperandum* was always my motto. I rode two horses all round Exeter, gave away four black pigs in a crate tied with a blue ribbon, and as a clown introduced my one wheel omnibus. I am happy to say I packed the house. Business improved and Sanger put up a large circus building.

The Sanger circus continued on its way. It toured from Scotland to Cornwall, with diversions into Wales, and set up its winter seasons at various locations. William had extended his abilities to include 'tumbling on stilts and blowing a feather out of a tube and catching it on my nose'. In Aberdeen, to drum up interest in a short season, he drove four pigs in harness through the town, and in Dundee he presented his 'Three Nations' act, coming on as, to start with, an English sailor, next as an Irishman, and finally as Rob Roy, riding the fastest horse, Tam O'Shanter. Mr Sanger, naturally enough, was always keen to recruit fresh blood and talent into the programme, and when he engaged Jim Mires, the star leaper, a contest was set up, William being no mean leaper himself. So far as William was concerned, any act that overlapped with his own talents tended to set off a keen sense of competition in him.

Sanger lined up for us to leap over three horses, three camels, three elephants and an upright man. Mires leaped as far as two elephants, but could not achieve the last elephant and the upright man; so it was left to me to clear them all. This I did and Mr Sanger increased my salary by 10s.

A rival performer whom William did feel sorry for was the American rider Frank Masterson. Masterson kept missing his somersaults because Sanger had provided him with a 'long-paced' horse when he was used to a 'short-paced' animal. William's own Indian riding act was 'working to perfection' at the time, and he feared that it showed up his fellow artist unjustly.

Another attraction to come into the repertoire was a drama on the theme of *St George and the Dragon*. Sanger, William and Lauretta all played in this, and on one occasion, when it attracted a capacity audience, they had just reached the finale when they were startled by a tremendous crash. The promenade had collapsed and thrown several of the audience down among the horses stabled underneath.

We managed to get everyone out and took those with the worst injuries to hospital. Sanger paid all their expenses and gave them money until they were able to start work again. One couple, the Millers, despite having arms and legs broken, would not take anything as they said Sanger had done all he could by giving £200 to the hospital and £150 to the soup kitchen.

By now William had been with the Sangers seven years or so, and a certain amount of mutual irritation was finding its way into the relationship. The final quarrel came when the circus was playing at Dover and Mr Sanger had taken the chance to slip across the Channel on a visit to Paris.

The ring was very wet [said William] and the horses kept slipping (we were riding two horses each standing up, with the ladies riding side-saddle). I wanted to buy a load

43

of straw to put in the ring, but Mrs Sanger refused and there was an argument. When Mr Sanger came back from Paris he was in a vile temper and said, 'William, I think we have been together too long.' When I told my wife, she said, 'William, dear, do what you think is best.'

As soon as the circus reached Norwich, William severed the association and went to Preston in Lancashire to team up with Bell's Circus. There he was given a fine horse called Granite – quite the fastest he'd ever ridden – and used him to open with his Indian act, which was as great a success as ever. There followed the sort of challenge that appealed to him.

I . . . then leaped against the other leading vaulters of the day. In a horse-leaping contest Mr Anson, known as the Arab Vaulter, refused to go over the eleventh horse, so I had the other ten horses taken out, leaving the eleventh where it stood, and cleared it with a mighty leap. Without boasting, I realized that I would be hard to beat, and this enabled me to establish a good relationship with Mr Bell.

At Leeds, William performed his 'Three Nations' act, while Lauretta danced on the low rope in baskets and wooden clogs, something, William claimed, never achieved before. They both played principal roles in the spectacles. When the question of a benefit arose, the problem of securing an extra attraction was especially important: Mr Bell's terms were for a shared benefit on a 50–50 basis. William took a train to Bradford and engaged the Yorkshire champion leaper, Mr Howard.

We performed together, leaping and vaulting over everything. We finished with Mr Howard leaping through the open doors of a mail coach and me somersaulting over the top. Once again it was a successful benefit . . .

We also put on a play called *Love in a Tub*. I played the lead as I was the only one who could perform the concluding trick – a back somersault out of the tub and a lion's leap over the 'Old Man'.

William's career was well-established by now. The offers began to come in for engagements in music halls and theatres, and the Matthewses came to London to play in pantomime at the famous Surrey Music Hall in Southwark Bridge Road. William played Black Clown and Lauretta Black Columbine, and they also performed 'the high ascent from stage to gallery'. For this they received a handsome salary of £25 and were talent-spotted by a Mr Abrahams for the Effingham Theatre, who booked them for a six-week season at £30 plus a half-benefit. He also booked them for the next pantomime season in a production entitled *The White Cat*. In this, Mr Abrahams himself played a wild character called the 'Cranky Girl', while Columbine, Harlequin, Pantaloon and Clown were played by a Miss Batty, a Mr Clarke, a Mr Finley and William respectively. A Mr Robinson had also been engaged, so Abrahams told William, 'to play the part of the "Flying Bluebottle" to do the traps in a new comedy scene he had written'.

For this my leaps were changed from four feet to five and a half feet. The scene was a garden with a large house, a glass house and a garden wall. My leaping board was let into the stage so that no one could see it. In the chase I ran up the path on to my board then into the first-floor window (ten feet high), then did a somersault out of the window. No sooner was I on my feet than the 'Flying Bluebottle' was to do the same leap. However, when he first tried it, he landed on his stomach in the window. I tried to teach him how to hit the board, but the next time the poor chap hit the window with his head and had to be taken to hospital with a broken arm and collar-bone.

So much for the 'Flying Bluebottle'. William felt guilty about poor Mr Robinson's injuries. He'd seen from the start that the man wouldn't be up to the acrobatics, but, he'd reasoned, to mention his doubts to Abrahams would only be to get himself accused of professional jealousy.

When the time for another benefit arrived, William heard that there was a certain Captain Hunt in the East London Volunteer Band who had always had an ambition to be a clown. He therefore proposed to Captain Hunt that he might indeed become one. In return, the band would play from Mile End Gate to the theatre, led by William in his clown's costume, driving his four trotting cats and cats' carriage. The captain accepted, the band bought two pounds'-worth of tickets, and, as an extra draw, Lauretta undertook to wheel young Laurina in a barrow up a rope from the stage to the gallery, then to carry a man on her back for the return trip down to the stage again. Hundreds had to be turned away at the door.

All the while the Matthews family had been growing apace. It reached the point where William confessed he'd lost count of the number of his children. At the earliest possible moment, each of the young ones would be incorporated into the family junior team, billed as 'The Midgets'. He also took on apprentices, including Freddy Griffiths, regarded as an honorary son and later to perform before King George V in the 1923 Royal Variety Performance. Freddy Griffiths and Theodore Matthews, the eldest son, performed an act as the Brothers Griffiths when Theodore was only six. When the bicycle first came in, its possibilities were spotted at once, and Freddy with another apprentice and the two Matthews boys put on the first bicycle-riding act to be dressed as animals – cat, monkey, dog and lion. They were, William claimed proudly, the top cycling act of the day.

They were in pantomime at Shoreditch when, in *Jack and the Beanstalk*, Theodore played the Lucky Sixpence and Freddy Griffiths the Goose, William taking his usual role of Clown. For his benefit night in the eighth week of a four-teen-week run, William managed to secure the support of no less a personage than the '*lion comique*', Mr George Leybourne, the original 'Champagne Charlie'; though the big novelty of the evening was, in William's view, 'Mr

46

Williams, the great tenor, riding on horseback as Garibaldi'. Lauretta 'ascended the high rope blindfolded and then danced the "Sailor's Hornpipe" '.

Through a combination of hard work and dazzling skill, the Matthews family grew to be a showbusiness clan whose varied talents were ever welcomed by audiences. William could proudly record that they once 'played in London for six years, with never a week out of work or on the road'. Before long, they embarked on their first tours of the Continent, where William used his guile to get round any problems arising from the employment of the younger children. At the opening night of a two-month engagement at the Eldorado, Paris, the gendarmerie came to inform him that he must report at the police station with his four children at eleven the next morning.

So . . . we got them all looking pretty and well dressed, and off we went. The first thing we were asked was whether they could read and write to which I replied they could do so in French and English. When the girls were asked to confirm this they replied in French. I was then asked if I had their birth certificates. I did not, but replied that I could get them in three days. The Mayor gave permission for them to work until such time as the certificates arrived. When the certificates arrived I took them to the police. I explained that I was very nervous about breaking the law and asked if I could have a permit for the girls to perform. They gave me one stamped with an official coat of arms. That evening the Mayor came to see the performance, and he told me that the permit was valid for the whole of France. So I went to the English consulate and was introduced to Lord Lyons who gave me an English certificate; then to the Spanish consulate for a similar letter to the French one. So we were now covered for England, France and Spain.

In Spain they opened at the Circe Madrid, and whereas other child performers were forbidden to appear, the Matthewses had their permit. The royal princesses attended the first night with their mother, and after the show the Queen sent round a message to say how much she'd like to meet Mr Matthews. She had, she told him, particularly enjoyed the children's act. Returning to England by way of engagements in Brussels and Bordeaux, they were playing at the famous Cambridge Music Hall when an American scout, who'd seen William's Clown in pantomime, approached them with the offer of an American tour. As a result, in 1871, the Matthews troupe, consisting of William and Lauretta, their sons, Theodore and William, and their daughters, Caroline, Lucretta, Laurina, Polynina, Lauretta, Leonora, Josephine ('Josey') and Ernestine, set out to spend over a year in the United States. The last four were billed as 'The Midgets'. They appeared initially at the Union Square Theatre, New York, where William was the first English clown to perform.

On 30 September, the *Sporting Times and Theatrical News* hailed the Matthews as 'the greatest stage-gymnasts ever to visit America, and [they] are in every way a success, being equally clever in song, dance and acrobatic feats'. The *Philadelphia Sunday Transport* for 3 March 1872 had this to say about their activities at Fox's New American Theatre:

> The Matthews Family has been the attraction and sensation during the past week, creating the most intense excitement whenever they appeared. Their performance is the most varied to be found in any single troupe, including as it does vocalism, dancing, pantomime, burlesque, and acrobatic and gymnastic feats. Mr and Mrs Matthews are formed on the Herculean scale, but are as easy and graceful in their movements as their more lithe sons and daughters. Master Willie is the Clown of the troupe, and his acting would do credit to an artist of more mature years. The family will remain another week and will introduce their trained dogs.

The *San Francisco Daily Evening Post* for 30 June 1872 recorded the visit of the 'Great Matthews Family', to its city:

This family, ten in number, who are now performing at the San Francisco Circus, Jackson Street, have fairly earned the proud distinction of being called the best artists in the profession in America. Californian audiences are pre-eminently just and the immense throng that congregates nightly at the Pavilion is proof that they are appreciated. The gymnastic performances of Messrs Theodore and Willie are truly wonderful; they seem to possess a finesse that no Americans attain. Master Willie gives promise of true greatness on the stage. Their parlour entertainments are very pleasing, laughable and unique. The graceful postures of Miss Leonora Matthews, the difficult feats of Theodore and Willie and the wit of the latter, keeps one's attention wholly engaged. We are sorry they are soon to leave us, for we would like to see more of them. We hope they will return to California after their next engagement. We congratulate whoever has been able to secure their services, for they are worthy of their hire.

Before leaving America, they played before Brigham Young and all his wives and children at Salt Lake City. They also did a season with P. T. Barnum for £100 a week, all expenses paid at the best hotels, though because of a technicality they had to appear as American artists. They gave their farewell exhibition at the famous Harrington's Opera House.

A decade of touring the world followed, culminating in a special engagement in Moscow on 6 June 1883 as part of the magnificent and legendary celebrations that marked the coronation of Tsar Alexander III; this was followed by a three-month engagement at the Hermitage Gardens, Moscow, and two months at the Arcadia Gardens, St Petersburg.

William and Lauretta Matthews certainly brought into the world an amazing and numerous family. Even more remarkable was the fact that, in a wandering life, they succeeded in raising them so successfully, taking them to church regularly and teaching them so much, for they were by all accounts fine linguists. To my great regret, despite much searching,

I've never been able to track down the subsequent careers and fates of all of the twenty-one children. Laurina, their first-born, was my own grandmother, born on 22 June 1852 at 6 King David Fort on the Ratcliffe Highway, and therefore a real cockney. During that 1871–2 tour of the United States, there was working with the troupe a young gymnast from Nottingham called Arthur Gregory. Romance blossomed. The young couple were married on 28 November 1872 in Boston, Massachusetts.

3

The Chevalier and the Cannon Queen

In the same year that the Matthewses had Laurina, the first of their twenty-one children, a boy was born in the city of Nottingham to John and Charlotte Mellors and christened Arthur. Little is recorded of his early days. He doesn't seem to have come from a showbusiness family, but like William Matthews he got bitten by the bug when young. He was apprenticed at a very early age to a Mr J. C. Gregory, and took Arthur Gregory for his professional name. He became a star performer on the horizontal bars and was known for his 'globe spiral', an act where a contortionist squeezes himself inside a globe that seems to take on a life of its own as it moves about and then up a spiral ramp and down again. In 1872, he was working in America for the then current Barnum set-up, probably Coup & Barnum, at the same time as the Matthews troupe, and so the way lay open for him to court and marry Laurina, which he did, as I've already told.

The young couple stayed with the Matthewses for a while and were working in Chicago when, a year later, the first of their own children was born: a boy, christened Raymond Daniel and destined to be a clown among clowns. Soon after this they parted from the family troupe and returned to Europe to found the Arthur Gregory Troupe of acrobats, with which they commenced to tour the world and in which Grandmother was billed as 'Madame Gregory, Cannon Queen'. The next of their children to be born were Leonora Catalina, in 1875 at Buenos Aires where they were touring with the Circo Equestro Sociale, and Laurina in 1876 at Mannheim, under the auspices of Hengler's circus; and finally there were Arthur and Melita, born in 1879 and 1881 respectively, though their birthplaces are unknown. Circus folk led such nomadic lives. Probably because of this, and their association with caravans, people thought of them as gypsies, but they weren't gypsies as a rule, though there have always been some real gypsies mixed up among them. The essential thing, when a child was born into a circus family, was for the mother to get back into business as quickly as she could. As happened with my brothers, sister and myself in the next generation, the Gregorys' babies were found foster homes until they reached the age of five or six. It was no use leaving it till any later to start training if they were to follow in their parents' footsteps.

Little Laurina was fostered by a family in Nottingham, but the poor child fell and scraped her knee, and the wound turned sceptic. Dr Lister's method of antisepsis, using carbolic acid, was not enough to save her in those days before penicillin. Melita, too, died as an infant – in her case in Schulma, Bulgaria. This was at a time when things were at a very low ebb for my grandparents. They couldn't even scrape together the money to pay for the funeral. A Greek conjuror named Aspietti approached my grandmother and offered, 'If you can pay for the ground, I will make the coffin.' As an illusionist, he was also a master carpenter, and he put his skills to noble use. Yet even then their troubles weren't over. The Greek Orthodox priest arrived to inform them that it was the funeral custom to leave the coffin open till the moment of interment. This they refused to countenance. As a result, they were ostracized by the local community and little Melita was buried in a vineyard. Not long after that, Arthur, the youngest now surviving, died of croup at Cagliari in Sardinia and was buried on the island among the rocks.

Out of my grandparents' five children, only two, my Uncle Dan Gregory and my mother Leonora, survived to be adult performers. Mother was in fact placed for fostering in Birmingham at a time when the Gregory Troupe was away on a three-year tour in India, working with the John Wilson Circus. Her foster parents were Mr and Mrs Cope, one of whose sons was married to a sister of Vesta Tilley. Early in 1882, Grandmother Gregory paid the foster home an unexpected visit. She found her six-year-old daughter in a state of shocking neglect – almost in rags and her body covered with sores. She took her away at once, and they decided, as soon as the little girl's health was restored, that the time had arrived for her to start her training. This meant she could accompany them on their next foreign trip – to South Africa for an engagement with the Fillis Circus. Before that came about, however, she made her début on stage at the Theatre Royal, Leicester, in a pantomime in which she sang two songs, 'Now Don't, Do Let Me Be' and 'Down in the Meadow Where the Green Grass Grows'.

Meanwhile Grandad Gregory had taken her to a gymnasium at a skating rink in Leicester, to start her training on bending and trapeze. He rigged up a trapeze with a net below, told her to hang on to the trapeze and to put her legs out into a sitting position. Then she was to let go. Of course, Leonora was frightened and hung on as long as she could. In the end, she had to let go, and dropped into the net like a ripe plum. It may sound like a cruel approach, but after the first shock (as with making a parachute drop for the first time), she knew there was nothing to fear even if the catcher missed her. In fact she came to enjoy the sensation of dropping into the net. Knowing the way to fall, with legs stretched out in front, was the important lesson. When it's done correctly, there's no chance of the knees jerking up to hit the chin and knock the head back sharply, which could be enough to break the neck.

The net, needless to say, has to be given the right tension to absorb the fall. On an occasion some years later, Leonora failed to check her apparatus properly. She came a cropper as a result – 'cropper' being a much-used word in circus vocabulary. She crashed down to hit the unadjusted net, which bounced her straight out on to the ground in the circus ring. 'Send in the clowns,' is the cry at anything untoward or unexpected, and on this occasion the clown sent in was Billy Reeves, who was the first to play the 'drunk' in Fred Karno's *Mumming Birds* sketch – a part later memorably taken over by Charlie Chaplin. Billy's brother was Alf Reeves, who worked for many years with Chaplin and became his manager.

But now to rejoin little Leonora on her first sea voyage with the family *en route* to South Africa. Her mother used the time to continue training her in an acrobatic act. One of her routines went as follows. A small fork was fitted to her heel in the manner of a riding spur. As she lay on her tummy, she'd spear an apple with the fork, then bring her leg over the top of her head and eat the apple. While she was still learning, she used to let her arms go, and her mother only realized that she was banging her eyes on the deck when, after some days, they became badly bruised. The ship's doctor placed leeches on her eyelids to draw the blood.

Learning to impress her brother Dan was another hurdle she had to get over. He was only two years her senior, but already a seasoned performer: tumbler, rider, violinist and clown. He teased the life out of her and called her a 'Jack the Josser', which in circus parlance means greenhorn. But Dan's scorn didn't last long. Leonora was quick to learn: trapeze, tumbling and ballet. In South Africa, the *Kimberley Diamond Fields Daily Independent* for 3 November 1885 gave her quite a write-up:

> The best thing of the evening was the performance of little Leonora Gregory on the trapeze which was a marvel of grace and daring. She is a pretty little child, full of pluck and showing a skill in all she does that would not disgrace an adult gymnast. Her feats on the trapeze received unbounded applause throughout, especially her flight called 'The Flight of Cupid', when she slid from the top

54

of the tent by her teeth while playing a small zither. Upon her being recalled Mr H. S. Caldecot stepped into the ring and said, 'I have been asked by Mr Bonamici to present this little lady with this handsome gold and diamond star in recognition of her début made on 23rd October, and I am sure you will join me in wishing her every success in her profession and in the future.' Then Mr Caldecot pinned the star on the little thing's breast, and she bowed her acknowledgement amid loud cheering and applause. And she was later called upon to present the Mayor with a bouquet of flowers at the opening ceremony of the Kimberley railway.

Chevalier Arthur Gregory – the title an award to him by the Chevaliers Sanveteurs des Alpes-Maritimes – had decided meanwhile that he'd like to become a circus proprietor himself, and entered into a couple of short-lived partnerships. Between these, however, a throat condition had begun to worry him, and he made a visit to London to consult the leading throat specialist of the day, Sir Morell Mackenzie, who diagnosed and removed a benign growth. After his second unsuccessful venture with a partnership, Grandfather took the momentous decision round about 1886 that he would run his own show and went to a firm of world-renowned tent-makers at Wisbech in Cambridgeshire to order his 'Big Top'. He also engaged a well-known American rider, Romeo Sebastian, whose specialities included a riding somersault act, and set about building up a team of ring and liberty horses.

The Gregory Equestrian Circus of the World was, as its title implied, always to have a strong emphasis on equestrian display, and Dan and Leonora had by now begun their riding lessons. The basic skills Leonora had learnt to start off her acrobatic career were also essential to her as a rider. At one time she had a very strict German riding master. When she developed the habit of sticking her little finger out while riding round, he, who'd warned her about it more than once, showed his own skill by catching the offending finger with his whip as she rode by. She soon learnt to keep the finger in. Just as well. She could easily have broken a bone in it while changing between standing and sitting positions on horseback.

Grandfather Gregory was finally putting his circus together at Cagliari, Sardinia, at the time when Leonora's little brother Arthur died. There was no leisure to dwell on the tragedy, and that autumn the brand-new circus set sail for Malta, where it was to give its first performances. From Malta the circus went to Gibraltar, then to Spain and back to North Africa. At Tunis, Grandfather bought Mother a fine horse. It became the custom for all the Gregory horses to be named after the places where the circus was playing when they bought them: Cagliari, Sassari, what have you. Circus horses were of many different types. The Spanish or Lippizaner breed represented the *haute école* of the equine world, though the liberty horses, with their riderless simultaneous movements, were its ballet dancers. When it came to voltage, though, you needed a horse with a broad back, the so-called 'resin-back'. For a stand-up rider there was nothing worse than a hunter, since that is a horse whose back goes up and down over much. Riders would often find themselves in great difficulties if they couldn't have their own horses with them and had to make do with whatever mount was available.

My mother loved all her horses throughout her career. As a child, she also had her pets, for circus children were usually allowed pets within the limits of a general rule that any animal must be trained to earn its keep. You did get the odd exception of a privileged animal. One of these came Mother's way through the family belief in the saying, 'When in Rome do as the Romans do.' On this occasion, though, the circus happened to be in Greece, where it was the custom for children to be given a baby lamb at Easter. It came about that Mother was also given a lamb, and that she called him Billy. Unfortunately, male lambs have a habit of growing up to be rams. Billy was no exception. He grew into a fine ram with an equally fine appetite. A particular fondness for sequins, or spangles, was to bring about his downfall.

It so happened that one of the acts had some beautiful

56

spangled covers among their props, that these were stored in the stables close to the ring doors, and that this was where Billy was tethered since he was now too big to be kept in a caravan. The owner of the covers, arriving at the stables to do some repairs one day, was horrified to find nothing but chewed and soggy rags. In a towering rage he turned to the nearest groom and screamed, 'Get rid of it!' The groom jumped to obey, and poor Billy was decapitated on the spot. When Leonora entered the stables a few moments later, she came face to face with Billy's head held in the groom's hand. Speechless with terror, she ran straight to Grandmother, who eventually managed to get the story out of her and marched directly down to the stables to confront the grooms over Billy's headless carcass. Billy's body, Grandmother commanded, was to be put in a sack, taken out to sea and dropped over the side. But she didn't stay to see her orders carried out, so I've always had my suspicions that mutton featured on the grooms' menu for some days after the incident.

One of the artists appearing with the Gregory outfit was a young man called Paul Canzi, whom Arthur had taken on as an apprentice. Paul, always known as 'Powell' after the foreign pronunciation of his name, became like a brother to Mother and Uncle Dan. He and Daniel were often to be seen together, as like as not getting up to some prank or other. Both became skilled in taxidermy. They'd collect and stuff lizards. One of their favourite larks was to catch mice, of which there was usually no shortage in the hotels where they stayed. They'd tie small bells round their necks before letting them loose again behind the wainscoting, the idea being to perplex the other hotel guests with sounds of spectral tinkling. Paul was particularly good with animals, and was the only one in the team who could master a clever baboon of uncertain temper that did a globe-rolling act.

The Gregory Equestrian Circus of the World was certainly a success in its day, which lasted approximately from 1886 to 1891. There were the inevitable ups and downs, and special moments of triumph. On 25 November 1887, for instance, when the circus was back in Malta, Grandfather

57

was requested to give a special show for HRH Alfred, Duke of Edinburgh, commander of the Mediterranean Fleet, for the eleventh birthday of his daughter, Princess Victoria. I still have a letter in its original envelope, embossed 'Admiralty House, Malta', which reads: 'Mr Richards is desired by the Duke of Edinburgh to enclose to Mr A. Gregory the accompanying cheque for twenty (£20) pounds for the special performance given yesterday at Mr Gregory's Circus.'

In December 1888, Gregory's took over for a season the Building Circus, a wooden structure and arena that stood in front of the Ottoman Bank in Cairo. There, on 1 February 1889, a show was given before the Khedive Mohammed Tewfik Pasha. The very next night was a Grand Military Night under the patronage of Major-General the Honourable J. C. Dormer, CB, in the presence of the officers of the army in Cairo and featuring the band of the Welch Regiment. By March the show had moved on to Port Said, where a benefit performance was given for the Lady Strangeford Hospital. Mr Strange, the English Chaplain and honorary secretary to the hospital board, sent a note of appreciation: 'On behalf of the Board of Visitors of the Lady Strangeford Hospital at Port Said I beg to tender my sincere thanks for the show you gave last night for the funds of the above institution.'

Back in Constantinople the next month, they were summoned to give a performance in the Yelditz Palace before Sultan Abdulhamid II – the last but one of the Ottoman sultans, destined to be deposed in 1909. Not only were they paid in gold sovereigns, but Grandmother and Mother were each presented with a gold medal as well as a *mijadia* or button-hole emblem. Whenever they wore these about the city, they'd be saluted by the Turkish policemen in recognition of the honour the decorations conferred.

The show itself had been memorable. Among its highlights was an animal trainer who presented a remarkable team of performing cats. This act in particular tickled the Sultan's fancy. Trained camels he understood, but cats were something else! He took Grandfather Gregory on one side and said, 'I would like to employ your cat trainer on a

58

A bill for Gregory's Equestrian Circus of the World, appearing in Cairo in 1888

permanent basis. I will recompense you for your loss and will pay him handsomely. He may have a suite of rooms in the Palace and whichever of my wives he fancies.' Grandfather agreed to approach the man, and said he'd not stand in his way if he was willing. So it came about that, when the circus left Turkey, the man and his moggies remained behind at the court.

For a time, it seemed, all went well, though the cats didn't prove too popular with the residents of the harem. One sultana in particular grew to hate them by day, and even more by night, for reasons readily imagined. The night came when, in desperation, she had them evicted from their fur-lined baskets and booted into the alleyways where, appropriately, it was raining cats and dogs. In an instant they were transformed from pampered performing pussies into genuine alley cats. It was no joke for the unfortunate trainer. The story went that, in fear and trembling, he scoured the city for his felines, fearful not only for the loss of his bread and butter but also for his head, Abdulhamid being famed for his absolute power and tricky temper.

Leonora and Dan enjoyed all aspects of circus life – performing, travelling the world, learning and speaking different languages, loving all the animals. The main blot on their general contentment with life was their father's habit of drinking and gambling. For Arthur Gregory, I'm sad to say, these recreations turned into very real problems. Many was the occasion when, before a performance, the children went out to search the bistros, bring him back to the caravan and dose him with black coffee. He was not only proprietor of the show, but also one of its star performers and so long as they could get him on to a horse, he was always capable of going through his routines flawlessly.

Arthur Gregory was a Freemason and a lover of good company, always ready to treat those he sought to impress. Whenever he needed a spot of ready cash he'd simply go to the pay-box and take out a fistful of sovereigns. As a result, it became impossible to keep the books straight. In the end, his behaviour unsettled my dear old grandmother to the extent where she started to drink too.

Grandmother was always a strong woman. When she'd worked with her own father, she'd carried on her shoulders both a cannon and the man who fired it. Before she married, she was the one who did the heavy work at home, leaving the domestic chores and cooking to her sisters. It was amazing how she and Arthur Gregory survived together when you thought about it – a woman who couldn't boil water and a man who was highly fastidious and a *bon viveur*, who thought nothing of eating a couple of pigeons for breakfast and who was inclined to throw any meal not to his satisfaction up to the ceiling in disgust.

When he was drunk, Arthur Gregory was generosity personified and would give anyone anything they asked for. The ticket staff always had to be on the alert to make sure he didn't sell the same seats twice. Once, when he was four sheets in the wind, he was offered a big sum for a particular box that was to be occupied the following night by a Very Important Person. Being Grandfather, he didn't want to disappoint the customer, but fortunately his secretary overheard and quickly stepped in to say, 'I'm sorry, but the boxes are all booked and we can't get in touch with the people concerned.' It saved Grandfather from falling into a trap. A bomb could easily have been planted in the box, assassination being then as much in fashion as it is today.

Time and time again Grandfather would sign the pledge, but all to no avail. As we harp on this theme, it brings us forward to one particular night in 1891. The circus ring is quiet and empty, except for the sound of animals in the background and four figures who sit at a lamp-lit table. A tense all-night gambling session is in progress. There's an occasional break for someone to light another cigar or draw another cork, Grandfather's favourite tipple being champagne. He's losing heavily, the first thing to go being the night's takings. After that it's the horses. Towards morning he throws down his last losing hand and rises from the table, realizing he's gambled away the entire show except for one horse, one performing donkey and his set of three-bars, which he's allowed to keep as a gesture of generosity on the

61

part of his gaming companions. You may imagine the feelings of his wife, son and daughter as they find themselves making their way to the nearest beach, all their former glory reduced to a horse and donkey. There on the sands Arthur Gregory erects his three-bars and starts into an acrobatic display, swinging atop the bars, then lowering a collection bag for the bystanders.

It was this event, I believe, that prompted Mother to strike out on her own. After working in continental music hall with her brother Dan for a short time, she returned to Britain to work with the Frank Bostock Circus. Mr Bostock was inclined to tour early in the season, while there was still snow on the ground. When they got to Burton-on-Trent, the animal trainer, Delhi, went to the bears' cage with snow on his boots, slipped and fell, and was killed by his charges. Shortly after this, she made the decision to go in with the well-known French circus, Cirque Diter. On 15 June 1892, Grandfather wrote a letter from St-Nazaire, Paris, addressed to 'Mr and Mrs Diter, Circus Director, Le Mans':

Dear Sir,

I beg to inform you my Daughter Leonora Mellors or Gregory so called in the circus line of business, is only a few Months over seventeen years of Age, so until she is 21 according to English laws, I beg of you to state the amount of salary you are paying her at the rate of Monthly salary as my Daughter as not sent my Wife and self 50 Francs monthly dating from the time we left your Circus and as your Wife and yourself as taken my Daughter away from her Home against her Mother's and Father's wishes as we have done for her for Seventeen years I wish to know what you intend to do as my Daughter's Salary is 400 Francs a Month for her talent. We cannot be left to starving in a foreign Country so if we cannot manage my Daughter must return to her Mother and Father at once. Awaiting your reply by return of post, truly yours

Chev. A. Gregory (Mellors)

It seems an understanding was arrived at. From that time

on, Mother continued to work independently with the top-line circuses. Children in that era were, however, expected to go on contributing to their parents' well-being. Boys and girls were minors until the age of twenty-one, and the old song, 'Twenty-One Today', gives a true picture. It was not until then that you had the key of the door and the chance to do as you wished. Dan was older than Leonora, but he still had to sign a legal guarantee to them:

Vice-Consul, St-Malo, Ile St-Villani, France
I, Daniel Mellors, undertake to give my father £1 per week while I am in work until I am 21 years of age, namely until August 23rd 1894. Witness my hand this 16th day of May 1893, Daniel Mellors.

I certify the above signature to be that of Daniel Mellors, a British subject, who has signed the same in my presence . . . Edward Kenneth Ways, Vice-Consul

Mother's career had meanwhile been flourishing. After working with several continental circuses, she went to join the Circus Oscar Carrée, the best-known Dutch circus of the day. It was while she was with them that she experienced the one and only romantic attachment of her life other than that for my father. The young man in question was Albert Carrée, son of the circus director, whose speciality was juggling on horseback. After Mother's death, we came across some poems she'd written at the time and kept all those years. These two verses provide a sample:

From thee, Albert, I must go and from my native shore.
The cruel fates between us throw as boundless oceans roar!
But boundless oceans roaring wide between my love and
   me
Never, never can divide my heart and soul from thee.

Farewell, farewell, Albert dear, the youth that I adore,
A brooding voice is in my ear. We part to meet no
   more!

But the last throb that leaves my heart while Death
    stands Victor by,
That throb, my dear one, is thy part, and thine the latest
    sigh.

Another reads:

Oh, time is ever fleeting by, destroying all that's dear.
On earth there's little worth a sigh and nothing worth a
    tear.
When I am far across the sea and you have someone in my
    place
Just let your thoughts be once of me
That I may lie not quite forgotten.

Not great poetry perhaps, but it reveals the depths of my
mother's feelings at the time. She was, after all, expressing
her first great romance, and she'd never had the advantage
of any formal schooling after the age of six. She first met
my father, Henry Whiteley, in December 1898 when she
was twenty-three years old and they were both working for
the Schumann Circus in Hamburg. Father had just then
unexpectedly found himself the head of the Whiteley troupe
following the death of his elder brother, Jack. Leonora
offered him moral support at this difficult time, and before
long they were going to church together.

It was the custom for performers to get together in a café
each morning for a game of cards. One morning my Father
was caught up in such a session at the same time as he had
an appointment with Mother. At a quarter past the arranged
hour of meeting she made her way to the café and rapped
on the window. When he looked up and saw her, he called
out, 'I'll just finish this hand and be right with you.' Away
she went in high dudgeon, and avoided him for more than
a fortnight. When he caught up with her and reproached her
over what he saw as her unreasonable behaviour, she said,
'If a game of cards means more to you than keeping our
appointment, we'd better call the whole thing off.'

'Well,' he said, 'if that's what's worrying you, I won't play cards again.'

And he never did. It was typical of his strength of mind. For years he enjoyed cigars, until one day his doctor told him to stop. He took a packet from his pocket, placed it on the desk, said, 'Thank you, doctor,' and never smoked again.

Mother had always declared, as a girl, that she'd on no account marry an acrobat, but that, of course, was just what she did. She was of age when she decided to marry. Even so, Father wrote to his future father-in-law, Mr Gregory, to seek his consent. This was the letter that came back:

317 rue de Pyreneus, Paris

Dear Sir,

Your letter of December 28th duly received, of which I have very few remarks to state in regards of giving consent to you and my daughter's engagement, as she has informed me that it is her wish to get married to you this summer, and it is not my wish to bar my daughter's future happiness to a good honest man as she is a good honest girl and has always done her duty towards her parents. I wish you to understand that we are poor and that my daughter and her brother are our only support and as my daughter states in her letter she wished always to be so, and as I am told you are a good son to your own mother, and this as a general rule makes a good husband, and as you state in your letter that you will do all in your power to make her happy, I hope you will keep your word and do so. I want you to understand that she is a good girl and deserves a good husband. Let me know when in the summer you are getting married. Mrs Gregory sends her best respects to yourself and to your mother. Now I conclude, wishing you a Happy New Year, yours truly

Arthur Gregory

And so it came about that Miss Leonora Gregory, daughter of Chevalier Arthur Gregory (né Mellors), lately proprietor of Gregory's Equestrian Circus of the World, was married by the state on 10 June 1899, and by the church on the following day at St Paul's English Church, Hamburg, and became Mrs Henry Allen Alexander Whiteley. She had married out of one circus family into another, as was very much in the family tradition. Her brother Daniel had already done the same, for his wife was Miss Lydia Maldavan, a member of a well-known Irish circus clan, the Duffys. The couple worked together for many years as Dan Gregory and Lydia, until she became an invalid.

Before leaving my mother's early years, I'd like to sketch you a picture of her when she was still Miss Leonora Gregory, a versatile performer as rider, trapeze artist, tumbler and ballet dancer. She was petite, only about five feet tall, with blue eyes and jet-black hair that she wore long – so long that, if she lay back while riding, the ends of her hair could be caught under the horse's hooves. Alongside her other talents she possessed a very good singing voice that once, in 1888, enabled her to sing the military song, 'On the Burning Plains of Egypt', with the band of the Scots Brigade. I remember the songs she'd sing to me when I was a child, including the following spirited number which she had sung in pantomime in 1885 at the Palace, Leicester, when she played the title role in *Jack the Giant Killer*:

> Down with the Giant,
> Down with his crew,
> I'm not much used to fighting
> But I will settle you.
>
> I'll hash him, I'll crash him,
> I'll bash him till he's dead,
> And then the sweet Princess
> I shall quickly wed.

There was another that she used to sing:

> Just behind the battle, mother,
> I was eating Irish stew.
> You should hear those cannons rattle –

Makes one feel uncommon blue –
If I only could skedaddle
I would hurry home to you.

I cannot tell you which battle was being referred to.

True to their word, Mother and Father continued to contribute to the Gregorys' livelihood and bought them a caravan. Finally, on the night of 22 October 1899, just eighteen months after his daughter's marriage, Grandfather Gregory left the Masonic Lodge in Paris somewhat the worse for drink and was apprehended by two gendarmes who took him to a hospital. There he was put into a straightjacket – a common precaution with drunks in those days, though today he'd be given a sedative injection. He fought to escape the straightjacket. In fact, he succeeded, but in the effort burst a blood vessel. So he died and was laid to rest in the Commune de Levallois Perret Cemetery in Paris, aged only forty-five. In the course of a short life, Arthur Gregory had achieved much in his profession, but in the end it was drink and gambling that brought him low. My mother would in after years enjoy the occasional glass of wine, although in general she hated anything to do with gambling or drink, as was quite understandable. I have to say, though, that I never heard her utter one word of condemnation or reproach in Grandfather's memory.

4

Old Crafty and His Progeny

And now we have another family history to unravel. The tradition of my father's people, the Whiteleys, began with one John Whiteley, born on 28 September 1823 in the Yorkshire village of Slaithwaite (pronounced *Slowitt* by the natives). He, my father's grandfather, appears to have become an acrobatic entertainer at an early age. How it came about that he was attracted to the profession and learnt his skills is not recorded, but he's mentioned as a well-known local character in a book by John Sugden entitled *Slaithwaite Notes Past and Present* (1902).

For some reason said to be connected with his ability to do the apparently impossible, the first John Whiteley came to be known as 'Old Crafty'. He played a one-man band (big drum on his back, bells on his hat, wooden pipes, cymbals and the like) and was a clever tumbler who could stand with his back to a wall and perform a back somersault or face a wall and do a front somersault. Travelling around with his band instruments and tumbling mat, he'd work the neighbouring streets and markets. As Mr Sugden tells it:

He went to all the feasts and fairs, being highly appreciated and largely patronized by the general public, with whom he was a favourite. Sometimes in mid-winter, under

68

depressing circumstances, he would come home to rest and refresh. He lived down Laith Lane . . . where he would practice (not to the glory of his neighbours) on the drum and the shepherd's reeds . . .

The [Slaithwaite] feast at that time lasted two days. After these two days the showmen would all fold their tents and go away, except 'Crafty'. This favourite stayed on for the week; and rare fun there was. Prizes would be given for eating hot porridge, and many scalded mouths have I seen by the foolish vigour of the contestants in too eagerly attacking the boiling beverage. To vary this, a prize pig would be offered, to run in with the evening's entertainment, which was enlivened and diversified by the smart sayings of Whiteley, who was no mean clown or wit.

In time John Whiteley left his native Yorkshire and headed for London. It's said that he married three times. His first wife was also in the busking line, though her speciality was tightrope walking. She was the mother of his two eldest children, John the second and Laura, 'a clever boy and a finer girl, who went to London afterwards in a good position, for which she had a special training as a splendid horsewoman', says Mr Sugden. The story told of their mother was that she went insane after losing £20 and was found trying to make soup out of pebbles. With that sad anecdote the curtain descends on my knowledge of the first John Whiteley, except that Mr Sugden tells us that he went 'home to die, and Slaithwaite harbours his remains after the many ups and downs of the troubled sea of a showman's life'.

John Whiteley the second, my grandfather, was born in Huddersfield on 19 April 1843. He started off by being apprenticed till eighteen to the circus owner Frederick Ginnett, and afterwards arranged another apprenticeship for himself to take him through till he was twenty-one. The training gave him the grounding to become a noted bar-act rider, clever forwards tumbler (he could go six times forward in a swing) and trampoline leaper (trampoline being the term then used to describe a springboard). One of his early appearances was at Astley's. Here, at the famous covered circus amphitheatre in Westminster Bridge Road, London, he struck up an association with the Delevantis, a well-known acrobatic troupe who were billed at the time as the 'Kings of the Carpet'. The association went even further. On 23 January 1865, at the church of St Martin-in-the-Fields, he married a young lady called Ellen Alberta Bowden – London born on 1 April 1850, and daughter of the Delevanti troupe's founder, John Bowden.

Old Mr Bowden (another of my great-grandfathers) worked under the stage name of John Delevanti and was himself an acrobatic champion, somersaulter and rider. One of his equestrian pupils, who appeared as George Delevanti and was remembered by the circus historian Thomas Frost for his 'marvellous leap through a series of hoops', later changed his name to George Crippen and became a famous actor. On the day of his daughter's wedding, John Delevanti's troupe was appearing at the Holborn Amphitheatre. As soon as they'd done their bit on the night show there, they had to dash round to Drury Lane to take part in the 'Harlequinade' with its acrobatics and trap work, John Delevanti playing Clown.

There were to be twelve children of the marriage. When my father made a list of them in the manuscript memoirs he wrote 'in the year of war 1944' when he was in his seventy-second year, he included for interest the places where they were all born, so I'll do the same. They were Ellen Edith (London), Mary Ann (London), John (Cologne), Margaret (Florence), Henry Allen Alexander (Modena), Thomas (Palermo), Madalena (Genoa), Rudolph (Genoa), Benjamin (Paris), Sidonia (Paris), Arthur (Lisbon) and Lina (Laibach). As you see, the country in which my father, Henry Whiteley, was born was Italy, the date of his birth being 31 March 1872.

John and Ellen Whiteley kept on with the Delevanti troupe for some time after their marriage. They travelled with them in Europe to work at such famous circuses as the Circus Renz in Germany and the Circus Emilio Guilleaume in Italy. In about 1870, Mr Bowden decided to return to England to remarry. He'd been a widower since shortly after the birth of his daughter Ellen. The Whiteleys stayed on in Italy, however, as Grandfather was offered a contract with the Guilleaumes. It was by all accounts a long and happy association. In due course his employers presented him with a heavy gold locket that had the letter 'W' picked out in small diamonds.

There were a couple of occasions when Grandfather Whiteley made an attempt to become a circus proprietor himself. The first happened in 1874, when he became one of four partners who formed the Circo Ecuestro Sociale. The enterprise started well, and he engaged, among others, the Arthur Gregory troupe of acrobats, but there were already signs of his health beginning to cause problems. He couldn't even think of accompanying the circus when it went to South America (during which tour a certain Miss Leonora Gregory was born in Argentina), and he sold out his share of the partnership.

The continuing deterioration in Grandfather's health meant that he had to stop performing his riding act in 1883 – a fact that led to George Sanger cancelling an important contract for the Whiteley troupe and lean times for them in general. Grandfather Whiteley's second venture into circus proprietorship, which followed in the next year, 1884, was even more of a disaster than the first. With the encouragement of his half-brother, Harry Whiteley, he bought a circus set-up formerly owned by the Brothers Levene of Nottingham. Unfortunately, the Levenes had a bad name with the public. Grandfather brought in an entirely new set of acts, and took on the task of ringmaster himself, but people still said as soon as they recognized the tent, 'Another Levene swindle under another name.'

That finished the John Whiteley Circus after five weeks' touring in the Midlands. Grandmother pawned her wedding ring and Grandfather departed to London to raise a loan. In a last-ditch attempt to salvage the situation, his brother Harry took the horse and riding goat to put on an act for the holiday-makers on Skegness sands. Harry had my Grandmother Ellen in tow, as well as his wife, Miss Lizzie Barnes,

71

who did a juggling act. They also had with them a young trapeze artist then going by the name of Aubrey, but who'd later be known to the world at large as Fred Karno. All efforts to salvage the situation ended in failure. The horse, the goat and the tenting gear had to be disposed of. The Whiteleys returned to working with other people's circuses.

My father had been born in Italy back at the time when John Whiteley was still with the Circus Guilleaume. His godparents were Henry Williams and Katalina Kasakova, a noted husband and wife riding team who accompanied the Circo Equestro Sociale on its South American tour. This gave Father the chance to write in his memoirs in 1944 that, when Arthur Gregory's daughter was born in Buenos Aires, 'her Godfather was Mr Tom Virello, and her Godmother Katalina Kasakova – the same lady [who] in 1872 at Modena was my Godmother, and 22 years later Miss Leonora Catalina Gregory became my dearly beloved wife, and as I am writing this, is sitting opposite me sewing'.

As a baby, Henry was considered delicate, which seems ironic when you consider that one of the leading features of his act in later years was to juggle with his feet a six-foot solid table weighing sixty pounds. (In fact, when he did his solo act, a notice would be put up at the front of the stage, stating that the table weighed sixty pounds. One night, when I was still very young, I was sitting in the audience and noticed that the stage staff had forgotten to put out the notice. I became most indignant and loudly informed the people sitting beside me, 'That's my father, and that table weighs sixty pounds!') At all events, at that phase of his life Father was sent back to London to live with an uncle and aunt in Clerkenwell, his earliest memories being of Saturday jaunts to the Angel, Islington, to buy fruit and meat pies, of flying a kite in Finsbury Park and of being taken to the Britannia Theatre, Hoxton, to watch a performance by the Mohawk Minstrels. He also saw one of the Britannia's famous pantomimes and had his first sight of a circus at the Agricultural Hall, Islington, where his uncle Harry Whiteley was putting on a riding trick act. He was particularly impressed by the men with pink legs who flew from trapeze to trapeze. 'I little thought at that time,' he wrote, 'that I should have pink and many other coloured legs.'

To start with, his ill-health interfered with his schooling. He made up for that when he finally grew stronger and could set out to rejoin his parents and family in Paris. There he found himself learning French in no time as his mother sent him out on shopping errands. He also began to practise his splits and bends. Inevitably he had to put up with being called a 'Jack the Josser' by his older sisters and brother. His father bought him a small risley, as the cushion on which acrobats rest their hips in foot juggling is called, a large ball and a small tranca, the cylindrical beam of solid wood also used by foot jugglers ('risley artistes' or 'antipodeans', as the billings of the time called them).

When in his seventies he wrote his recollections of those early days with his family, Father's powers of recall were quite remarkable. His memoirs contain names and details of all kinds of fellow acts – equestrian, juggling, clowning, high-wire, trapeze, performing animal. There are so many that there could only be space here to list a fraction.

I'd especially like to pass on to you what he says about a team of five members called the Bozza troupe. It gives such a good idea of the variety and inventiveness of the acts of those days. The Bozzas performed a musical kitchen act in which they played 'plates, saucepans, frying pans, etc.'. They were also 'the first to introduce the road menders act, playing on paving stones with tuned hammers, and then . . . beating the stones into place'. These stones were large imitation stones 'each containing two notes' so that when they were pressed down they 'played small trumpet notes'. The implements used for pressing down were camouflaged cornets, as were the handles of the wheelbarrow, and 'for finale all played and marched out'. Another innovation of the Bozzas was the first electric musical act; 'using dry batteries' they provoked reactions in 'different things placed in different parts of the auditorium: a small train set in motion, a little house set on fire, and whistles and trumpet played'. The five Bozzas dressed themselves as demons for this act, the middle one perching on a small table to set off the

73

tricks while the other four 'played very long posthorns and cornets'.

And who could have resisted Arturo Magrini's troupe of performing dogs:

> featuring shot dog lying dead, then funeral coach drawn by two dogs, four dogs in long black coats and hats, two each side of coach on hind legs, in their mouth, on a stick, a lantern, another dog dressed as a priest on hind legs with book, coach drawn very slow until trainer shouted, 'Go home, all run home' (à la maison), the dead dog jumping out of the coach.

Despite his health problems, Grandfather Whiteley continued to manage the family troupe. Once, when they were on the bill at the Royal Aquarium in London, a violent thunderstorm shattered some of the thick glass in the roof. Everything was grist to Grandfather's mill. He asked for some of the glass, had it cut into strips and tuned three sets for the boys to play like xylophones.

Not long after the débâcle of the John Whiteley Circus, Grandfather secured an engagement in Naples with the Brothers Amato Circus. They had a difficult journey across France because of the late arrival of a money order for travelling expenses, and when they arrived at the Italian frontier on the other side of the Mount Cenis Tunnel, discovered a cholera scare in progress. The carabineri took them off the train and ordered them into seven days' quarantine under canvas high in the Alps – 'in the daytime the heat was terrific', Father remembered, 'but at night very cold'. When they did reach Naples, the cholera outbreak was having a bad effect on business and the Amatos appealed to the players to continue on half-salary. On this basis they completed a tour of Italy before getting away to Alexandria, where they were put into five days' quarantine this time, and had their luggage fumigated and all the property boxes opened and sprayed with disinfectant, which tarnished the spangles and the gold and silver trimmings on the costumes and equipment.

They arrived in Cairo just at the time when Kitchener's expedition was being mounted to relieve General Gordon in Khartoum. As a result, there was a strong military presence in the audiences and, when it came to their benefit night, the Whiteleys sang a topical version of the song 'Far, Far Away', of which this was one of the verses:

> Where are our gallant troops?
>   Far, far away.
> They are now on the Nile,
>   Far, far away,
> Dispersing fast the Mahdi force,
> Braving the Nile's swiftest course.
> McEwen's beer will then in force
> Be not far away,
> Far, far away.

On Christmas Eve, Grandfather told the boys to fetch their handbells, and they went in a cab to ring sets of chimes outside the headquarters of the C.-in-C., the residence of the resident, Sir Evelyn Baring (later Lord Cromer), and the various army barracks. On Christmas Day, Grandfather and the bell-ringers were invited to dinner at the sergeants' mess of the 19th Hussars. After their act in the matinée that afternoon, they were presented with a large Christmas pudding 'with Sir Evelyn Baring's compliments'.

They returned to Italy via the Greek islands and Trieste, this part of the tour seeing the birth of my youngest aunt, Lina, at Laibach, and the departure from the profession of my eldest aunt, Ellen Edith (Nellie), at Genoa, when she married Mr Carlos Salinas, a member of the Alexandria stock exchange. The Whiteleys were now established on the Continent, even if the ebb and flow of fortune did mean they were sometimes paid in IOUs rather than hard cash.

'We became,' Father said, 'great favourites wherever we went with our musical act, especially Tommy, with his natural gift for silent droll comedy.' Tommy was particularly brilliant as a young clown. Clowns, of course, never let other clowns see their props. If they do, the others will

75

know at once which particular entrance is going to be used and may go on first and steal the entrance. Grandfather and the boys had been caught out like this on several occasions, and one day he decided they'd get their own back.

At the time, in 1887, they were performing as 'los Hermanos Whiteley' with the Circo Alegria in Spain, where one of the Spanish clowns' successes was the cod bullfight. This, needless to say, was always looked on as the Spanish clowns' prerogative. Grandfather, however, took Tommy to meet a retired bullfighter, who gave him lessons in handling the cape, banderillas, sword and muleta, while Jack and Father practised hard at being a bull, getting the movements and quickness as lifelike as possible. Then, one night, after the Spanish clowns had given their bullfight, the boys followed it with their version. Tommy was every inch a toreador, though there weren't too many inches of him, and his movements were perfection. The response from the audience was overwhelming. Forgetting the performers were only children, they threw cigars into the ring. It caused, said Father, 'a lot of jealousy among the clown element'. But when the Whiteleys put on their main acrobatic act, Spanish audiences took to shouting, '*corridar, corridar!* and wouldn't let them go until they had given the bullfight parody'.

Grandfather was by now in very poor health, and although he was able to be with the company for Christmas 1887, he left for England in the New Year to stay with his sister in Walthamstow and try to recoup his strength. All that spring, the news from London sounded bad, and on 11 April, just as he was about to go into the ring, Jack was handed a telegram saying 'Come immediately'. He left there and then with Grandmother, but they arrived too late to see Grandfather alive. Only seven months after that, the news came from Alexandria that Ellen too was dead, leaving a little daughter. The child, sad to say, was never acknowledged by her father's family, they being Jewish and her mother a Christian. Grandmother Whiteley was back in London for good by that time. She took a large house with some sixteen bedrooms, and these she let to members of the profession. The address was 29 Brixton Road, or 'Greasepaint Road', as it was often called, for many showbusiness families had their homes in that district of South London during the times when they weren't travelling. Among these, in Coldharbour Lane, was the family of Tom Major, an acrobatic comic who was destined to be the father of our youngest twentieth-century prime minister before his career was over.

Many of Grandma Whiteley's family were to die young, including Tommy and Arthur. Jack, who married into the Alegria family, and became equestrian director and manager of the fine Circo Barcelona in the Plaza Cara Luna, died in Frankfurt at the age of twenty-eight in 1897. This was the tragic event that helped to bring Father and Mother together, as has been related in the previous chapter. Meanwhile Father had, with an eye on the variety theatres, formed with his younger brothers the first Five Whiteleys act, which for some time performed abroad. While they were playing in Breslau, Ike Rose, an American impresario who'd brought Harry Houdini to Europe, was impressed by them and asked why they didn't play in England. Father replied that he'd written many times but didn't seem able to attract any bookings. 'Leave it to me!' Rose said simply. True to his word, he used his influence to get the act four weeks of bookings, starting on 6 May 1901 at the Tivoli, Birmingham. The presentation was a great success, and from then on the family were able to get good bookings in their home country.

In 1904, they played the Alhambra, London, for six weeks, so let us imagine we are attending that theatre at the time. The rich have arrived by horse and carriage (another year on, and we might even be seeing someone arrive in a Rolls-Royce – the original 'Silver Wraith'). The gallery patrons have travelled on one of the early motor buses, or by shanks's pony. We shall assume we're privileged, and take a seat in the stalls. There's a continual buzz in our ears, for a full theatre has a sound all its own. As we look towards the stage, we find ourselves reading the advertisement cloth: 'Cockerell's Coals for Comfort'; 'Freeman's Real Turtle Soup, 2d. a cup' – delicious consommé prepared from the meat of West Indian turtles; 'Gordon & Dilworth Tomato Catsup, 3d., 6d., 9d.'; 'Panshine, 1d. a packet', and so forth.

All at once, there is a complete hush. We notice the orchestral players are in their places. The conductor enters. He faces the audience and bows, turns and raises his baton. The musicians of the orchestra, some eighteen or twenty of them, start in with an abbreviated overture, perennial favourites being *Poet and Peasant* or the *1812*. The audience looks down at its programmes in excited anticipation. A number comes up on either side of the stage. Who's opening the show, then? Why, it's the Five Whiteleys. The orchestra begins to play lively music, but the curtains do not open immediately. Instead there's a sudden noise from the back of the stalls. Two gentlemen appear, wearing the smart top-coats of the day, and two ladies. Did we but know it, one of the 'ladies', Rudolph, is a gentleman who on this occasion is working as a lady. Each of the four carries a suitcase, as if they've just arrived in a rush from the station. Behind them comes the comic, supposedly the groom, or general factotum, who carries everything but the kitchen sink and whose burdens include a tumbling mat.

As the group moves down the aisle towards the stage, the curtains do open at last, and we see the wire for walking already in place. In the twinkling of an eye, the acrobats' coats are off, revealing gorgeous costumes underneath; the mat is down and the act is away. The 'lady' shows 'her' skills by jumping over four chairs on the wire. The *pièce de résistance* comes as Ben Whiteley holds a long pole called a 'pen' for Henry Whiteley to climb. It has a square board at the top, on which Henry lies on his back to go through his antipodean act. The climax to this, the table-juggling routine, is a masterpiece. Afterwards the three principals hold handbells and, to the accompaniment of a specially arranged tune, turn back somersaults and play the bells in time. The act ends in a fast and furious tumbling finale.

The pinnacle of any act's career was to play the London Palladium or the Coliseum, the latter theatre having opened on Christmas Day 1904, with its vast stage and the first revolve in the country. The Five Whiteleys played a six-week season there in 1907, and in the same year started an Australian tour. Father was, in fact, the first foot juggler to play in Australia, and, appropriately enough, his antipodean tricks went down well among the antipodeans. The Five Whiteleys and Henri Alexander, Father's solo spot, opened at the Opera House, Melbourne, on 21 September, *The Age* reporting that they were 'certainly a wonderful quintet'.

> They have practically revolutionized the acrobatic business, and during their whirling occupation of the stage they have the house in a state of bewilderment. The troupe consists of three male acrobats, a very funny clown, and a young woman who is the most versatile of them all. The Lady is not individualized in the programme, but the presumption is that she is Miss Whiteley. Whoever she is, she is a living wonder, and the sight of her performance is all that the most ardent advocate of women's rights needs to clinch the argument that woman is man's equal at anything, even hard work . . . She and another Whiteley perform almost incredible things on a slack wire with nothing but an umbrella to preserve their equilibrium, while 'Miss Whiteley' alone jumps over a row of chairs on the wire with as much ease and certainty as if they were on the ground. She catches a 12 st. Whiteley (he looks every ounce of it) with one hand as he bounds into the air in a somersault, and elevating him high above her head carries him round the stage with no other aid than the other hand upon which she catches him. Other Whiteleys are thrown aloft by this astounding young female with ridiculous ease . . . As the Whiteleys are most of the time in a state of violent agitation it is practically impossible for one pair of eyes to keep track of half the things they do.

Unhappily for women's rights, 'Miss Whiteley' was my Uncle Rudolph. The troupe went on to play at all the principal cities, topping the bill at the Tivoli, Sydney. Returned to England, the family troupe's career flourished with never a week out of work. They were playing at the Ardwick Empire in the week in May 1910 when Edward VII died, and so entered another reign. That 31 October, they were

79

at the recently opened Empire Theatre at Kingston-upon-Thames on a bill that, according to the *Surrey Comet*, 'catered well for all tastes'. In the theatre's 'second week of bidding for public support and appreciation', the entertainment provided was 'calculated to appeal to predilections as varied as the turns which follow one another in quick succession'. The musical-comedy star, Miss Evie Green, topped the bill, and beside the Five Whiteleys, who 'severally and together, accomplished several wonderful acrobatic feats' of wire walking, there was, amid the rich and varied fare, the 'accomplished *siffleur*, Mr Arthur Slater, "The Whistling Man in White"', whose imitations of birds are so realistic his efforts won him cordial applause'. The opposition in the town that week consisted of a dramatization in three parts of *Uncle Tom's Cabin* at the James Hall; a play, *The Woman in the Case*, at the County Theatre; and, at the Cinema Palace, the two-reelers, *Between Love and Honour* and *The Way of the Red Man*.

It was strange how neither legitimate actors nor variety artists considered the cinema to be a threat overshadowing their livelihoods. This was certainly true of Father, who had wandered by chance into a show shop in Calais back in 1896 and seen the Lumière brothers' pioneering cinematic achievements only a few months after they were first unveiled to the public. For a long time, he was sure it was a passing phase, and only much later did he and others of his generation awake to the danger signals.

Another item in the same issue of the *Surrey Comet* was about local cinemas wishing to open on a Sunday. When permission was refused, Mr Robinson, the manager of the Palace, let the customers in free of charge, made a collection and gave the proceeds to charity. The report indicated that the public did not want Sunday opening:

It is contended by local Picture Palace directors that they have followed the example of hundreds of other cinemas in the provinces. This defence exactly reflects the tendency that is so much to be deplored. One fails to see where it will all end. In what school of Morals or Sociology, we wonder, have managers of Picture Houses graduated? But Mr Kendal Robinson still retains some of his ancestors' puritanism and says he will only show certain films on Sunday.

The theatre is still divided over Sunday opening. The traditional way round it has been, when a show is allowed, to call it a 'Sunday concert'. The following rules used to be enforced: no make-up, costumes or double patter. A well-known comedian, when he turned up sporting plus-fours, was told he couldn't appear in comedy props. Another time a yodeller, who used the name Van Lutin and appeared in Dutch dress, though he was as English as they come, was instructed not to appear in costume. With great presence of mind, he affected a broken accent and explained he was in the everyday wear of his country.

But, to return to the Five Whiteleys, as 1910 drew towards a close, matters were running less smoothly between the brothers. Even in the best-regulated families, there can be a period when discontent and quarrels grow frequent – an indication that the time has come to make changes. Although Father had signed contracts for return dates at several top theatres, he handed these over to his brothers, and it was on 26 August 1911, at the Empire, Dewsbury, that the original Five Whiteleys played their last date together. Father lost not a moment in forming a new act, the Henry Whiteley Trio, with Mother and a nephew, and they opened at the Victoria Hall, Cowes, on the 28th, for a salary of £10. It was, wrote Father in his memoirs, a 'quick, clean, smart act', but, he added, 'one trouble always follows another'.

By the end of November, Mother had to retire temporarily to Brixton, the 'family reason' for her retreat being that I was on the way. Father's sister Madalena stepped in to fill the gap, but then the nephew backed out, his place being filled by Mother's cousin, William Matthews (a grandson of old William Matthews), who had previously worked with the Five Whiteleys. Rudolph and Ben continued for a while with the Five Whiteleys act, working with their two wives and a young Dutchman, Conn Dekker. Conn, incidentally,

81

became a very fine performing acrobat and later worked for many years with his wife as Dekker and Pam.

Mother, needless to say, rejoined the trio as soon as she was able, and worked with it whenever she could. If they ever had to be apart for any reason, Father always wrote three letters a week home to Mother during the time he was away. A few extracts from his letters will show both what a pound was then worth and how the troupe never knew where it would be from one week to another.

20 March 1914: I have done no business here, and after next week I have the week out, then work following week, then two weeks out, but I hope something will turn up. I have been to Slay's Office. He has taken my dates. He saw the act at Morecambe and liked it. Also went to the Beresford and Pearce Variety Agency. They saw us Tuesday night and hope to book us.

23 March 1914: I am pleased to say we have got an early turn, unless they alter it tonight.

It perhaps needs to be explained that, by this time, it had become more difficult for speciality acts to top bills. Acrobatic acts were usually given the dressing room at the top of the building, and brought the show to a close. When Father asked an agent why speciality acts were always used to open or close a show, he received this reply: 'Well, Mr Whiteley, we have to put a good act on last so that the audience leaves with its last impression a good one. These two spots are always the hardest on any bill to fill.' Which may have been so, but the artists doing the filling were rarely paid accordingly.

24 March 1914: Saw the boys [his brothers] for a few minutes at Manchester station. I have settled next week, Earlestown, near Liverpool. It is a good job as the following week is Leigh, Lancs., only a 1s. 5d. [7p] journey: but the following week is right down to Penzance. I tried

82

without success to get it altered as the fares will be around £8, so must save towards it.

April 1914: I have a matinée tomorrow, so rushing to catch the post and send you the money £1 9s. 8d. [£1.49] to Mother for the room and 21s. [a guinea, or £1.05] for yourself.

The previous year, my eldest brother Harry had reached the age of fourteen and replaced Will Matthews, who wanted to form his own act by that time. Less than a year later, on 1 February 1915, Ben too was able to join the act, which became the Henry Whiteley Four and opened in ciné-variety at Blake's Picture House, Hitchin. By the time Harry's call-up for the army came through in early 1917, the third son, Harold, was ready to take his place.

Both Ben and Harold [wrote Father in his memoirs] we dressed as girls, using their own hair grown long and curled every night – according to our view, girls in tumbling was more effective. But I am afraid my Sons did not agree, having to wear their hair rather long.

Brother Paul, aged eleven, and Leonora, nine, were by then, of course, travelling with them and learning the profession, and although Father would never apply for a licence for the younger ones to work before they reached the proper age, theatre and cinema managers were seldom averse to an extra performer being slipped into the programme, provided it cost nothing. Paul and Leonora sometimes got to go on for, perhaps, a Friday first-house performance or a Saturday matinée, Leonora doing a toe dance on Father's juggling table and Paul showing off a few acrobatics. This was the state of things with the family troupe at the time when, as I have already told in the opening chapter, I came to join it from my foster home in Eastwood.

5

Family Round-up

Before I leave the earlier generations of my family behind, I must cast back and forth in time to tell you what I can of their individual histories.

I knew only four of my father's brothers and sisters: Mary, Benjamin, Rudolph and Madalena. Uncle Ben married Peggy Fame, who was really a Miss Wright for her father was Harry Wright, a song-writer and music-hall entertainer whose act was to invite members of the audience to give him a subject on which he would make up a song spontaneously. Her mother was Nellie Gannon, quite a famous name as a singer on the halls. Harry used to write Nellie's songs for her, such as 'Only a Few Miles of Water':

> For there's only a few miles of water,
> Only a stretch of the foam,
> Lies between Mother and daughter,
> In Ireland, my own native home.

Towards the end of September 1900, Nellie and Harry appeared separately on the same programme at Sadler's Wells, she billed as 'a Braw-Limbed Lass of Weight and Worth, tipping the Beam at 13 stone, yet as lightfooted as a fairy', he as the 'Ready Rhyming Referee and Topical

Tipster on all Sporting Events, Social Struggles and International Shindies from here to the Indies'.

Madalena married a well-known French circus performer, Alfred Delbosque – Auguste clown, tumbler and rider. The marriage unfortunately broke down and they were divorced in 1926. Their three children, Nella, Alfred and Rita, my first cousins, all followed the profession as Delbosques. Nella became a wardrobe mistress, dressed a lot of stars, and on her eightieth birthday was given a fine party by many of those she had dressed. Rita married and went to live in Las Vegas. Alfred was ringmaster with a lot of famous circuses, and married Heidi Lorsch, whose family were known for an acrobatic springboard act, making leaps on to each other's shoulders until the last (the third or fourth) lands seated on a chair held by the one second from the top. At the outbreak of the Second World War, they were working in Germany, but managed to escape to France. The Lorsches were Jewish, and eventually they were betrayed to the Gestapo. Somehow Alfred managed to rescue his wife at the last minute, but most of the rest of his in-laws perished in the gas chambers.

Aunt Mary married an Italian artist, Emilio Spampani, who, under the name of Clown Niny, performed a clowning and tumbling act with a donkey, pig and leaping dog. Together they took a circus out to Java, then a Dutch colony. As I hardly need to tell you by this time, circus knew no language barriers. They worked together out there for quite a few years, and also played adjacent islands, such as Sumatra. They did very well, and for a long time had no competition; not that circus was unknown there previously. In 1897, when he was only six, my uncle Dan had also been in Java, clowning with the Gregory troupe on a Far Eastern tour.

Aunt Mary suffered from the scourge of the times, tuberculosis, and she had to have one of her lungs collapsed. But the climate in Java seemed to agree with her, and when her husband died, she remained there to carry the circus on with another business partner. Once, when the lighting in the circus failed, a leopard jumped out into the audience and mauled a child. The partner managed to pull it off and hold its jaws until someone could bring a gun and shoot it.

85

Eventually Mary returned to Europe, first to Paris, then to London. She brought with her a very clever toy terrier. It would stand on its front paws on her fingers and, when she said 'Valse' would jump down and pirouette all around her. Realizing that it would fret if it had to go into quarantine, she smuggled it on board ship in her muff, and took it off the same way. She died in London and the little dog, her constant companion, did not long survive her.

After the break-up of the original Five Whiteleys, Uncle Rudolph joined the army in 1916. Once the war was over, he teamed up with Ernie Allan, a former performer with the high-wire act called the Four Holloways (whose senior member was Captain George Holloway, father of James Holloway, otherwise known as Jimmy Nervo of Nervo and Knox). Ernie and Rudolph formed an act called the De Havillands for a couple of years, after which Rudolph took up stage management and toured with several shows, including Fred Karno's *Mumming Birds* revue, which was still doing the rounds. In fact, in May 1919, the Whiteleys had played on a programme at the Cheltenham Coliseum that featured *Mumming Birds* at the top of the bill. Before his active acrobatic career finally came to an end, Uncle Rudolph worked with Florrie Zetina, daughter of a family of acrobats known variously as the Zetinas and the Clevelands, and helped to found a famous troupe called the Zio Angels. After that he settled down to be stage manager to the famous Windmill Theatre, where the Van Damm management ran its continuous variety show, *Revudeville*, from 1932.

On the occasion of the Windmill's twentieth anniversary, one press write-up said how Rudolph Whiteley had helped to keep the Windmill 'milling merrily for twenty years'. The Windmill, of course, was mainly noted for its nude tableaux and its proud wartime motto, 'We never closed' – usually altered to, 'We never clothed' in popular parlance. The nudes of those days were not allowed to bat even an eyelid; under the Lord Chamberlain's rules, they had to remain absolutely still. From ten o'clock onwards each morning, there was always a mainly male queue waiting for admission. Uncle Rudolph told me how strictly the girls who posed were supervised, while elaborate precautions were taken to make sure that no unknown males angling for a pick-up got past the stage door. The Windmill was also a launching pad for a host of young actors and comedians: Kenneth More, Peter Sellers, Jimmy Edwards, Arthur English, Michael Bentine and Harry Secombe, to name but a few. In his autobiography, *Kenneth More or Less*, Kenneth More mentioned Rudolph several times, but was under a grave misapprehension when he stated that he had begun his career as a stage carpenter. Readers of the present book will know otherwise.

As I have already mentioned, I never was able to trace all of my various great-aunts and great-uncles, the twenty-one children of William and Lauretta Matthews. Even though there was, early on, a certain feeling that circus folk who went to work in the music halls were letting the side down, the Matthews family were pioneers in this respect, as a review in *The Era* for 1 November 1869 bears witness:

> The Matthews troupe, nine in number, have made their reappearance in London after some time. They did as follows on the night of our visit. First a sharp little boy and a pleasing girl cracked jokes in a couple of duologues. They were followed by three girls of greater age in a terpsichorean and acrobatic performance which was lively and pretty. Finally the little boy first referred to and three others leaped and tumbled with great daring and agility in conjunction with their trainer and director, Mr Matthews himself. They are all clever acrobats. The smallest boy performs some novel and exceedingly difficult feats which excite great applause. The hall is being decorated and promises to look quite elegant.

The hall in question was John Wilton's Music Hall, 'The Handsomest Room in Town', in Grace's Alley, Wellclose Square, London E1, where the Matthews troupe had made its London stage début some years earlier in 1864. Alas, the stage on which the Matthews performed was destroyed in the fire of 1877, but Wilton's rose from the ashes and has survived as a precious if dilapidated relic from the golden age of music hall through being respectively Wesleyan mission hall and rag warehouse. Efforts to bring it to full restoration have continued against enormous difficulties, and I wish the enterprise well. There are those who enjoy the luxury and privilege of driving a vintage car. I would be delighted to see a vintage music hall revived and cared for just as lovingly, to provide a uniquely living link with our not so distant past.

But to return to the amazing and numerous family of William and Lauretta, my knowledge of them, in addition to the apprentice, Freddie Griffiths, who was always looked on as a son, runs as follows. The roll-call as I have it is: Laurina, Harriet, William, Theodore, Polynina, Lauretta, Josephine (known as Josey), Leonora, Leontine, Ernestine (known as Ernie), Frassetti, Madeline (known as Maddie), Clementine, Clare, Caroline and Lucretta, which means there were five more to whom I cannot even give names.

To begin with Freddie Griffiths, he went into partnership with a man called Ridgeway to perpetuate the double act the Brothers Griffiths, their specialities being animal parodies. They did an excellent lion and lion-tamer, but their most inspired creation was probably the Blondin Donkey. This was a parody of the Blondin Horse: a horse trained by an Italian performer, Corradini, to walk a twelve-yard rope above a net. (In fact, in the original act, the 'rope' was a board about nine inches wide laid on iron rods and with padding underneath simulated to look like rope.) The Brothers Griffiths were, it goes without saying, much in demand for pantomime. The Blondin Donkey featured in Augustus Harris's Drury Lane pantomime of 1887, *Puss in Boots*, and so they unknowingly played before Joseph Merrick, the Elephant Man, on the occasion when he was smuggled into the theatre to watch the show concealed at the back of the Baroness Burdett-Coutts's box.

After Mr Ridgeway's death, Freddie brought his son, Fred Griffiths Jun., into the act, which was introduced by his daughter, Miss Lutie, 'animal trainer'. In 1923 he scored a great success with his last creation, Horse Pongo, at the Royal Command Performance at the London Coliseum, as a result of which he was dubbed in the papers 'the man who made the King laugh'. After Freddie retired, Fred Jun. carried on the act with his sister Lutie and Harry Tate Jun.

Lauretta, Josephine, Leonora and Ernestine Matthews were the four sisters billed as 'The Midgets' who in due course formed the core of a noted act, the Seven Sisters Matthews – joined in this by Leontine, Frassetti and Madeline. They were all clever and versatile performers in their acrobatic displays, and the high musical point of the act came with all seven of them playing on xylophones or other instruments. The original four at one time also played the old-fashioned 'Harlequinade': Lauretta as Harlequin, Leonora as Columbine, Josey as Clown and Ernestine as Pantaloon. Josey, in fact, was the first lady tumbling clown, and Ernie was one of the foremost lady tumblers, renowned for her achievement of turning fifty flip-flaps on a table with her hands and feet tied.

At the Theatre Royal, Bolton, on 2 February 1891, the Sisters Matthews made a sizeable contribution to the benefit night of a fellow artist, Mr Lonnen Meadows, before the Mayor of Bolton, Matthew Fielding Esq. 'For this night only', ran the bill, the Halliwell Brass Band had 'kindly consented to appear' to play a Verdi selection and make 'Their First Appearance in Public in their New Uniform, specially made by J. Breen, Esq., of Huddersfield'. 'For this night only', Miss Ernestine Matthews would 'attempt the feat of throwing 30 Flip-Flaps with hands and feet tied. If she accomplishes it she will be presented with a Purse of Gold by a few of her Bolton Admirers.' After this came the 'Screaming Sketch', 'Have You Seen the Dog?', featuring the comedian Mr Meadows and carrying a guarantee that 'the number of Needles and Thread that will be required next morning to sew on the buttons that have dropped off through the yells of laughter, will be something alarming. Don't Miss It!' Then Miss Florence Carlile sang 'Lo! Hear the Gentle Lark', followed by the Sisters Matthews, in this case, Josephine, Leonora, Leontine and 'Flossett' (the bill printer's failed attempt to cope with the name Frassetti),

Josephine and Madeline advertise a Sisters Matthews double act in an
elaborate letterhead

playing the 'Vivandière March', then 'creating such a furore in Paris', on their mandolines.

So it continued, every item on the bill being exclusive to the night in question. Miss Leonora Matthews sang 'The Beautiful Mexican Girl' in full costume; Mr Fred C. Biron ('The Baron') sang a descriptive song, 'Outside the Cri'; Mr Lonnen Meadows sang a new song, 'The Ills of Life'; Mr Will Harvie gave his celebrated musical entertainment; Miss Lilian Mackley danced her 'Pas de Seul'; and 'the Canine Wonder, "Blood-drops" ' had 'kindly assented to appear'. And that wasn't the end of it. The audience could still look forward, after the interval, to the whole of the pantomime, *Cinderella*, written by Mr Meadows and starring himself as Buttons and Clown. I told you right at the start how much variety there was in variety. Do you believe me now?

Of those two clever little Matthews boys mentioned in the Wilton's review, Theodore, the eldest son, married a Miss Susie Harvey, who came from the Harvey family, another successful act on the international circuits. He died at the early age of thirty-three, in India where he was running his own circus. The second son, William, also died at thirty-three, in his case in Belfast. He had married Miss Annie Wilson, who was a daughter of the circus proprietor, John Wilson (with whose circus the Gregorys were touring in India at the time when my mother was being fostered in Birmingham). William left three sons, Edward, William and Theodore, who acquired a stepfather when Annie remarried, to Dan Fanning, a marionette man. Later Dan formed a partnership with his stepson Edward and daughter-in-law Jenny and her family, the Goddens. Together they presented the well-known act, Delvaine's Marionettes, founded by the son of a Dublin Cathedral organist in 1877.

Clementine, born with spinal trouble, was unable to follow the profession she loved so dearly. Her father bought her a little cottage in Billericay, Essex, where she and her husband ran a modest business selling firewood from a hand-cart. By all accounts, they were an exceptionally happy couple. Harriet married in the United States and died in the San Francisco earthquake of 1906. (A family link with the past was renewed many years later when her grandson came to London as a GI during the Second World War.) Frassetti toured the States, having formed with her first husband a refined harp and piano musical act, 'Les Frassettis'. She eventually settled in Los Angeles with her second husband, Ernest Bridgeman. Her sister Polynina also married in the States; in her case to a Mr Bates.

Madeline joined a show of world-wide repute, the circus of William F. Cody or 'Buffalo Bill', who will always be remembered for his Wild West shows, associated with such famous names as Chief Sitting Bull, Buck Taylor and Annie Oakley. She married 'Mustang Jack', or Jack Andrus, a rough rider with the show, her part in the act being to race the horses on a bicycle. They travelled together on some of the famous Cody tours of Britain. As the often-told story goes, when Cody first arrived on these shores, he found that George Sanger was running an item in his circus called 'Scenes from Buffalo Bill', featuring 'two real buffaloes, a number of unreal Red Indians, some good mules, and a rickety stage coach', to quote Sanger's own account. Cody took out an injunction to prevent Sanger using the number – an injunction Sanger defied. Cody took him to court, and lost his case. Sanger, however, had been greatly irritated by the constant references in the court record to 'The Honourable William Cody', and declared, 'Hang it! I can go one better than that, anyhow. If he's the *Honourable* William Cody, then I'm *Lord* George Sanger from this out!' And so he was, and the public loved it. The matter was even discussed in Parliament, but since Queen Victoria herself had gone along with calling him 'Lord George' when being shown around the Sanger menagerie, the honorary title remained with him till the end of his days.

After coming from the States with the Cody outfit, Madeline and Jack stayed on in England. For a time, Jack joined forces with Billy Burke, a famous Barnum & Bailey clown, to form an act called Burke, Andrus and Frisco, Frisco being a performing mule. The theatre historian W. Macqueen-Pope remembered seeing the act at the Argyle Theatre, Birkenhead, at the time of the Boer War, when it included 'a

92

delightfully pretty red-haired girl' who recited Rudyard Kipling's poem 'The Absent-Minded Beggar' very appealingly and was paid a guinea a week. This was Burke's daughter Billie, destined to be a star of musical comedy and Mrs Flo Ziegfeld, besides appearing in various films, one of her best-remembered movie roles being the good witch Glinda in *The Wizard of Oz*.

Eventually Madeline and Jack retired from the hectic life of a cowboy act, and, reverting to their non-stage name of Bleasdale, settled in Wales, where he became resident stage manager at the Palace Cinema, Britton Ferry, Glamorganshire. The Bleasdales had two daughters, Lorelai and Elvera. The former achieved brief fame when she swam out and rescued a pilot trapped in his cockpit during one of the Schneider Trophy seaplane races.

Now we come to Lauretta, who was always referred to as 'The Duchess' in the family – a very prim and proper lady from the first. She married a Mr Winn, who had been apprenticed to the Holdens, the most famous marionette act of its day. Naturally he therefore developed a similar act, called Haydee's Marionettes, and this suited Lauretta down to the ground, for marionettes were considered to be one of the most 'genteel' types of act. The Winns were successful and played all the No. 1 theatres. They had three sons, Victor, Henry and Harold, and since Lauretta wanted only the best for her family, she sent all the boys to boarding schools. Unfortunately Harold, a nervous and highly strung lad, could not stand up to the bullying and fagging and was soon marked down as a target. He died from a broken neck when he was tossed in a blanket. Not long after this tragedy, Lauretta suffered a further disaster. She broke both her legs when the 'bridge' on which they stood to manipulate the marionettes collapsed. In the end the family settled in Paris.

Leontine, like all her brothers and sisters, tried her hand at a great many things, but eventually settled down to a career as a violinist. Late in her life I met her in Manchester. While talking to her about playing the violin, I mentioned the chin-rest, and she said, 'Oh, you mean the feather bed. I prefer to feel the grip of my chin.' She was a very stout, bejewelled and jovial old lady by that stage. I didn't know it, but she was suffering from dropsy, today termed oedema. She died, alas, in very straightened circumstances, and was buried in a communal grave. The only thing of value she left was her fine violin.

Most circus people married within the profession, and Josey was no exception. Her husband was Baptiste, one of the three Brothers Léotard, an acrobatic team. His grandfather had run a gymnasium in Toulouse and his father was the famous Léotard, the originator of the flying trapeze routine with double somersault. Léotard Senior had originally practised over a swimming pool, with the help of his father, who swung the spare trapeze. Finally he perfected his timing. He was engaged to give his first display in the summer of 1859, but an attack of typhoid fever delayed his début until November, when his achievement was revealed to the world at the Cirque d' Eté in Paris. By later standards, his act was quite simple, but we do need to remember that it was a solo act as the idea of having a 'catcher' had not yet evolved. He was the first 'daring young man on the flying trapeze' and the forerunner of all subsequent aerial acts as well as the inspiration for George Leybourne's well-known and often revived song of that title:

> He'd fly through the air with the greatest of ease,
> A daring young man on the flying trapeze,
> His movements were graceful,
> All girls he could please,
> And my love he purloin'd away!

For Léotard's act, his father designed for him the special costume that came to be known as a léotard: the garment now universally used in ballet and dancing schools as well as by trapeze artistes. Sadly, he was never anything except a young man, for he died in his late twenties, probably from smallpox. But Baptiste and Josey carried on the family trapeze tradition for some years. Later, Baptiste took a job with a bank, and they settled in Paris, close to Lauretta.

Their only daughter, Hettie, also worked in the theatre until, in Russia, she met and married a Welshman.

Great-aunt Ernie was married by proxy to the comedian Tom Foy. As it happened, Paul ('Powell') Canzi, Arthur Gregory's former apprentice who had been like an elder brother to my mother, worked with Tom Foy and the Foy family in an act billed as 'The Five Foys – Fun in a Fiacre'. The Five Foys were booked some time in the 1900s to appear at the Argyle, Birkenhead, the renowned theatre run by the astute Mr Denis J. Clarke. (Mr Clarke had launched many careers, including that of Sir Harry Lauder, and held Lauder on an optional contract to play the Argyle each year for a fixed fee when his salary was rising astronomically elsewhere – though it is said that he voluntarily paid Lauder above the contract rate. Clarke also helped to pioneer the showing of films in variety theatres, since he arranged a demonstration of Edison's Vitascope projector to marvelling audiences back in 1896.)

On the occasion of the Foys' visit to the theatre, Mr Clarke came round to the dressing room beforehand and said, 'One of the acts is unable to appear. Can you help me out by doing another spot?'

'Well,' said Tom, 'I could put in a comedy sketch I've written, if it fits the bill.'

The Five Foys went down well, as they always did, but Tom's sketch, with himself playing the principal comedy part, was a sensation. By word of mouth alone, the theatre was packed nightly, and Tom received rave notices. 'Why waste time on the act?' said Clarke to Tom. 'You're a great comic. I'll book you a regular date here for the next five years.'

But Tom, perhaps thinking of the stories told of Clarke's hold over Lauder, said he would love to play the Argyle again, but if he did it would be on a separate contract. And so Tom, billed as 'The Yorkshire Lad', became a star comedian in London as well as the provinces. The following write-up from the north-east is typically fulsome:

Had the South Shields Empire been twice the size it is

doubtful if it could have accommodated all the people who sought admission to both houses. The theatre was completely packed out. A better programme for a holiday night could hardly have been devised. Tom Foy is undoubtedly the funniest artiste in his particular line of business who ever performed in South Shields. Paying a return visit, his reception last night was enthusiastic in the extreme. The famous little man appears with a company of several artistes (his wife Ernestine, etc.) including a remarkably knowing donkey in his sketch 'The First of April', one of the most comical turns that could be imagined. Tom and his donkey are outstanding figures in the sketch which owes its success primarily to the wonderful mirth-making proclivity of Foy. Indeed it would give a Sphinx some difficulty to keep a solemn countenance. Foy exploits the Yorkshire dialect to great account, and this adds not inconsiderably to the success of his remarkable fooling.

Tom quickly became one of the highest paid entertainers of his time, both in variety and pantomime, in which he played Dame. He was one of the first comedians to use a catch-phrase: 'What did I say when I coomed in?' His main sketches, as a Yorkshire lad in London who couldn't find the circus in Oxford Street and the famous donkey sketch, were recorded on wax discs for His Master's Voice. His last pantomime was in 1916 at the Opera House, Kingsway, in which a fellow star was Fred Emney Senior. Both men were dead not long afterwards. Tom had accomplished much in such a short time. He was only twenty-eight when he died in 1917.

Tom had bought a farm in Billericay, Essex, together with a pony and trap for recreation, but, like so many dedicated performers, he had no head for business and had never invested anything for the future. Well, he was still so young, so who could blame him? Everything he owned had to be sold, and all his widow ever received was the royalties on his records. Ernestine, having known more wealth in her few short years of married life than any other member of the family, moved to a basement flat in Paddington, where she kept house for a nephew, Jack Brennan, and accompanied him on his pantomime tours, for Jack was one of the most notable pantomime cats in the business. I remember Great-aunt Ernestine taking me to Hyde Park to see some celebrations associated with George V's birthday. A lovely lady, she lived to a great age, always cheerful so long as she could have a glass of Guinness at her elbow and a game of cards in hand. She was in her eighties when she upset a kettle of boiling water over herself, and was badly scalded. It was the pneumonia setting in after the shock that she died from.

As a *grande dame* of the family, Leonora was second only to Lauretta. I remember how, in my childhood, whenever Mother said we were off to visit Great-aunt Leonora, I knew I was going to have to be on my best behaviour. Leonora had been born on 20 October 1868 at Windmill Hill, Snenton, Nottinghamshire. Although she soon became a working member of the Matthews clan, it was dancing that was to have the greatest influence on her own career. In this she was inspired by an American dancer she had seen performing when she was a young woman. This was Loie Fuller (born in 1861 as Marie Louise Fuller at Fullersberg, Illinois), an actress, playwright, singer and dancer. In her dancing, 'La Loie Fuller', as she was often billed, was self-taught – an 'expressionist' dancer much admired in Art Nouveau and Symbolist artistic circles, her work and reputation in many ways prefiguring those of Isadora Duncan. Loie Fuller became a star turn at the Gaiety Theatre in London as well as all over Europe, and was famous for her 'serpentine dances', to which she gave titles such as 'Butterfly Clouds', 'Lily' and 'Fire'. The presentation involved the expressive movement of the body amid diaphanous flowing silks in front of magic-lantern slides and the use of experimental lighting effects.

Inspired by this example, Leonora put together her ideas for the kind of act she intended to present. She was already a trained ballerina, having studied under Enrico Cecchetti, who gave his own first solo performances at the age of five at La Scala, Milan, and who was a strong influence on the development of the Russian ballet. He had created two of the leading roles in Tchaikovsky's *Sleeping Beauty* and was ballet master to such stars of Diaghilev's Ballet Russe as Pavlova, Karsavina and Nijinsky. Later, when he had a studio in London, his pupils also included Ninette de Valois and Marie Rambert. Leonora therefore had the best possible grounding as a dancer, and added to her talent an artistic temperament as well as an unshakeable confidence in her own ability. She had her costumes made and employed an electrician to operate the magic lantern.

To supply the exotic touch of class she felt to be necessary, and taking advantage of the Foy connection through her sister Ernie's marriage to Tom Foy, Leonora adopted the stage name of 'Mademoiselle La Foy'. And she did indeed become a star as a classical picture dancer. The *Brighton Herald* for 19 January 1907 was extravagant in its praise:

A performance like that of La Foy . . . lifts a music-hall entertainment to a high level of merit . . . For sheer riot of colour, indeed, La Foy transcends a tropical sunset. She whirls through the whole gamut of colours – from dainty heliotrope to vivid green, then to a palest pink deepening to ruddy crimson, from flaming orange to a brilliant shimmering gold – until the dancer seems to be actually revolving in a fiery zone of gorgeous tints . . . The effect is to present a series of pictures absolutely dazzling in their brilliance. The snowstorms dance is a thing of delight; while the final tableau of La Foy bending over a glittering fountain strikes a note of repose which affords a beautiful contrast with the orgy of colour which had preceded it.

She was especially famous in Germany and Austria, and much sought after for commercial advertising, on cigarette cards and advertisements for soaps and shampoos and so forth. In February 1898, her portrait had been painted by the German artist Franz von Lenbach, who was known as the portraitist of Bismark.

Around this time she was also courted by and married Paul ('Powell') Canzi. Powell had, besides his work with the

98

Foys, continued to build on his talents as a clever animal trainer, first revealed during his period as an apprentice to Arthur Gregory from the age of six till he was twenty-one. At one time he was booked for a highly lucrative tour of America with his remarkable chimpanzee, Mish-Mash. Mish-Mash was kitted out for the voyage with a smart suit – jacket, trousers, waistcoat and so on – and once he got his sea legs began to enjoy the crossing. He was often to be seen turning somersaults on deck or sitting smoking a pipe in a deck-chair, and was a great favourite with passengers and crew alike. Unfortunately, it was decided to repaint the funnels during the crossing. Mish-Mash, not quite human enough to understand that the paint could be poisonous, licked some off and died. Signor Canzi arrived in the States without an act! There was to be no more animal training for Powell after marriage, however. Instead, he was to become 'Mademoiselle's' manager, besides taking over from the electrician as the magic-lantern operator. And since it was professionally necessary for Leonora to remain 'mademoiselle', Signor Canzi was always introduced to the public as her brother.

By the time I was taken to meet her in about 1921, Leonora had become a dancing teacher at the Royal Academy, where she made sure no one knew anything of her former connections with the circus. Drama, opera and ballet were legitimate art; music hall and circus were not. She had been a pupil of the great Cecchetti, and that was what counted. She was residing in Ackland Mansions, Cricklewood, and I remember a notice on the door that read, 'Please wipe your feet', and all the furniture being covered in dust-sheets. She took one look at me and said, 'Stand up straight! You're going to be round-shouldered.' She then produced a walking stick and proceeded to show my mother how to put it under my arms at the back to make me hold my head up at the correct angle.

After she became legitimate, Leonora took steps to organize a correspondingly respectable position for her husband. The story went that one morning she announced, 'Powell, I've arranged for you to go to Harrods for an interview.'

'Whatever do you mean?' he asked.

'They are advertising for interpreters. You should do that very well.'

'But they won't accept me,' protested Powell. 'I've no formal education. What on earth did you tell them?'

'I told them you had been with Thomas Cook in Paris. They expect you tomorrow.'

Knowing it was useless to argue, Powell agreed to go. He was certain he would be turned down as he had made up his mind to tell the truth about his background. When it came to it, however, he was given a chance to demonstrate his skills. After holding various conversations with the many foreigners working in the store, he was, much to his astonishment, accepted for the post. Being a man with a most pleasant personality, he remained, as Mr Foy, with Harrods for some ten or twelve years, dealing with visiting royalty and meeting such celebrities as Rudolph Valentino when they were in London. A testimonial card sent from the Hôtel Majestic, Paris, in July 1928 wished Harrods to know that a lady named Elrina Costa de Sala had been 'very well attended by Mr P. C. Foy, interpreter. She begs you to remember her his merits and take into account his intelligence when occasion would come.' I remember Powell as a gentle person who was never so happy as when he could call round, talk with my parents about the old days with the continental circuses and discuss philately with my father, their foreign travels having left them with a mutual enthusiasm for stamp collecting.

On 22 June 1931, my parents had gone up to the Theatre Royal, Coventry, but my brother Harold had stayed behind to spend a few hours with Great-aunt Leonora. By that stage she was a widow in her sixties, living in a flat in Bloomfield Road, Maida Vale. They went out for a walk together, and were standing on a traffic island when Harold let go of her arm to transfer the coat he was carrying on to his other arm. Leonora stepped off the kerb without him, and the next moment was thrown into the air by a motor-cycle, breaking both her legs and sustaining other injuries. With that misfortune, her career as a teacher at the Royal Academy came to an end. We thought she would never teach again, but, with typical Matthews determination, she fought back and within two years was taking private pupils.

Ten years after her accident, when I was in the RAF at Blackpool, training as a wireless operator and gunner and doing my 'square-bashing' on the promenade at Stanley Park, a letter arrived. Aunt Leonora would be in Blackpool to stay with her nephew, Ted Matthews (of Delvaine's Marionettes). She was delighted to see me in uniform, for she was nothing if not conservative and patriotic. Ted told me how they had sat on the promenade one morning, watching a corporal drilling his squad. The corporal had sought to impress the squad with his fitness by performing a handstand and some simple acrobatics – whereupon Auntie went up to him and began to advise him on the best way to improve his performance. The unfortunate drill instructor got the lot: the whole rigmarole of her days in the circus, how she and her sisters had been introduced to the Tsar of Russia and his family and were a star attraction at the reopening of the London Pavilion; and how she became a professor of dancing at the Royal Academy in 1914.

The old lady returned to London and resumed her private teaching, but it was not to be for long. Her career had been everything to her and there must have been much sadness for her in teaching other people's children, for she had no family of her own. She grew to be very melancholy and to suffer from insomnia. Eventually, she entered a private nursing home. On 17 July 1944, the house matron went into her room to find an empty bed and an open window. Great-aunt Leonora had made her last exit.

And what of William Frederick Matthews and his wife Lauretta, the founders of the remarkable Matthews clan? They spent their latter years together far from the sawdust and spangles, for William became a country gentleman on his farm at Billericay, Essex. There he would have had plenty of time to think as the memories flooded back. He had outlived three reigning monarchs and seen twenty-one prime ministers, from Peel to Asquith, come and go, and the great expansion of the British Empire. His thoughts were less likely to be of these things, however, than of his own world of circus and the changes, and the artists, he had seen: the mainly equestrian shows prior to 1850, the great days with P.T. Barnum not long before the outbreak of the American Civil War. The beauty of circus was its variety and internationalism. German tumblers were notable for their precision and military bearing; the Italians were graceful, the Spanish inventive; the British were fast and funny. But when it came to whirlwind tumbling, there were none to compare with the Arabs, while the Japanese, inventors of the perch, were poetry in motion.

If he thought of jugglers, those most likely to come to mind were two who could perhaps be equalled but never surpassed. First there was Paul Cinquevalli, originally a trapeze artist and later an acrobat. After a fall, he switched to a less demanding act, as did so many circus artists, though few were as successful. His most famous trick was to place a stemmed wine glass in his mouth. In this he put a billiard ball, and on the ball he balanced a regular-sized billiard cue, point downwards. Finally, he balanced two billiard balls on top of the cue, one on top of the other. He also performed a trick in which he caught a forty-pound cannon ball on his neck. A fraction out, and his skull could have been shattered like a nut. But if Cinquevalli was peerless, Rastelli could run him a close second. He could juggle nineteen objects at the same time – nine balls and ten plates. His greatest feat was juggling with ten footballs. Like so many other circus artists, he died young – at the age of thirty-one.

If William thought of leapers, it would be with considerable pride, for had he not beaten Jim Mires, the acknowledged biggest leaper of his day? William, moreover, had never used the long-run springboard from the ring doors: all his leaps were made from a small inclined deadboard, so small on stage that it could not be seen by the audience.

William had travelled the world, using virtually every means of transport then available: horses, horse-buses, trams, trains, sailing ships, steamships, paddle-steamers and the Underground (steam in 1853, electrified some thirty years later). But although he lived into the age of flight, he never flew. When, in 1909, Blériot flew across the English Channel, William drew his old-age pension. He also gave a talk on circus life, published in the *Evening News*. In this he expressed his feelings about how sad it was to have seen the passing of such men as Barnum and Bailey, though it made him happy to hear that his old employer, Lord George Sanger, was still in good fettle. (Only two years later, Lord George was brutally murdered, in his mid-eighties, by a crazed ex-employee.)

William and his dear wife Lauretta used to enjoy their trips to Brighton. They would go down in their pony and trap, a gift from the generous Lord George when he finally decided to retire in 1905 and auctioned his entire circus under the hammer, as auctioneer, of Tom Norman, 'The Silver King', famous among showmen for having brought Joseph Merrick, the Elephant Man, to London for exhibition in his freak shops.

Returning to Billericay from one of their trips to the south coast in 1915, William said he was feeling tired and thought he would go to lie down on the sofa for an hour. There, after sixty years of marriage and more then eighty-five adventure-packed years of life, he passed gently away. Some time after he had been laid to rest in Abney Park Cemetery, his wife and family commissioned stonemasons in Italy to sculpt a bust to go on his tombstone at a cost of some £300. Unfortunately the ship with the bust on board was torpedoed on its way to Britain, and a second one had to be made, this time by English stonemasons. It remains as his monument in the cemetery to the present day.

Apart from the farm, William also left in his will a butcher's shop, 414 High Road, Leytonstone, and the set of four terraced houses christened Lauretta Villas in Third Avenue, London E17. You will remember that it was at her home at Lauretta Villas that I met my great-grandmother during the First World War; it was there that she died, as peacefully as William ten years before, in 1925 at the age of ninety-one. I am confident she was reunited with her life partner. Lauretta Villas were sold for £200, and the butcher's shop went for

£700. The family solicitors were Porter & Crust, Bank Buildings, Billericay, Essex. They were still handling the family business in 1942 when my brother Harold took them to place in their vaults for safety a valuable coffee set willed to a niece in Los Angeles by Mademoiselle La Foy.

By founding the Matthews clan, with its many offshoots and branches, William and Lauretta gave pleasure to millions in the life of rings and curtains. Small wonder if, wherever I travelled, at home or abroad, my relatives seemed to spring up like mushrooms.

6

Three, Four, Five Whiteleys

Christmas 1920 was another I would never forget. My brother Paul, just fourteen, had taken his place in the act, so Mother wasn't working. When Paul came in with a mighty turkey slung over his shoulder, the landlady said, 'I can't cook that. I haven't a baking dish big enough.' So we bought one and presented it to her for Christmas. Our tree reached almost to the ceiling, and at its very top was a miniature violin. When it came to drawing for our presents on the evening of Christmas Day, I kept looking at the violin and hoping I would be the one to get the lucky ticket. It came to my turn to draw, there were only two tickets left, and, yes, I drew the violin. You can imagine my delight when it was handed down to me. What I didn't know at the time was that it had been intended for me all along. The winning ticket had been 'planted', so no one else could draw it. I didn't know either – nor could any of us – that it would be Paul's last Christmas.

On the following 6 June we travelled north to play the Empire Theatre at Seaham Harbour in County Durham. By this time the act, billed as the Henry Whiteley Four, consisted of Father, Ben, Harold and Paul. Paul had proved a very smart performer and Father's hopes were high for the future. He felt he now had a good act, 'quite out of the ordinary', with possibilities for 'good dates and increased salaries'; unless, as he added, God proposed otherwise. We didn't reach Seaham until six in the evening, so Father went straight to the theatre with Ben and Harold to set everything up for the act. Our landlady, when she met us at the door, told Mother that she was rearranging the sitting room as a bedroom for us because two of her children were ill. Mother said ever afterwards that she did not know what made her ask, 'Is it diphtheria?' No, no, the landlady replied, the doctor had said it was only tonsilitis. With that reassurance we decided to stay.

On the Tuesday night, at dinner, the landlady startled the family by saying she was very sorry, but it was diphtheria after all. I remember going to play on the beach one evening after the show, when Paul was listless and didn't join in. On the Thursday evening, during the second house, he complained of a sore throat, and by the next morning was very ill. The doctor came, declared that there was no sign of diphtheria and left him some gargle and medicine. But Paul grew steadily worse, and on the Sunday Father tried to summon another doctor. None was available. It had to be the same doctor as before, and this time the man said that it was diphtheria, gave an antitoxin injection and arranged for Paul to be admitted next day to the cottage hospital. I was packed off with Ben and Harold to Nottingham, where we stayed with a great-aunt.

On 20 June, as Father recorded in his memoirs, 'God took our Paul to his heavenly home.' The sad news reached us in Nottingham by telegram. Paul was the only one of those affected to die in the outbreak; the other children all recovered. At the Seaham Empire, a fellow performer announced the tragedy to the audience and a collection was taken up, amounting to £5 – a generous sum in those days. The townsfolk showed a lot of sympathy, and many of those who had seen Paul perform and had heard of the doctor's negligence and of the landlady taking us in when she shouldn't have done, turned up at the cemetery to pay their respects at the funeral. There was one kind soul who tended the grave for many years, and who regularly placed flowers

106

on it for us. But though a curtain may fall on one scene, it has to rise again for the next. Mother went back into the troupe until such time as Leonora would be old enough to take her place. To add to the family's troubles, Leonora fell off a wall and broke a wrist; and not long after that she developed whooping cough, though she soon recovered.

As the sad and upsetting year of 1921 drew towards its close, I can't say we were looking forward to the Christmas season which we were booked to spend in Roker, Sunderland. When we arrived at our lodgings, though, we found the decorations already up and a roaring fire awaiting us. The Christmas dinner was so perfect, the table so beautifully laid, that it would have been ungracious not to do it justice. Our landlady, Mrs Rowell, and her husband, a ship's pilot and football enthusiast, became great friends. After that, whenever we played in Sunderland, we always returned to the Rowells.

The only regret in the Rowells' lives was that they had no children. There came the occasion when Mrs Rowell told us, 'I've got a surprise,' and went to fetch a baby about a month old. It had been brought in a blanket by its real parents, and handed to Mrs Rowell for adoption. They christened the child Inga, her parentage being Danish, and over the years we saw her grow up into a delightful young lady in that warm-hearted household.

There is a saying in the showbusiness that if you've not played Ireland, you haven't lived. I can bear out the truth of the saying, because later on in my career I was to have some first-hand experience of working in the Emerald Isle. One aspect of the uniqueness of the experience was that few towns in Ireland possessed theatres, so most performances had to be put on in town halls or under canvas. Another aspect was the general sense of timelessness. Out in the countryside, a show might be scheduled to start at 8 p.m., but there wouldn't be a soul in sight as the clock came round to the hour. Gradually, however, there would be glimmers of light in the distance, like an invasion of glow-worms. This was your audience. Most of them were walking, their paths lit by candles in jam-jars. Others were on bikes, and the upper echelons came by horse and cart or jaunting car. By nine o'clock the tent would be full. As a local saying went, 'Don't worry, there's always tomorrow, and it's not been touched yet.' Ireland certainly had a character and life-style all its own, especially deep in the countryside, and playing the villages and hamlets among the peat bogs and semi-wildernesses brought one close to nature in the raw.

It was round about this time that the family toured in Ireland with Fossett's Circus, though the name was changed to Circus Heckenberg to get round the anti-English senti-ment existing in the country. On this occasion I wasn't with them, but my brother Harold noted down some of the stories of their adventures. Circuses in Ireland were certainly not among 'the greatest shows on earth'. The caravans were small, and it was impossible, said Harold, to go out in the night to relieve yourself without waking up everyone else. It was tenting at its most difficult, travelling daily, putting everything up, giving two shows, dismantling and packing everything away so as to be back on the road by six the next morning. It would usually be well past midnight before anyone got any sleep. The tent hands slept either in the 'big top' or under the caravans. Nevertheless the Irish circuses, like Duffy's, put on good shows with full performances, and the performers did wonderfully well, appearing in the ring with their costumes looking as fresh and clean as new in those days before washing machines and spin dryers. All you had to do the job was spit and polish. Mother would aim to change her riding clothes almost nightly. She also made satin riding-pad cloths to match each dress. (One of her dresses – whaleboned and in blue plush – was still in such good condition eighty years later that my wife was able to wear it as a costume for an old-time music hall.)

Medical attention, if needed, was difficult to come by, and the Whiteley caravan came to be known as 'the dispensary', since Mother always made a point of travelling with first-aid equipment and medicine to cover any routine mishap or malady. Because of this, she found herself acting as doctor and nurse combined. In that farming countryside, it was often easier to find a vet than a doctor, and as a result the animals in the show tended to be better catered for than the human beings.

Once, when they played at Lisdoonvarna in County Clare, in a circus field that stood on a hill overlooking the pleasant spa town, two drunks arrived just before the matinée performance was about to begin. The boss refused them entry, foreseeing they would be certain to disrupt the programme, and that evening the circus played to a full house and excellent audience. Then, just as the company started to take down the tent, they found themselves under attack from a group of six men throwing large stones into the site from the surrounding darkness and shattering many windows in the living caravans before trying to cut the main guy-ropes.

If the king pole had fallen, there could easily have been a fatal accident. All that the circus people could do was bring the circus lorries up to the front with their headlights full on and hope to dazzle their assailants while they continued packing. A member of the company who went to the local police station to ask for protection found he was apparently completely invisible and all his requests were ignored. Luckily, apart from one of the circus children, who was cut by broken glass, nobody suffered any injury except for minor bruising. They managed to harness the horses, start the engines and be on the road by 4 a.m., driving in the dark all the way to Corifin. There they learned that the two men refused admission were local butchers who'd got a gang of their pals together to do all the damage they could.

The Irish roads were certainly more suitable for mountain goats than transport, and the horse-drawn vehicles found the going easier than the lorries and trailers. Harold, who was driving a lorry with trailers, said he would never forget one morning at Ballycastle in County Antrim.

I was feeling particularly happy as I hitched up my three trailers and started to drive through the most delightful scenery, up and down the switchback roads. Passing a local postman, I bade him a bright, 'Good morning!' 'Hey, mister!' he shouted back, 'ye're on t'ree wheels.' I accepted this as typical Irish humour until, arriving at the market

109

square in Bush Mills and getting down from the driver's cab, I discovered that I was indeed on three wheels, and had driven into town on the axle bar. I found my missing wheel two miles down the hill from where I must have lost it. By good fortune, a local garage man saw the funny side of it and said he could repair the damaged hub. In two hours I was back on four wheels. He charged me £1 and a packet of Player's cigarettes.

On another occasion, when they were in the Protestant north, Harold had been left to cook the Sunday lunch while the rest of the family went to attend the service at a little local church. Before long, one of them was back with the message: 'You're wanted at the church.' He guessed why at once. The organist hadn't turned up and Harold was quite a good keyboard player. He protested that he could hardly cook lunch and play the organ at the same time, but there was a clown called Tommy Binsent who was sharing the Whiteley hospitality as he had no wagon of his own and slept in the back of a lorry. 'Just tell me what to do, and off you go,' said Tommy.

Everything was already prepared, so Harold explained carefully exactly when and how it should all be put in the oven. After that, it would only be a question of keeping watch as it cooked. Harold left for the church and played the organ throughout the service as brother Ben pumped the bellows. The vicar thanked them profusely afterwards, and they made their way back to the 'tober' (a piece of circus slang; it means pitch). As they neared the van, keenly antici-pating their Sunday meal, they saw smoke pouring from the top and bottom of the door. Tommy had fallen fast asleep and the food was a burnt offering.

Another time, after an early 5 a.m. start, they finished a long journey at the small town of Ahoghill in County Antrim. The circus had some sixty horses in its convoy, for the king and queen poles alone needed four horses to draw them. They found that, this time, the tent was to be erected in the market square itself, and that even after it was up they couldn't relax. The town's children came from far and near, 'screaming, banging on our living wagons, chasing the poor ponies'. Since any hope of a rest before the performance was out of the question, they decided to attend the service in a small mission tent also erected in the square.

The preacher tried his best, but, owing to the noise, he was fighting a losing battle. Desperately he asked the Almighty to let the service proceed in peace. Then, over the noise, there came another sound, at first a quiet pitter-patter but getting louder and louder. Rain! The other noises grew quieter and finally ceased. The rain again softened to a gentle pitter-patter and the service continued in peace. Coincidence! Well, who knows! Ireland is, of course, famous for its twelve-month rainy season.

They had a graphic illustration of the Irish weather down in Cork at Bantry Bay when a reservoir burst its banks and flooded the circus field. As it was an emergency, the town council allowed them to erect their tent on Bantry harbour square.

Fighting against the high winds, we eventually got it up, but, no sooner had we done so, than all hell broke loose! It was a real hurricane. We pushed our caravan to the side of the square and lashed it to a lamp-post. The next thing we heard was a crashing sound. The harbour wall had broken, and the tent, king pole, queen pole and all were in the sea. We managed to pull it all out, but it was a never-ending nightmare. At 2 a.m. we heard screams. The big trailer had been blown over with five bandsmen inside. We had to get them out of the windows. The following morning, naturally, was beautiful, and, with everything in need of repairs, we bade a sad farewell to Bantry Bay.

There was still a lot of superstition in the remote country districts, and although people were prepared to pay the circus a visit, they still confused circus folk with gypsies and tinkers and placed them among the Devil's people. In certain villages you might get there to find the village pumps padlocked

111

against your arrival. This would place you in desperate straits, since the pumps were the main source of a water supply and you had many travel-weary animals to water, apart from your own needs for cooking and washing. It was also necessary to deal with the fathers, the local priests, on many occasions. At one location the boss had words with a priest whose 'request' for payment he turned down as being extortionate. 'In that case,' said the priest, 'I shall have the bells rung and no one will come to your show.'

My brother Ben, who was acting as manager, protested, 'In our country we would call that blackmail.'

His indignation made no impression on the cleric. The bells were rung and no one came to the circus. The locals would never have dreamed of going against the father.

The situation could have its more humorous side. As a rule, it was agreed that, rather than a set sum, the circus would pay according to its receipts in that particular place. On one occasion, when the local father asked the inevitable question, 'Well, now, and what will the Church be getting out of it?' Ben replied, 'Well, father, it all depends on what sort of a day we have, but our boss is a fair man.'

The circus proved a good draw and, after the last show, the boss put a £5 note in an envelope and handed it to a tent hand to take round to the father. (Five pounds, of course, was no mean sum in those days.) Having opened the envelope and seen the banknote, the father asked the tent hand, 'And where would you be going next?' The tent man told him. 'Sure,' said the father, 'I know the father there very well. I'll write you a letter and you can give it to him.'

The tent hand brought the letter back to the boss, who, although it was sealed, decided to open it. Frustration! The letter was written in Gaelic. One of the tent hands knew Gaelic, however, and eventually a translation was produced:

Dear Father Murphy,
    It will be all right as regards letting the circus appear. They were no trouble, and it was worth a fiver, so I'm sure there is no doubt you will get the same.

★

112

Ben and Harold had been agitating for a while for Father to secure the act some engagements on the Continent. Eventually he was able to do so, and when he did it marked the start of my own travels abroad, with tours to Belgium, Holland and France. While we were in Paris, we lived off the rue Montmartre in a hotel called the Babylon. True to its name, it catered for the artists of every nationality who appeared at the Moulin Rouge, the Cirque d'Hiver, the Cirque Medrano, the Alhambra, the Olympia and the Petit Casino. Again, in Paris, I met relations: Father's sister Mary (the one who'd once had a circus in Java), Great-aunt Josey and her husband Baptiste Léotard, and Great-aunt Lauretta. Leonora and I also discovered that the theatre called the Cigalle was featuring a personal appearance by our heroine of the silent screen, Pearl White. In no time at all, we were round at the stage door, armed with our autograph books and asking where we could find her. 'At the Hôtel Carillon,' they told us. We made our way there and marched up to the reception counter to demand, in what was still our very limited French, to see Pearl White. They had to summon the hotel interpreter to find out what it was we wanted, and he agreed to ring through to Miss White's suite. 'Two English children to see you,' we heard him say, and five minutes later a lift door opened and there she stood.

We produced our books and asked her to sign her autograph, which she did, and then she asked us why we were in Paris. We explained that our family act was appearing at the Olympia Theatre. 'What do they do?' she asked. 'They're acrobats,' we replied. 'Are they real good ones?' she asked, shaking me by the shoulder. Then she added that, if we came to the theatre, she would see we got some seats.

Well, of course, we arrived back at the Babylon excited beyond measure, but Mother would hear none of it. On no account was she going to allow us to go to see the show. Naturally we were furious, but Mother did not see fit to explain her reasons. The bare fact was that the Cigalle, like many another Parisian theatre, was noted for its nudes. A little later on, short skirts and bra tops, leaving the midriff exposed, became standard chorus girls' attire – and certainly

113

trimmed back wardrobe costs! But when an agent suggested to Mother that she and Leonora should wear a costume on similar lines to liven up the act, she was most indignant and said, 'Bare midriff today, bare all tomorrow!' History was to prove her prophecy accurate.

When I was some years older, we played the celebrated Bal Tabarin, once one of the haunts of the painter Toulouse-Lautrec and famous for the can-can. By then I was a part of the act, which had thus again become, to Father's pride, the Five Whiteleys. (My own début was made at the Worksop Gaiety.) At the Bal Tabarin, a number of the dancers were English, but the spectacle ladies were all French and were booked for their nude posing, beautifully and artistically produced with special lighting and settings. In these more blatant times, it seems a pleasure to return to the days when it was the quality of presentation in an act that counted, and not achieving the maximum vulgarity, as so often seems to be the case today. The Five Whiteleys, incidentally, were very well received at the Bal Tabarin.

It delighted Father when he was able to arrange a six-week tour of Italy, the country of his birth, but the first difficulty we ran into was a problem with the Italian railways. They would not accept any item of luggage six feet long, and this meant that Dad's juggling table had to be cut in half. As a consequence of this, a centre board then needed to be made that could be bolted back together again. All of this added quite a bit to the weight we had to carry with us. Since the charges for excess baggage were quite an expense, we put as much as we could into our hand luggage. We even tucked angle irons inside our violin cases. It's surprising how a few extra nuts and bolts can drag you down, but all travelling performers were natural adepts at this sort of cost-cutting exercise. Back in Britain, you paid excess on the railway for anything on wheels. As a result, bicycle acts always made crates to take their machines. We had a pram as a part of our act. When we reached a station, one of my brothers would take its wheels off and pack it away in a hessian sack.

Our Italian tour was all set to begin in Bologna at the Arena del Sole, a new theatre. We were full of excitement, and had a good spot on the bill. Whether we were early or late on a bill, however, we always liked to leave plenty of time in hand so that, once we were dressed and made up, we could loosen up and relax. On the first night, as we sat in the dressing room, we heard the sound of stamping feet and whistles. English audiences whistle for more. Not so the continentals. With them it means getting the bird! Our excitement turned to apprehension, we went to the wings to see what was causing the rumpus. On stage was a German called Baron who performed a hopping act on his head, including a jump down from a table. This remarkable act was being booed from every direction for no good reason that we could conceive.

A local star came next: Ada Primavera, an Italian ballerina. Her performance was well received, and for her final dance she was given a standing ovation. Having taken four or so curtain calls, she retired to her dressing room. Still the audience shouted, 'Encore!' but she had no more to offer them and refused to return. Ours was the act that followed. Pandemonium! The Italians certainly don't do things by halves. They even ripped up the seats. It was a nightmare in which we stood not a chance of putting ourselves across, though we battled through to the end. By that time the stage was littered with every removable object the audience had been able to lay hands on. The next morning Father was summoned to the manager's office and paid off with just the one night's money. The rest of our dates were cancelled.

As we discovered later, an opposition theatre had sent in a claque to create a disturbance. In certain countries it was the custom to plant a claque in the audience to set the applause and laughter going when required. Each act would then be approached, and those that did not agree to pay up found themselves being shouted off the stage. In our case, the opposition had paid a claque to start trouble and wreck the evening. It was real Mafia stuff, and only the star ballerina, being Italian, was exempt from persecution. Father's one regret was that he had never addressed the mob in his fluent Italian. If only he could have got his presence of mind together he would have liked to say, 'I was born in this country, not many miles from here, in Modena, and I have played all over Italy. After many years away, I have returned with my family, telling them what a wonderful country this is, and how appreciative its audiences are. But times change, countries change, and yours certainly has, so it is with regret that I bid you, "Arrivederla!" [Goodbye], rather than, "Arrivederci!" [Till we meet again].' In fact, this was to be the last occasion when Father ever did return to the land of his birth.

So there we were, stranded in Italy. We decided to make the best of it and stay out the week since this was our, the children's, first visit to the country and we had a kind landlady. The landlady's daughter, a beautiful girl of about eighteen, undertook to be our guide and introduced us to the province of Bologna within the Emilia-Romagna region on the northern edge of the Apennines. Among the other sights she showed us, we saw, along the ancient vias or stradas, chess boards laid out in black and white mosaic on stone tables. We took a twelve-mile walk, ever upwards, with forests of Christmas trees on either side of us, to reach the magnificent church of San Petronio at the summit. We also learnt to exist like the poorer Italians on a diet of macaroni and a maize-based pudding called *polenta*. In the meantime, Father had been in touch with our Paris agents and established that there would be work waiting for us there when we got back to France.

At the end of the week we returned by way of the Simplon tunnel, travelling fourth class – dreadful, but cheap! By the time we booked back in at the Babylon we were virtually penniless and there was only a fortnight to go till Christmas. However lean our fortunes in our world of rings and curtains, though, we never let anything get in the way of the seasonal celebrations. Mother bought some bread puddings from Félix Pontin and a pound of turkey from the market, these to be cooked on a paraffin stove, known as a *flamme bleu*, that we had in our hotel room to do our own catering on. (The adjoining wallpaper was covered to protect it from the grease.) We could not afford a Christmas tree, but the spirit of improvisation blossomed as strong in us as ever.

116

We went round the market picking up any broken branches we could find and tied these to a broomstick. Mother, as always, had the decorations with her in the luggage, and once we'd finished the decorating the effect wasn't bad at all.

It is often remarked that the actor and the priest seem to have much in common. In February 1926, when I was fourteen, I was taking lessons in the Catechism leading up to confirmation. These were arranged for by a society called the Actors' Church Union (the ACU). (Its Catholic equivalent was the Actors' Guild.) Ministers and priests would visit theatres and circuses, meeting performers in their dressing rooms, praying with them and offering christening, confirmation, wedding or even funeral services when required. In those days, the ACU had a fine headquarters in Shaftesbury Avenue, the heart of London's theatreland. At its head was Father Kingsbury, a wonderful personality, a polio victim. He was unable to walk without sticks, but would always travel to wherever he was needed, no distance being too great. The ACU possessed a model theatre, perfect in every detail from flies and lighting switchboard to the advertisements for Bass beer on the dressing-room mirrors. This model was regularly toured around to raise funds for the ACU's continued services to the profession, which included grants for acting and dancing schools.

While we were appearing at the Theatre Royal, Hepburn-on-Tyne, the Revd Marr of St Cuthbert's Church, who was giving me final instruction, arranged for me to be privately confirmed by Bishop Henson, the then Bishop of Durham. After I had been confirmed in Durham Cathedral, the bishop invited us all to tea at his palace. It was a painful experience. We had all recently been vaccinated, and the bishop, a hearty man, was given to emphasizing any point in his conversation by slapping whomever he was addressing on the arm. He showed us a picture of one of his predecessors, a distinguished looking man who carried a sword. He had been a prince as well as a bishop, Bishop Henson explained, and while he had, as a prince, been able to kill in battle, he had,

117

as a bishop, been able to grant himself absolution. Then the Bishop gave me a book of advice he had written, called *Letters to a Godson*. From this I learnt that his nephew was Leslie Henson, the musical-comedy star and actor-manager. My brother Paul, who had died in such tragic circumstances, was confirmed by the Bishop of York (later Archbishop of Canterbury), Cosmo Lang, and Dr Lang was a cousin to Matheson Lang the actor, long remembered for his roles in *The Wandering Jew* and *The Chinese Bungalow*.

Father had taken the plunge to become confirmed at the age of fifty-four, so once I was confirmed as well we could all, to Mother's joy, take communion together. Her own first communion was to have been in Turkey when the Gregory Equestrian Circus of the World was appearing in Constantinople. The English vicar there had become friendly with the family and arranged to prepare her for confirmation by the Bishop of London when he visited the country at the end of a European tour. Unfortunately, the Moslem month of Ramadan then created difficulties for the circus which they hadn't foreseen and it left Turkey before the bishop arrived. Not until ten years later, when she was appearing with the renowned Circus Carrée, did the chaplain of the English church in Amsterdam arrange for her to be confirmed and take her first communion. To carry these links and coincidences (if there are such things) further, this was the church where I now took mine, since we were booked to play at the Flora Theatre in the city. I therefore knelt at the same altar as Mother had done about forty-five years before, and the same clergyman, by that stage a very old gentleman, officiated.

While we were still in Holland, the vicar of the English Church in Rotterdam asked us to give a show at the Sailors' Rest. Would it be possible, we asked, for someone to pick up our props and tumbling mat? 'Oh,' said the vicar, 'you won't need a carpet. You'll have the honour of performing on the carpet from Captain Wyatt's cabin' – Captain Wyatt being a famous hero who had rammed a German submarine during the First World War.

Returning from the Continent, we opened New Year 1927

in Sunderland, where we stayed, as usual, with our friends the Rowells. The following March we struck a bad patch. We played in Greenock, but then had a couple of vacant weeks without pay before going on to the Pringles Cinema, Edinburgh. There, after the Monday-night opening, Leonora said, 'I don't feel very well.' Neither did I, I chimed in. We were both complaining of sore throats, and that was a particular worry to Mother, who was troubled with her own throat for years after losing Paul from diphtheria. The doctors of those days told her that she suffered from a 'sympathetic throat'; today they would explain it as psychosomatic.

At one point in the act Ben stood on Harold's shoulders as they both played their violins, and I, also playing the violin, stood on Leonora's shoulders as she played the piano. When it came to this spot on the Tuesday night, Leonora's shoulders were shaking and my legs were like jelly. Mother sent for a doctor, who said we had severe tonsilitis and certainly shouldn't work. Father then needed to negotiate with the management to make the Five Whiteleys act into a trio, and needless to say also had to agree to take a cut in salary. By the Thursday, Leonora and I had both came out in a rash. The doctor returned and pronounced our trouble as scarlet fever, then still an illness to cause concern, though it has since lost its virulence. We were both packed off to the Isolation Hospital at Collington, outside Edinburgh, and the following week Ben joined me as a fellow sufferer in the men's ward. He was able to tell me that Mother had sent little Raymond off to Father's sister in London, and that while he was there, the health authorities had called, examined him and discovered that he was a carrier though himself completely fit.

It was then decided that we should, while still in hospital, have our tonsils out. I remember being wheeled into the operating theatre and surrounded by a ring of masked faces before my own face was covered by a mask on to which ether was poured. It was a frightening experience for anyone, let alone a child.

Poor Father, with most of his act in sick bay, was not at

119

this point even able to plan ahead. There was no access to the dole or such things as supplementary benefits in those days. Harold meanwhile, having escaped the fever, went round to the theatre to check if there was any mail for us. While he was there, he met an act we had worked with before, a man known as Egoes the Armless Wonder. Egoes travelled on his own and could do a great many things with his feet, such as shaving, playing the accordion, drinking – so long as the cup had a handle – and drawing lightning sketches. Besides his stage act, he was an accomplished painter who enjoyed royal patronage. Queen Mary would meet him personally off the train, and drive back with him in a pony and trap to the stables at Sandringham, where he painted portraits of the royal horses. He had also been responsible for designing the war memorial in his home town: Heacham in Surrey. Egoes asked Harold to give him a hand with his act – the joke being unintentional – and said he would pay him for the week; and Harold was most grateful for this piece of employment at a time of financial hardship for us.

At last we were due to be discharged from hospital, but before that could happen we had to take what was termed the 'end of fever'. This was a special bath that made the skin peel off, much like a snake's (the medical term is desquamation). With that done we re-emerged, after six weeks, into the world and Father was able once more to look to the future. During our first week back at work, we found we were turning in a rather shaky tumbling performance, but by the end of the week we were practically back to normal.

The signs of decline in circus were still not too obvious at this period. As you will have gathered, the silent cinema did not affect the livelihoods of live performers too adversely and ciné-variety provided a lot of work for vaudeville entertainers, even if there was no big money in it. The wireless, too, did not really constitute any sort of a threat when it came in during the 1920s. In fact we all became radio enthusiasts. I purchased an attaché case from Woolworth's and got the components together bit by bit as funds allowed: variable condensers, fixed condensers, power triode valves, grid bias

120

accumulators that had to be charged, Daventry cells. What an excitement it was when I finally had it all assembled and it actually worked! I felt a very clever lad. It seems a far cry from my portable briefcase wireless to today's ubiquitous Sony Walkmans.

There was at this time a Mr Grapho who thought highly of the family and with whom we worked a great deal. He put on a fine pantomime, *Beauty and the Beast*, in which we featured. The first half ended with a patriotic finalé: flags, historical personages, 'Rule Britannia' and a bulldog that sang to the tune of 'Land of Hope and Glory'. This dog was an absolute menace. If it caught you sitting down, it would jump into your lap, after which you did not dare to move a muscle unless you wanted your hand bitten off. All you could do was sit there petrified until it decided to get down of its own accord. Mr Grapho was the only person who could stroke the animal with impunity.

Mr Grapho also ran revues and summer shows at Clevedon and Saltburn, and so it came about, after the pantomime season of 1928, that we began to work in revue, however apprehensive we may have felt about being on the same bill as the aforementioned bulldog. Now the word *révue* is French, of course, meaning 'survey', but according to Father there had long been a revue type of entertainment in Spain, though the Iberian revue tradition was mainly satirical and had political overtones, as did so much of European cabaret. The English and American revue tradition was never so political, though it was adapted from the French pattern, and originally took off in the 1890s. Broadway was first in the field with *The Passing Show* in 1894. The very first true English revue, entitled *Pot-Pourri*, was produced in 1899, and in its wake the great names in London revue were to follow and flourish: Harry Gabriel Pélissier (who was Fay Compton's first husband, and who died in 1913), Albert de Courville, Alfred Butt, André Charlot and C. B. Cochran. In the United States, *Ziegfeld's Follies* had its first edition in 1907, and the next year in London Pélissier put together a revue that was an instant success with the public. The company for *Pélissier's Follies* all wore pierrot costumes, a style of presentation that sprang from the beach and 'end of the pier' shows of late Victorian England. As soon as the idea of a revue was established in the capital, revues began to spring up at theatres and concert-party entertainments all over the country.

Many of these provincial revues were very successful, though they did tend to have a strong regional flavour and not to travel well, especially in their comedy elements. But every revue, whether it was metropolitan or provincial, followed the same sort of format: dancers or chorus, comedian and straight man, speciality acts, full-length sketches (one in the first half and another in the second), blackout cameos and picture numbers. The blackout cameos were a series of three or four very short, snappy sketches, of which the following might be a typical example:

[On stage a box-office mock-up with a notice board advertising *The Miracle*]

MAN [speaking in broad Scots dialect to GIRL in box-office with the COMIC standing in the queue behind him]: I'll have twa of your best seats, if you please, and a box o'chocolates.

GIRL: Will this box do?

MAN: No, nae the small one. I want the biggest and most expensive box you've got. [Takes it and moves off stage]

GIRL [to the COMIC, who is next in the queue]: Have you come to see *The Miracle*?

COMIC: No thanks, I've already seen it.

[BLACKOUT]

The picture numbers usually closed the first half. They would consist of the company in costume – gypsy, Spanish, French, Dutch or whatever, or perhaps dressed for an occasion like Derby Day – for a song and dance medley, with the comic putting in a comic song or a gag in the middle. Tin Pan Alley was a great supporter of revues. Such song publishers as Feldmans, Francis Day & Hunter, Walsh Holmes, Irving Dash and Brons were ever ready to provide full orchestrations for anything from 'Three Blind Mice' upwards. No matter what country was used as the background for a picture number, there was always an appropriate piece of music available. This service was free to producers and performers, the music publishers relying for their pay-off on the advertising impact the show or act had on the public, who would then hopefully want to go out to buy their piano arrangements or hit-song music sheets. Today's music, with its emphasis on sound and the so-called 'beat', has so much less to offer stage performers.

During the run of Mr Grapho's revue, we learned that he had booked it to play for a week at Seaham Harbour. We had never been back to perform in Seaham since Paul's death, which had made it a fateful, ill-omened sort of place for us. Father decided that it would be better for Mother and all of us to take that particular week out. He explained our reasons to Mr Grapho, who said he quite understood. One of the ladies in the show offered to take some flowers to place on Paul's grave on our behalf, and we gladly accepted. As we were carrying the flowers up the stairs to the dressing room, we passed the kindly Mr Grapho, who remarked how beautiful they were. And so we remained behind as the show went on its way to Seaham Harbour. During the week, Mr Grapho became ill, and that weekend he died, seven years after the death of my brother. Since he was a Liverpool man, Mrs Grapho arranged for his body to be taken from Seaham to Liverpool by road. She sat all the way on one side of the coffin, and the bulldog sat on the other.

Mrs Grapho in fact continued with her husband's business, and we played in another Grapho pantomime at the City Varieties Theatre, Leeds, in 1929. At about that time we also worked in revue with Harry Russell. Revues could also have linking ideas or themes, and this particular show was *Try This One*. It was so titled because Mr Russell had an arrangement with the Radiance Toffee Company of Doncaster, who supplied boxes of caramels that also featured the title of the show, thus serving to advertise both their toffees and the entertainment. Toffees would be thrown to the audience at each performance and, needless to say, none of us went short of sweets during that particular run.

The theme in this case was built around a chase after a top-secret toffee recipe. This allowed licence to shift the action from one part of the world to another – to incorporate a comedy bullfight in Spain, the can-can in France, and so on. Comedy involving cars was also quite popular at this time, as in the well-known sketch 'Motoring', with Harry Tate and his waggling moustache. The car we used in *Try This One* still had its running board but no engine. The back axle was put through the wheels off-centre so that, drawn across the stage by a wire, the vehicle lolloped like a tank. During the sketch it had carpets beaten on it and dustbins emptied into it among other indignities, and at one point the comic, Mr Russell, had to emerge from under the chassis with his wig on fire. This effect was achieved with a special methylated spirits gadget. It was my job, hidden behind the car, to work the special effects, explosions and whatever, and set the wig alight. One night the gadget had broken slightly away from the wig, the meths leaked and the whole wig went up in a spectacular blaze. Mr Russell rushed off-stage a bald-headed man, but came back to finish the scene with a full head of hair. 'You must try my hair restorer some time,' he told the audience.

Back in 1927 an ominous event for us had occurred in America when Al Jolson first spoke on screen in *The Jazz Singer*. After that, the rush was on to produce the talkies, and Alfred Hitchcock's *Blackmail*, the first British film with a soundtrack, came out in 1929. The silent films had been all very well but the public had continued to expect music and song as a part of their entertainment. The talking pictures sounded a death knell, however, not only for many stars of the silent screen who could not adapt, but also for many stage acts who needed their ciné-variety dates to keep them going. Theatre and cinema managers up and down the country were quick to realize that all they required now to bring in the crowds was a talking-picture projector and a projectionist. They no longer needed to have to stand the expense of an orchestra, a stage manager, stage hands, flymen and all the other members of the team involved in putting on live acts. They could hardly be blamed, especially when, in the smaller provincial towns, touring revues were often playing to empty seats. However could such shows have hoped to go on competing with anything of the nature of MGM's first spectacular musical, the '100% All Talking, 100% All Singing' *Broadway Melody* of 1929, which ran at local cinemas continuously from one in the afternoon until eleven at night, seven days a week, and had a sequence in Technicolor?

The first performers to be hit hard by the advent of the talkies were the musicians. At about that time we were staying in London in Kennington Park Road, next door to the Kennington Theatre (formerly the Princess of Wales Theatre), with its fine frontage and eighty- by fifty-foot stage. Like many another theatre, the Kennington had converted into a cinema and foregone its licence for live performance. It was a mournful sight in July 1929 to see, after the last of the silent screenings, the little band of musicians coming out for the final time. Billed for the following week was the sound film, *My Man*, featuring one of the new queens of the cinema, Fanny Brice, who had first risen to stardom on stage as a protegée of Flo Ziegfeld's in the *Ziegfeld Follies* revue series.

Talk of Kennington reminds me of another curious 'theatrical digs' story, about the time we entered a somewhat grubby kitchen in search of a cooking utensil but found not a pot or a pan in sight. The reason for this marked absence was that provided instead was a collection of every conceivable type and size of empty tomato can. I have often wondered how many of those who stayed in that particular lodging realized they were coming so dangerously close to a severe bout of food poisoning. Another time, when we were staying not far away at St George's Circus, Waterloo, we encountered a strange gentleman as a fellow lodger. He would walk about carrying an Angora rabbit that seemed to be his sole companion. We arrived home one night from the Surrey Theatre, where we were playing, to find the landlady in a terrible state. She had gone out into her garden in the moonlight, and there encountered her lodger in a drunken frenzy waving a carving knife. In the other hand, he held the struggling rabbit by the ears, and before her very eyes proceeded to decapitate his beloved pet before himself falling to the ground. When he came to his senses, he was literally heart-broken. It emerged that his name was F. Brooke Warren and that he was author of a celebrated melodrama of the 1880s, *The Face at the Window*.

In that same year of 1929, Ben, my second from eldest brother, was married at St Mark's, Kennington, the church in which all the family had been christened, except for Harry, the eldest, who was born in Germany. Ben's bride was Laurel Wynne, a dancer, whose mother ran a dancing troupe, the Wynne Juveniles. It was a real circus and theatre wedding, the guests including Whiteleys, Gregorys and Duffys. The reception was held at Pam Pinoli's Restaurant in Wardour Street, and afterwards the happy couple set off to honeymoon in Paris. I shall always remember Ben's wedding for one reason in particular. At that time it was customary for shorts or knickerbockers to be worn by boys until they were twenty-one. This I resented, and, although I was still only seventeen, I set up a campaign of protest against stiff opposition from the family, especially from Mother. Happily Ben's bride-to-be, Laurel, proved a staunch ally and took up the cudgels on my behalf. Thus I attended the occasion in a full suit with long trousers and never wore knickerbockers or shorts again.

Meanwhile, despite all the changes that were coming to pass in the world of entertainment – silent pictures, radio, talking pictures – there were still a good number of theatres and circuses in operation, and there were some cinemas that changed back over to panto at Christmas time, since pantomime remained a great draw during the season. Pantomime still had and still can have its magic. I was taken to see my own first pantomime in 1922–3. It was *Beauty and the Beast*, starring the comedian Bunny Doyle and featuring the Whiteleys as a speciality act. To this day I can remember two of Mr Doyle's comic songs, though I was only eleven at the time. The words of one of the songs ran:

In our little garden sub bub,
Far away from the noise and hub bub,
There you can grow stewed rub bub,
Have a bath in the old rain tub bub.
So leave all the hub bub, the pub hub and club hub,
And grow your own grub bub in our sub bub.

The other was an audience participation song with the nonsense refrain, 'Wy ky walla walla up bar bay'. Comic songs were commonplace in those days. In the present time they have become rarities. Whatever the reasons for this, long may pantomime survive to take people, regardless of age, out of themselves and for a few moments into the land of make-believe. Pantomime is, from a performer's angle, very different from any other kind of show. Sad to say, there are many today who do not understand or respect the traditions of pantomime and who strive to modernize something that cannot be modernized. Yet, if you stay true to its traditions, pantomime is still capable of casting a spell. What is it all about, then? Well, if you would care to join me in a brief digression, I will treat you to my personal view of it.

7

Pantomime – a Digression

Mime – to me it's the most descriptive of four-letter words: the language of sign and gesture, perhaps the first language known to primitive man, and an international mode of communication. The last great popular flowering of mime came during the era of silent cinema, particularly in the silent comedies. Today mime is maybe looked on as a rather specialized branch of theatre, but it always was at the heart of that curious hybrid which is said to perplex Americans generally and foreigners at large: the traditional English panto. Of course, today and for many years past there has been a lot of talk going on in pantomime, which, before we go any further, might seem like a contradiction in terms. In his book *Christmas Pantomime* (1934), Mr A. E. Wilson tells how he was showing some German visitors round London.

We paused to admire the portico of the Lyceum, which they recognized as part of the old home of Irving. They looked at the posters and were interested to see that pantomime was being performed.

'So you have pantomime in England,' said one.

'Yes,' said I, 'pantomime with words.'

'Pantomime with words? That is very funny. In England they have pantomime with words.'

128

The astonished foreigners roared with laughter at this excellent example of English eccentricity.

For the roots of English pantomime, we have to go back to the form of theatre known as the Harlequinade. This was derived in turn from the Italian *commedia dell'arte*, which came to England by way of France during the seventeenth century and, in the course of its travels, underwent various transformations. The *commedia dell'arte*'s long list of stock characters included such personalities as Arlecchino, Columbina and Pantaleone, all of them known by their masks. Another of these characters, Pulcinella, arrived on our shores during Restoration times and evolved into the Mr Punch of the English puppet shows.

Theatre historians still mull over such questions as to who it was who first presented Harlequin as a character on the English stage and how the character of Clown came to be introduced. Clown in fact seems to be an English innovation in the simple comedy drama of the story of Harlequin's wooing of Columbine against the wishes of her father, Pantaloon, and the mischief and chases that are then set in motion with the help and hindrance of Clown. But while the story may seem to be basic, a wealth of variations have been wrung from it over the centuries.

In the history of pantomime, one thing that is certain is that it was John Rich, a theatre manager and actor, who invented what he called his pantomimes – entertainments, often based on classical themes, that were woven around and about the character of Harlequin. Rich was the first producer of John Gay's *The Beggar's Opera* at his Lincoln's Inn Fields Theatre in 1728, and with the money made from that smash hit of the day, he built the first Covent Garden Theatre. Here Rich himself took the lead role of Harlequin and famously played him in dumb show under the stage name of Lun in various productions. The great actor David Garrick wrote of Rich in action:

When Lun appeared, with matchless art and whim
He gave the power of speech to every limb;

Tho' masked and mute, conveyed his quick intent,
And told in frolic gesture what he meant.

What better description could there be than this of the
magic of mime? The masks in Rich's day were still full-
faced. By the start of the nineteenth century they'd become
the domino half-mask. Convention had it that, if the mask
was up, the character was visible, if down invisible. Other
changes to come about by the 1800s were more elaborate
plots into which the Harlequinade business could be incorporated. The great comedian Joseph Grimaldi then transformed the part of Clown, hitherto a subsidiary role, into a
star attraction. So famous was Grimaldi's Clown that the
white-faced clown has in general ever afterwards been called
'Joey'. It will be remembered that my great-grandfather,
W. F. Matthews, also played Clown; and that my Great-
aunt Josey was the first lady to play a tumbling Clown.

There are clowns for all occasions. They can range from
the poor fool in *King Lear* to Feste, wise enough to play the
fool, in *Twelfth Night*. There are sad clowns, happy clowns,
tumbling clowns and musical clowns. There is also the
Auguste, with ragged hair and baggy clothes, who acts as a
foil to the more elegant and stylish white-faced clown. It is
said that the Auguste's originator was Tom Belling, acrobat,
rider and juggler, when he was playing in Germany with
the Rentz Circus. There was a rule that any artist who failed
to be in his or her dressing room by half an hour before the
performance must enter by the box office and pay top price
for admission. Tom, who was in the habit of lingering over-
long in beer halls, was constantly caught out by the rule, so
one night he disguised himself in a red wig and put his coat
on back to front before he tried to enter unrecognized. As
he attempted to sidle in, he bumped straight into Mr Rentz
himself and fell through the ring doors in surprise. The
audience roared, and Tom, being a superbly instinctive artist,
played up to the laughter. Then someone shouted out,
'Dummer Auguste!' (the German for 'stupid clown'), and
'Auguste' became the descriptive term for a clown of that
type.

130

Clowns are often recognized by their appearance and a clown's make-up has become something individual to him alone. All clowns have their own tricks or idiosyncracies. That of Raymond Daniel, the Gregorys' own baby clown, was to tie his hair in a top-knot – a trick I often copied. My brother Harold's own special creation was Clown Rainbow, known for his costumes of many colours; the name was taken from the *Rainbow*, the children's comic of our youth. But it is a mistake to think that clowns need make-up or make-up makes a clown. With the decline of circuses in size and number, a tendency has crept in to put make-up and costume on tent-men and grooms and send them into the ring. It has been a sad deceit.

As the nineteenth century got under way, pantomime began to be associated more specifically with the Christmas and New Year season. Previously pantomimes had been put on at any time of year. Grimaldi's greatest hit was *Harlequin and Mother Goose; or The Golden Egg*, presented at Covent Garden for a triumphant season from 29 December 1806. Grimaldi played Squire Bugle and Clown, and Mother Goose was played by a Mr Simmons, so we can see that the male Dame tradition also goes back a long way. It was no doubt inevitable that, with the passing years, the Harlequinade should gradually lose its pride of place. Attempts were made to preserve it as an ever-dwindling component, notably in the great Drury Lane pantomimes under Sir Augustus Harris's management in the 1880s and 1890s, and later at the famous Britannia Theatre, Hoxton, which was said to be the last home of the true Harlequinade. Eventually it disappeared altogether, but its spirit – and this is the real point of what I'm saying – is still there behind every pantomime that's true to the tradition. Perhaps the day will come when we shall see the mime put back into pantomime in some form or other, for the very oldest things in theatrical tradition do have a way of coming full circle for new generations.

Of course, pantomime has always been open to change and innovation. It would be ridiculous to suggest going back to candles for lighting. But while it may be necessary to keep up with the times, it is also the essence of theatre to follow tradition. The apparatus introduced by Kirby's Flying Ballet early in the twentieth century, with its line, hook and safety harness, represented a great technical advance on its predecessors but still conformed to the spirit of the original: fairies were intended to fly, and no one is likely to object if they start to fly better. By tradition, the forces of evil (such as the Demon King) enter left, and the forces of good (such as the Fairy Queen) enter right. By tradition too, there should be a happy fairy-tale ending as the Prince and Princess are the last two characters to enter down the palace steps for the grand finale. When such traditions are broken by star comedians or so-called media personalities coming down last and upstaging the grand finale, or by vulgarizing the 'immortals', then to my mind it amounts to a sad state of affairs.

Many years ago, when he brought in famous comedians from the music halls to play Dame and other comedy parts, Augustus Harris was severely criticized. This intrusion might, it was feared, introduce unsuitable material, with dubious songs and suggestive dances. To some extent, this did happen, but eventually the two elements blended satisfactorily and, indeed, proved an immense success with Dan Leno in his famous dame roles and Little Tich performing his big-boot routine, balancing on the tips of his long boots and leaning forward at an acute angle, as if nailed to the stage.

Drury Lane's *Humpty Dumpty* of 1891 must have been memorable for all those who were fortunate enough to see it. Little Tich took the title role, Herbert Campbell and Dan Leno were respectively King and Queen of Hearts, and Fanny Leslie was principal boy. The *travesti* role of principal boy was also by then long established in pantomime and could, like so many other elements, be traced back to some of the most ancient roots in the theatrical tradition, besides artfully providing a bit of a treat for the fathers. But children always were an important part of the appeal of pantomime. When Drury Lane became the great home of pantomime in central London, they used, it is said, to take children, many of them nearly starving, from the streets to appear in the shows. Joey Grimaldi's cry of, 'Here we are again!' every time he made a fresh appearance, was aimed at catching the attention of the children in his audience.

All comedians were, at one time, expected to learn the tricks necessary to pantomime – to take a fall, for example, and to take the 'knap', meaning that when one gets slapped one makes the sound by slapping one's own hands in a way that's convincing to the audience. The brokers' men, the Chinese policemen, the robbers in the wood were all expected to provide a comic acrobatic speciality and to link it in with the narrative of the panto. Whenever I played Buttons in *Cinderella*, for instance, I would work in a valid reason for performing my own speciality act by explaining that, as I was going to have to entertain the Prince at the ball, I would first just like to try out my routine on them, the audience.

One feature that never failed to engage the children was the chase, a Keystone Kops type of extravaganza involving the use of traps. There are two kinds of trap. The first are the stage traps, where players are shot up from below stage or swallowed down through the floor; and the second are the scene traps – windows, revolving doors, collapsible stairs. The finest exponents of this sort of fast comedy were the Lupinos, a truly theatrical family of pantomimists descended from an Italian puppet master who came to England in the seventeenth century. A Lupino had been apprenticed to John Rich at his Lincoln's Inn Fields Theatre, and a later generation was closely associated with the pantomimes at the Britannia Theatre, Hoxton. The 'Old Brit', as it was known, was founded by Sam Lane and run by his widow, Sara, for many years after his death. Sara's favourite niece, Charlotte Robinson, married Harry Lupino, and their son, Henry George Lupino, was given the name Lupino Lane to honour his Great-aunt Sara. The Lupinos of that generation learnt much of their business from working at the Britannia, which had the largest stage in the country and was noted for its stage traps. My mother, incidentally, possessed a fine brooch that had been given to her by Sara Lane.

133

The Harlequinade was a considerable rarity by the time the Doncaster comedian and producer, Harry Russell, decided to revive it for the 1930–31 pantomime at the Theatre Royal, Huddersfield. On this occasion it was performed by the Whiteley family and the Olvas Brothers, my brother Ben playing Harlequin to my sister Leonora's Columbine. I landed the part of the errand boy. The show made much use of the scenic traps, which were fitted with catches at the back to secure them when they were not in use. You ran and dived through them off-stage (breaking your fall on tables with mattresses), and then rolled out of a lower flap to come back on stage facing the audience. Our safety depended on the efficiency of the stage staff. It doesn't take much imagination to think of the consequences of taking a dive at a trap which had the catches unreleased, or of going through a window and finding there was no table and mattress in position to land on.

Thankfully, negligence was the exception. Responsibility for a resident production lay with the theatre's stage manager, and in the case of a touring production the company's stage manager needed to rehearse the local staff. Inevitably, mishaps did occur, but one developed a sixth sense for something being amiss and realized it within a second, breaking the fall and hopefully escaping with only a few bruises. I have never weighed more than nine stone, and when I was a youngster I weighed less. On one occasion during the Huddersfield pantomime, I took my dive and landed safely on the mattress, only to have one of the Olvas Brothers, who weighed about twelve stone and who was playing Clown, follow immediately behind and land on top of me. Result: one flattened errand boy.

Another trick that looks easy is the collapsible stairs, but it can be dangerous if it isn't done correctly. Timing in breaking the fall is all-important. Traps that rise from below stage depend on the team-work of the pullers. The traps must come up strictly on the level so that the performer is shot up as straight as a ramrod. Leaning sideways at the wrong moment could quite possibly result in the loss of an ear. There is the story of an old actor, booked to play the

Demon King, who arrived at the theatre for rehearsal only to find that his first entrance would be up through a trap to deliver the line, 'Behold, I am the Demon of Blood!' It was a trick he had never performed before, and he took things very slowly and nervously in rehearsal. When it came to the opening night, he was shaking in every limb as he waited below stage. Up went the trap and down came the actor, wobbling like a jelly but declaiming in a loud, clear voice, 'Behold, I am the bloody Demon!'

Where would pantomime be without its animals? Where would Dick Whittington be without Tommy the Cat, Mother Goose without Priscilla the Goose, Mother Hubbard without her bow-bow, or *Jack and the Beanstalk* without Buttercup the Cow? It has always been rare for the pantomime animals to get the credit they deserve, even though they are, in children's eyes, the true stars. Their billing has generally been down among the 'wines and spirits', even though the animal concerned is often a title role.

One of the finest, perhaps I should say most realistic, pantomime cats I ever saw was Jack Brennan, the nephew of my great-aunt, Ernestine Matthews. Jack's feline movements were near to perfect. He was on the books of the Bertram Montague Agency for many years, and the last principal boy he worked with was Pat Kirkwood. With all due respect to those who play the animal roles today, or who may hope to do so in the future, it seems to me doubtful if they can ever hope to match the performances of the past. The reason is simple. In so many families of players, the animal tricks were handed down, besides which most of the animal performers were tumblers, contortionists or dancers during the rest of the year. Take Tommy the Cat, for instance. The Highgate Hill speciality spot, when Dick Whittington turns back towards London, always featured a wealth of tricks and antics for Tommy. Today it consists, as often as not, of only his traditional playing with a balloon, which was no more than a small detail in the old cat actors' routines. Several times in recent years I have seen bills for *Dick Whittington and His Cat* where the Cat does not even rate a mention, whereas King Rat, always a minor role, has been

135

prominently billed because of the television rating of the personality who's playing him. No wonder pantomime is in decline when it so often seems to be in the hands of people who do not understand its nature.

The first time I played in pantomime on my own, outside the family act, I was Tommy the Cat in *Dick Whittington* for a famous comedy duo of the day, Hatton and Manners. Ethel Manners played principal girl, that is to say, Dick Whittington himself, and Will Hatton was Idle Jack. My cousin Jack Brennan had taught me everything there was to know about creating a good feline impression, and my own Highgate Hill routine went more or less as follows.

Dick Whittington turns to Tommy and says: 'I'm so tired I can go no farther.'

Tommy meows. (I had a very convincing *meow* in those days.)

'Poor Tommy,' says Dick Whittington, 'you're hungry,' and throws down a fish.

Tommy starts to eat it, sneezes and indicates by a combination of mime and cat language, 'Too much pepper!'

'Don't be so fussy,' says Dick Whittington, and throws down a stale crust of bread which breaks in pieces.

Tommy pretends to play draughts with the fragments, complaining, in cat language, 'It's stale!'

Dick Whittington puts down a trick saucer and pours milk into it, which disappears as Tommy laps it up before showing the empty saucer to the audience. Next a balloon is thrown on stage for Tommy to start his 'play' routine, which ends with him doing a belly-flop on to the balloon and bursting it. Tommy starts to meow again and, holding up his paw, goes over to Dick Whittington where he is sitting on his mossy bank.

'Why,' says Dick Whittington, 'you've got a nasty thorn in your paw. Let me get it out for you.' Quite a bit of comedy follows, with Tommy making a terrible fuss until Dick Whittington finally gives a big pull. 'There, it's out!' he says and, taking out a handkerchief, proceeds to bandage the injured paw. Then Dick says, 'I'm so tired, I really must try to get some sleep, and you should do the same.'

As Dick Whittington goes to sleep, Tommy unwraps the handkerchief from his paw and tries to cover his master with it – a gesture that wins a wealth of *ahh*s from the audience. Then, with Dick Whittington out of the way, he prepares to go to work in earnest. He moves down to the footlights where his violin and bow have been planted, and begins to take an interest in them. To start with, he plucks on the strings and runs away in fright at the noise. Then he picks up the fiddle and blows on it, sending up a cloud of dust. His *pièce de résistance* follows: an acrobatic routine, during which he plays a violin solo with the bow held between his knees before bringing it to a climax with fast tumbling timed to end with a back roll on to the bank, where he promptly falls asleep beside Dick Whittington.

To sleep I always turned upstage so I could craftily raise the mask to take in some breaths of air and allow some of the sweat to evaporate. Traditionally it was the fairy ballet, representing Dick's dream, that always followed this spot, and this gave me a good opportunity to rest. The interval, however, didn't mean I could take a break, for this was when I would go into the audience and walk round the circle rail, stopping to make friends with the children before, at the end of the interval, climbing into the stage box and jumping from there back down on to the stage. As I made my way round, the children would offer 'Tommy' a sweet or a chocolate, and since I could hardly hold on to all of these with my hot little paws, I had a small bag made to put them in. Then, to my surprise, I found that various children who had no sweets would ask their dads for money to put in 'Tommy's' bag. The coins could be anything from sixpences to half-crowns. I sometimes found that my collection even exceeded my salary. In the end, it caused a certain amount of backstage jealousy, so I arranged to donate a percentage of whatever I was given to the RSPCA.

There still remained a lot of work for me to do in the second half, the highlight here being my fight with King Rat, which might be described as a combination of Kung-fu, all-in wrestling and acrobatic antics. There was always a roar of applause from the children when I finally placed my foot triumphantly on King Rat's lifeless corpse. I can truthfully say animal parts are the hardest. Some years later, when I was engaged to play Idle Jack in a touring production of *Dick Whittington* in Wales, I persuaded my wife, Pauline, to play Cat and taught her, in turn, all the techniques that Jack Brennan had taught me. A double violin acrobatics act that we did together was incorporated into the shop scene. The poor girl did not realize what she was letting herself in for and suffered agonies of stiffness. Her reward came, however, with the march down at the end of the show. On many occasions she received a greater ovation than the principal boy and girl. When she finally took off her mask to reveal a pretty young woman with long dark hair, there would always be a gasp from the audience and people would say, 'Ooh, it's a girl!' Such moments made me very proud. With us in that production was Harry Worth as Captain, a role into which he managed to work the ventriloquist act he did in those days, before television made him famous.

Another pantomime animal that I played when I was a young man was the Dog in *Mother Hubbard* on a northern tour for the Hanko Agency. One of the other characters was the Squire, played by Jerry Gold, a very stout party who must have weighed some eighteen stone. A running gag in the show involved Dog for ever getting under everyone else's feet and tripping them over. Big Jerry, I'm sorry to say, made a dismal attempt to simulate his falls, and one day the producer asked me if I couldn't help to make things more lifelike. That night I positioned myself perfectly so that my shoulders caught him exactly at the bends in his knees. Down came Jerry with a crash that shook the stage, and it took the help of other members of the cast to get him back on his feet again. In the dressing room he called me everything except a gentleman, and I could see poor Jerry's point. It could have been a serious matter. But in those days, with the enthusiasm and thoughtlessness of youth, my attitude was still 'anything for a laugh'.

Having played Cat, Dog and the back half of a cow, I eventually decided to take life more easily and turned to playing principal comedian, Simple Simon, Wishee Washee,

Idle Jack or, my favourite of them all, Buttons. As Buttons I once introduced a real baby piglet called Pip whom I used to feed from a baby's bottle. Pip and I became great friends, and whenever I arrived at the theatre he would grunt until I paid him some attention.

One season, after I was properly and securely married, and was playing my favourite role of Buttons, I noticed that there were two girls in their early teens who sat in the same stage box almost every evening. As I was collecting my post one morning, I found a parcel that contained a silk tie. A few days later there was another parcel, this time with a silk scarf and an anonymous little note saying, 'Love and kisses.' So it went on until, after a matinée performance, the resident stage manager announced, 'A young lady's here who'd like to see you.'

My wife was not working at the time, but had come to the theatre to be with me. 'Let the young lady come in,' I said to the stage manager, and into the room, very shyly, sidled one of the teenage girls from the stage box and stood looking at me a moment. 'Thank you for your gifts,' I said, 'but you mustn't do it again. And now let me introduce you to Mrs Buttons.'

The crestfallen expression on the poor girl's face was a picture, but she stayed to have some tea with us in the dressing room. We had a feeling that her father's and brothers' ties and scarfs must have been mysteriously disappearing for some time. The 'romance' was obviously over, and it was all very flattering, but equally obviously I looked more boyish in my stage make-up than I really was. Buttons is always a lovable character to touch the tender heart, and the young woman had felt sorry for the poor lad who is spurned by Cinderella in favour of the Prince.

Before I was through I did play one more animal that might be said to be of the pantomime type. This was the dragon in a Children's Film Foundation feature, made in 1966, called *Danny and the Dragon*, and while the part called for some pantomime business, it was more strenuous than anything I'd ever experienced on stage. The dragon's skin was insured for £20,000, and I needed to be heavily insured as well. The film was shot during a mightily hot summer and the head alone weighed some twenty pounds. Wearing the suit was like being incinerated in an oven, on top of which the smoke was liable to backfire to choking effect. I could only endure shooting for a few minutes at a time, and then had to clamber out of the suit to cool off before starting all over again. The location was a pleasant place to be on hot summer days, though: Wisley Woods in Surrey. The end product was an excellent children's film that I imagine will go on being shown time and time again.

It is many years now since I last played in pantomime, though I did once catch a glimpse of 'myself' on stage when I saw Tony Blackburn play Buttons in my old costume. Even now, though, I cannot watch a pantomime without fidgeting in my seat and longing to be up there on stage in the thick of the action. But time has moved on. We must bid pantomime a fond farewell, or, preferably, 'Au revoir'. In my experience, there was never a performance during a pantomime season that was more satisfying or moving than the one falling on New Year's Eve when, at the end of the show, cast and audience would join together in the singing of 'Auld Lang Syne'.

8

Bandstands and Fit–ups

Back to the beginning of 1932. I was nearly twenty, my sister some three years older. In the old theatrical and circus families it was expected, as you will have gathered, that the children stayed with the act even after they were married. However, Lenora and I were of the 'new generation' compared even with our elder brothers and had ideas of our own. We put an independent act together, called ourselves 'Jack and Lee' and launched into the great unknown to try our luck. And where else to go but London?

The act as we plotted it out opened in Viennese costume. We played piano and violin and Leonora danced the 'Blue Danube'. A quick change for a trick violin and acrobatic routine then had us transformed into two skeletons. This was achieved by wearing overall-type garments on which we had painted the skeleton bones in luminous paint, and then putting on skull masks. After that, a blacked-out stage and white focus gave the desired spooky effect. I also had a pedestal some eight feet high made, and from this I would, as a skeleton, dive down to the stage as if diving into water. It was a difficult trick to bring off, and I've not seen anyone attempt it since, but at least we had our act together and could begin to go round the agents. But we needed to break the act in, and the only way to test an act is by getting an audience reaction.

The first stock question the agents asked was, of course, 'Where can we see you working?' This meant that, until we were working, we couldn't interest an agent. We had very little money and many times walked from Brixton to the West End, saving our coppers for a cup of coffee and hoping to find someone who'd give us a break. In those days, everyone in the theatrical profession used to gather in Charing Cross Road at the Express Dairy, which as a result came to be known as the 'Expro's Dairy'. As you may imagine, it was a good place for hearing in-jokes of a theatrical kind, of which the following two are typical samples.

After the first novelty of the talking pictures wore off, there was a modest revival of variety in cinemas, but usually only on a Friday, which was designated 'Variety Night'. These were known to the acts as 'ten bob and a cup of tea' bookings. As the first story goes, a certain small cinema decided to include variety, and the manager, who was new to the idea, phoned a theatrical agent. 'Is that you, Mr Finkelstein?' he asked. 'I want to put some acts into my cinema. It's the first time. What'll it cost me?'

'Well,' said Mr Finkelstein, 'that depends on how many acts you want. Let's say three or four good singers – one pound. Acrobats – thirty bob. Conjuror – around fifteen shillings. Of course, it'll cost more for a star name.'

The manager paused for thought. 'All right,' he said. 'I'll try out the acts next Friday. Just send me three pounds' worth of mixed.'

On another occasion, a strong-man called on his agent. 'Business is bad,' said the agent gloomily, but then he added, 'I'll treat you to a cup of coffee.'

As the two men walked along the street towards the café, they saw a crowd gathered. A horse and cart had overturned. The unfortunate driver was trapped under the cart and several men were struggling to free him. 'Stand back!' called out the strong-man and crawling underneath the cart he lifted it clear.

Fortunately the driver was unhurt. He brushed himself

down, turned to the strong-man and said, 'Thanks, mate. Here's a quid. Have a drink.'

As they walked away from the scene, the agent said, 'Well, Samson, that's the easiest eighteen bob you ever earned.'

There were many variety artists who were paying an agent's 10 per cent on a day's crowd film work – £1 a day plus travel fares – and glad to get it. Father felt that agents had gained altogether too much influence over the profession. They were dictating to artists what to do in their acts, and what to wear, and even persuading them to change their names. They had proliferated like mushrooms and made the Charing Cross Road the new 'poverty corner' (the former one having been south of the River Thames in the Waterloo and York Roads where the older generation of agents had their offices).

To find work, unless you were one of the favoured few – the top liners – there was nothing for it but to tramp along to the Charing Cross Road and do the rounds wherever you saw the sign 'Theatrical and Variety Agency'. Up and down you went, and by the time you'd finished you had, as Father wrote, 'walked several miles, and climbed a few hundred stairs'. The days when an agent informed a client of bookings by sending a simple postcard were over and done with. 'No postcards today,' wrote Father. 'Agents can go to their offices and be sure that practically every artist doing the round will give them a call.'

There was at that time a man named Tony Gerrard who used to run talent-spotting contests long before the days of Carroll Levis. When Leonora and I heard that he was running one at the Canterbury, we decided to use it to test out our act. The Canterbury Arms in Westminster Bridge Road, Lambeth, had been one of the first pubs to be converted into a music hall – by Charles Morton, the 'father of the halls', in 1852. It seemed an auspicious location for launching us on our career. We had to push all our props on a barrow for the three or so miles from Brixton to Lambeth, knowing full well that we'd have to push them all the way back again after only one performance. The act went reasonably well until I undertook my dive from the pedestal and we went into the acrobatic dance finale. I had been aware of a sudden tearing sound, and very soon the titters from the audience developed into outright laughter. The luminous paint had rotted the material and precipitated a split in the seat of my dungarees. Since I was wearing pink underpants, I must have looked, to the audience, like a skeleton with a bare bottom. By the end of the act, we both had faces as pink as the offending underpants and wanted nothing so much as the stage to open up and swallow us.

Eventually we obtained our first paid engagement through Dr Walford Bodie's Tours and Enterprises agency. The family had on many occasions worked on bills with Dr Bodie, the Laird of Macduff (born in Aberdeen in 1870 as Samuel Brodie), who some called genius and others called charlatan. No one disagreed, however, over the description of him as one of the greatest showmen of his day. His act was sensational in every sense. His 1903 London début was made at the Britannia, Hoxton, when the billing read: 'The most remarkable man on Earth, the great healer, the modern miracle worker, demonstrating nightly "Hypnotism, Bodie force and the wonders of bloodless surgery".' With his electrical tricks and stunts, he made the stage flash and crackle like Frankenstein's laboratory, and among his props was an electric chair that had allegedly been used in the first execution by electrocution of a criminal, the murderer William Semmler, in Sing Sing in 1890. In this chair brave members of the audience would be invited to sit and sample a high-voltage charge. The electricity, being of the 'static' kind, was, of course, perfectly harmless – as Dr Bodie knew, though his audiences didn't necessarily share his knowledge. He was also a very good ventriloquist.

Dr Bodie was seldom at a loss for words. During a famous court case brought against him for misrepresentation, and heard before Mr Justice Darling, cross-questioning Counsel asked him, 'You have continuously represented yourself as an MD, have you not?' 'No,' replied Bodie, 'only on one occasion. It means Merry Devil. Theatrical managers have called me that.' (Laughter in court.) On another occasion, in Glasgow, medical students had packed his audience to

144

scoff and jeer. As they hissed and booed he walked to the footlights and shouted, 'If you kept quiet, you might learn something,' and then quoted Robert Burns, ' "They gang in stirk and come out asses" ' – meaning those who go in like young bullocks end up as asses.

The most controversial parts of his act were the healing sessions, involving hypnotism and electric shocks. I can vouch for the fact that it was very remarkable and dramatic to see cripples walk on stage wearing calipers and walk off afterwards without them. If the victim was a small girl, she would be presented with a big doll. Bodie was a man of military bearing who, like my father, sported waxed pointed moustachios and who possessed a great deal of what can only be called Old World charm. His eyes were certainly hypnotic. He simply needed to walk into a room to become the centre of attention, especially for the ladies. In the pamphlet entitled *The Whiteley Tapestry: A Century of Entertainment*, dating from the early 1940s and printed privately for the Whiteley family, the author, 'Harlequin', remarked:

> It is a curious thing, to me, that women players have the greatest affection for 'the Doctor'. In speaking of him they all say, 'The old darling'. Several theatrical men of my acquaintance use terms that could not possibly be construed into 'Good Old Sergeant'.

I still have one letter that Bodie wrote to my father on 19 September 1931:

> Dear Mr Whiteley,
>
> Just a note to confirm the two weeks' bookings – Palace, Bradford, October 12th, Hippodrome, Warrington, October 19th, at £16 weekly. Please confirm. Also send me your vacancies. Kindest regards to yourself, Mrs, and all the family, especially your Bonnie Girl.
>
> Yrs aye,
> Dr Bodie

The 'Bonnie Girl' in question was my sister Leonora, of

whom Dr Bodie was very fond. The first date he obtained for Leonora and me was for a live variety week at the Raneleagh Cinema, Barnes, at a joint salary of £5. Out of this we had to find the agency's 10 per cent and our daily fares from and to Brixton, but at least it was a start. The applause I got for my skeleton diving trick didn't, on the whole, come up to expectations and seemed a small return for the risks involved and the bruises it got me. As they say, you live and learn. The trouble with ciné-variety audiences was that they were the least responsive sort of all. They had grown used to sitting and looking at a film and giving out no response, and were apt to treat live performers in much the same way as the shadows they saw on the silver screen.

The bookings began to come in, and the act evolved into Jack Le White and Leonora. Then, during March 1932, we decided to travel down to Bedford to see the family playing the County Theatre, having been offered a lift by a Mr Zola, a circus clown. By that time my little brother Raymond was a fully fledged part of the Whiteley act. The car we went in, bought in London, was in need of certain repairs, and Zola had agreed to drive it down to Bedford for this purpose. Outside St Albans the car broke down and needed to be towed to a garage. Zola asked me to take the wheel, and I didn't like to admit that I'd never driven a car in my life. I didn't realize that correct steering was still essential even on tow. The car began to vere wildly to left and right at the end of its tow rope, and eventually we were struck a broadside by another vehicle. I was very shaken and could only say, 'Thank God', when I saw the other car's occupants emerge safely. Cars had proper bumpers in those days. Then I turned to look at Leonora, who was sitting beside me in the passenger seat. Her face was covered in blood. She had hit the windscreen and there was a terrible gash in her chin.

At St Albans Hospital they put in seven or eight stitches and allowed her to leave, though she was still in a very shocked state. Luckily the other car was only slightly damaged, but Zola had to remain with his vehicle at the garage. As usual, we had very little money with us, and so I phoned Bedford and Father agreed he would go down to the railway

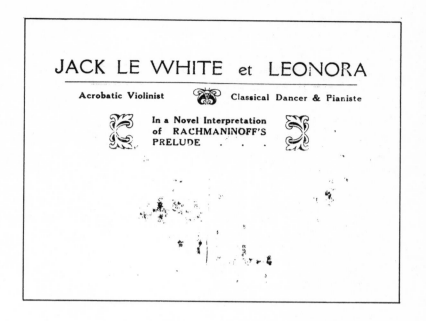

JACK LE WHITE et LEONORA

Acrobatic Violinist   Classical Dancer & Pianiste

In a Novel Interpretation
of RACHMANINOFF'S
PRELUDE . . .

The letterhead printed for the Jack Le White and Leonora partnership

station and guarantee our fares. The message was sent through to St Albans station, and in that way, in the end, we arrived at Bedford. Leonora was unable to work for some time after the accident. The wound turned septic and she suffered a great deal. Fortunately, although the hospital had put in the wrong kind of stitches, she was ultimately left with only a tiny scar.

I always did seem to be jinxed when it came to cars. While I was working a summer season at the Baths Theatre, Lytham St Annes, I developed an escapology act for the first time, in emulation of Houdini, who had always been one of my heroes. At the same time I bought the first and last car I ever owned. It was a Singer 8 and cost me £15. I took a few lessons and drove into Blackpool several times during the season. Bursting with confidence, I then sat my driving test. Early on in the test the engine stalled, and by the end I knew I'd failed. There I was, stuck with a car and a great deal of theatrical baggage and escapology props, all of which

147

I had to get back to Hornchurch in Essex, where Father and Mother had by that time bought a home for their retirement.

I decided to take the risk and drive regardless. I strapped my huge trunk on to the luggage grid at the back that my £15-worth of 'Rolls-'Ardly', as I christened it, was provided with. Then, having ditched the wretched L-plates, I left Lytham St Annes in the early-morning hours and set off southwards. I was still only a short distance outside Preston when I became aware of banging noises and stopped to see what had happened. The weight of the huge trunk had proved too much for the grid, which had buckled until it was touching the road surface. I forced the grid back up as far as my strength allowed, lashed ropes to the grid and the car doors and gingerly resumed my journey – every mile a mile nearer home. At last I crossed the county boundary into Essex and got as far as Romford. Hornchurch was only three miles farther on.

As I came to a roundabout, the car sputtered and coughed, the engine died. There was a garage just the other side of the roundabout. There was also a policeman coming towards me. I decided to take the bull by the horns and went to meet him. 'Ah, constable,' I said, 'I wonder if you'd mind giving me a hand. I've just finished my summer season at the Palace, Blackpool' (well, he'd never have heard of the Baths Theatre, Lytham St Annes, would he?) – 'and my car's decided not to go any farther. If I release the handbrake, would you help me to push it to yonder garage?'

The policeman, bless his little cotton socks, or whatever socks he was wearing at the time, happily helped the stranded traveller out of his fix as we propelled the car into the garage. I was gasping with relief as I hopped on a bus for home and vowed that in future I'd rely on public transport.

The accident at St Albans marked the end of my partnership with Leonora for the time being, and thereafter I was on my own while she went back to the family act. Father was pleased since it meant he could keep the Five Whiteleys on the road for a while longer. Their last appearance was at Easter 1936, at the Theatre Royal, Castleford, Yorkshire. After that, Ben, Harold and Raymond formed a trio called

Tom, Dick and Harry (or sometimes, when Laurel, Ben's wife, was standing in as the third member of the troupe, Tom, Dick and Harryette). This utilized the acrobatic violin routines, tumbling and table sliding. Leonora set up as a single musical act, using her skills at singing, dancing and playing the accordion, violin, bells and tambourine. And I was established by then as a solo act under the name of Jack Le White. It grieved Father that the old name of Whiteley, 'the descendants of John Whiteley, the one-man band and tumbler busker', was seen no more on the bills. But times change as times have done since time began.

In his novel *Under the Greenwood Tree*, Thomas Hardy tells the story of the 'Mellstock Quire', whose instrumental musicians are displaced by a new-fangled organ. Something very similar had begun to happen in the cinemas at the end of the 1920s when the cinema organ came into its own, a mighty descendant of the pipes of Pan. In fact the first organ specifically for a cinema in Britain was built in 1919 and installed at the Palace Theatre, Accrington. After the advent of the talkies, cinema organs soon found their way into almost every big cinema. The names of the makes of instrument – Compton, Hammond, Wurlitzer – spring evocatively to mind, as do the names of the great exponents who played them – John Ferguson, Sandy Macpherson, Reginald Dixon and Reginald Foort, the latter a household name in Blackpool for many years. There was also one well-known female organist, Ena Baga, in what was primarily a male preserve. The spectacular Wurlitzers were American organs and only the more prosperous cinemas could afford them, because of the import tax duty.

Who among the moviegoers of that generation could forget how the organ would rise up from the orchestra pit in a blaze of light during the interval and the organist launch into a robust musical medley, playing as many notes with the feet as with the hands? There might also be an invitation to the audience to join in the popular choruses, the lyrics being projected on to the screen and a little white ball of light moving from word to word. In the meantime, the

HIPPODROME

CHESTERFIELD.

WEEK COMMENCING MONDAY, OCTOBER 28th, 1935.
6-40 —— TWICE NIGHTLY —— 8-45.   'Phone 2335.

Direct from the London Palladium !

NICOL & MARTIN

in " FOOLING FOR YOU."   WHAT FOOLS ?
The biggest laugh on the stage.

LES GOLFUS
Golfing Equilibrists in " FUN ON THE LINKS."

THE 4 EMERALDS
Expert Novelty Dancers.

Those Two Boys at the Piano	Music Hath Charms !
# EARLE and ASCOTT	# PHILLIS and GILES
Recording Artistes from H.M.V. Decca, and Zonophone.	The Musical Farmyard.

BETTY WHEATLEY
The famous " Auntie Betty " of the Children's Hour.

The Quaint Comic !

TOMMY DIXON
Have you ever seen a dream walking ?

THE FIVE WHITLEYS

Present——" EASTERN ANTICS."
The Super Acro-Risley Musical Pot-Pourri.

NO INCREASE IN PRICES.

Orchestra Stalls	Stalls	Pit Stalls	Balcony
1/6	1/-	9d.	6d.

TAYLORS, Theatrical Printers, Wombwell, Yorks.

The Five Whiteleys feature on a bill for the Hippodrome, Chesterfield, in 1935, the year before the act's final appearance

W.F. Matthews (*rear*) with his troupe in the United States, *c.* 1871: (*left to right*) Harriet, Freddy Griffiths, Willie, Laurina, Theodore, Arthur Gregory

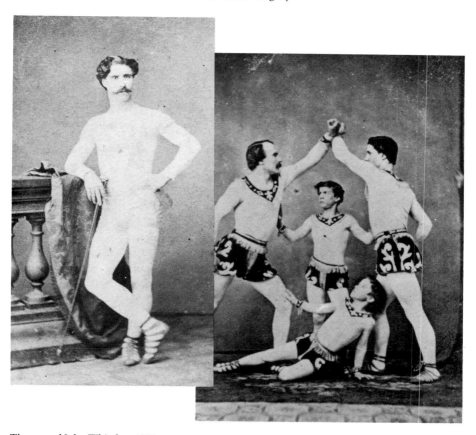

The second John Whiteley, 1873

The Matthews troupe

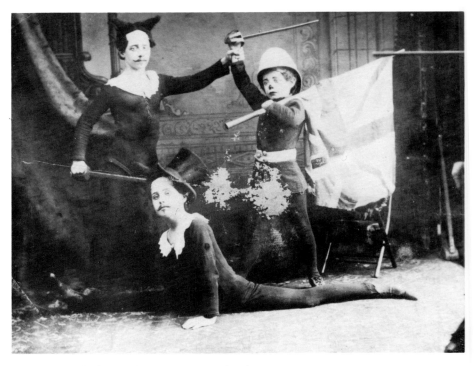

Three young Whiteleys, (*left to right*) Henry, Jack and Tommy,
dressed for a patriotic acrobatic presentation

Tommy Whiteley as a young clown

Tommy as part of a double act

The Gregory troupe: Arthur and Laurina (*centre*), Dan and Leonora (*behind*), with apprentices Talbot (*left*) and Paul ('Powell') Canzi (*right*)

The personnel of the Gregory Equestrian Circus outside the wooden-sided circus building in Cairo, *c.* 1888

Dan Gregory, winner of the First Prize at the Bombay Exhibition, 1879

Leonora Gregory in South Africa, 1885

W.F. Matthews in retirement at his farm in Billericay

W.F. and Lauretta Matthews in their old age

Tom Foy plays Dame
in a London pantomime

Paul Canzi, Arthur Gregory's former
apprentice who married
Leonora Matthews

Leonora Matthews (Mademoiselle La Foy),
dressed for one of her improvised dance presentations

Dan Gregory with his wife Lydia (*right*)
and his sister-in-law

Dan, in the character of Clown Ping Pong,
bows his fiddle from between his knees

Leonora Gregory, in a riding dress,
adopts the 'third position'

Leonora (now Mrs Henry Whiteley) in
Columbine costume

Mr and Mrs Henry Whiteley with
their first-born son Harry

Their daughter Leonora

Four Whiteleys: Henry and Leonora
dressed for an act with their sons,
Harold (*left*) and Ben, in drag

Albert (*left*) and Raymond Whiteley in their foster home at Eastwood, Notts, during the First World War

Albert (*right*) with Raymond during the Second World War

Raymond and Albert perform a cross–talk act in the revue *Variety Vanities* at Silloth, 1946. The fire-damaged curtains behind them have been cleverly repaired

In the Auxiliary Fire Service,
1939: (*from the top*) Raymond,
Albert and Ben

Pauline Fairchild and Leonora Whiteley perform as
Peta and Paula, 'The Little Maids from Moscow'

Publicity card for the acrobatic act, Tom, Dick and Harry, with (*inset*) Henry Whiteley
in Mephistophelian costume

Pauline Whiteley,
née Fairchild

Jack Le White as Buttons in *Cinderella*,
with Pip the piglet at Rotherham

Enter right, with sword: Jack with Charlie Stephenson prostrate on stage. The pantomime is *Babes in the Wood*; the venue the Astor Hall Theatre, Deal, 1952–3. Pauline (*centre*) is Principal Boy

The same pantomime catches Jack in one of his rare Dame roles, chastising Charlie Stephenson

Line-up at Clacton-on-Sea: Gordon Henson, producer and compère (*left*), Frank Penrose, pianist (*right*), Jack and Pauline (*third and fourth from left*); remainder of players unidentified

In action on the Pier, New Brighton: (*left to right*) Bert Seal, pianist, Minna Ward, soubrette, Lloyd Hughes and Dog, Pauline and Jack, unidentified singer, and Bert Lydon, light comedian

WHITE AND SIMONNE
• • • "Comedy in Cameo" • • •

Le White and Simonne: 'Comedy in Cameo', a twelve-minute quick-change act (one sketch every two minutes)

Le White and Simonne perform for the Lucan and McShane Show, using the family trick with violin bows

Jack Le White with Frank Windsor (*standing*) and Stratford Johns (*right*) in a *Z-Cars* strip story, published in *Radio Times*

Jack Le White as the chair-mender
in the film of *Oliver!*

The family clown tradition comes into its own for an Armour Star Corned Beef
commercial, made by British Pathé

old displaced cinema musicians continued to congregate in Archer Street, outside the Musicians' Union headquarters, and look for 'gigs' – one-night stands for dance halls or private parties. The pianists would seek work as audition musicians or as accompanists at dance schools.

But, as the saying goes, if one door closes another opens. The 1930s ushered in the new phenomenon of the stage bands. These were not to be confused with the more specialist jazz bands, but were bands that were capable, with one or two speciality acts, of presenting a complete evening's stage show. The best-remembered British band of this type was probably that of Jack Hylton. He turned his dance band into a highly successful stage band, and his catch-phrase, 'Jack's back!' was known nationwide. I met him once at the long-gone Holborn Empire, little realizing that he would later become one of England's best-known theatrical impresarios. In the United States, a famous stage band was that of Paul Whiteman. Each member was a top instrumentalist in his own right. The band was featured in the early musical movie *King of Jazz*, a genuine collector's item, and the violinist, for example, in whom I was naturally particularly interested, was Joe Venuti. Among Paul Whiteman's singers, of course, were Bing Crosby and the Rhythm Boys.

At that time it seemed that the stage bands were springing up everywhere overnight. There was Henry Hall's, Roy Fox's, Debroy Somers's and Billy Cotton's, and there were female bands led by Dorothy Holbrook and Ivy Benson. There were also various styles and specialisms within bands: the accordions of Jack Kitson, Troise and His Mandoliers, the Tom Katz Saxophone Six, Younkman's Gypsy Czardas Orchestra, the Ten Loonies Comedy Band. Even the humble mouth-organ was upgraded into the harmonica and we had harmonica bands.

I myself became a part of the Teddy Morris Band, which was one of the first bands to broadcast over Radio Luxembourg. There were twenty musicians, some of whom could also contribute speciality acts. I contributed my trick violin and acrobatic routine, while another member blacked up for a whistling and dance solo. All the players were good

151

musicians and their backgrounds ranged from symphony to jazz. Each of the two trumpeters had a speciality: Jimmy Beale played the triple tongue solo and Jack Doyle did the laughing trumpet. Jack was later to form part of a double act, Hackford and Doyle. Nothing was more enjoyable than to hear the band off-duty, when the musicians extemporized and let their hair down in a jam session.

The leader of the band, Teddy Morris himself, was an excellent showman with an innate sense of timing in his conducting. He was no musician, though, and it was his pianist, Buddy Mellor, who provided the musical drive and was the band's arranger. Teddy was certainly a larger than life character, and a real ladies' man. There was a popular song of the time, 'Why Do They Fall for the Leader of the Band?' They certainly fell for Teddy. The 'band boys', as they were always known, were seldom stumped for female company on tour, but if Teddy so much as looked at your girl, she was as good as lost to you. If you wanted to hold on to your job, you accepted the inevitable and determined that you'd keep the next girl to come your way out of Teddy's sight. These situations were continually arising, despite the fact that Teddy's wife and daughter often travelled with us. They were both performers, and Mrs Morris, whose stage name was Lily Hartley, was fully capable of taking over the band, and sometimes did.

When Lily toured with the show, she made an effort to keep Teddy on the straight and narrow, but was seldom too successful in her aims. Teddy would every now and then turn the band show into a revue he called *Mickey Mouse*, which conveniently featured a female chorus. From the line-up he'd then take his pick before allowing the band boys to make free with the rest. Not that all the band boys were the same. Some had fiancées and several of the married men took fidelity far more seriously than their leader. As for me, I was still very naïve and couldn't understand why, whenever I did manage to go out with a local lass, she was unwilling to follow it up. Eventually the more experienced Casanovas told me what was wrong. I wasn't making the right promises. Once, when we were playing at Torquay, there was a young lady named Iris who'd throw pebbles up at my window at seven if it was a sunny morning. Then we'd go down to the beach together and enjoy the swimming. The moment she suggested I might settle down and manage her hairdressing business in Wimbledon, however, that was enough for me and I backed off. I was strictly a showbusiness man and the thought of having a nine-to-five job made me shudder.

Teddy Morris was a top-of-the-bill attraction for many years, and he should have been able to afford to retire comfortably at the end of his career. Unfortunately, the pursuit of wine, women and song is not one to guarantee security in the latter stages of life. He was often so hard up that he'd only be able to pay his acts and meanwhile his long-suffering musicians had to wait for the ghost to walk. I started out thinking I was lucky since he always paid me, but as time went on I came to realize, first, that I was underpaid; secondly, that he held on to me because I did a solo spot and variety was an essential ingredient for a stage band; and finally, that he had to pay at least a number of his people if he was going to be able to touch them for a loan during the following week. In a typical Friday-night scene, he'd be in the dressing room surrounded by his musicians, all threatening to 'do him'. 'Go on then, hit me!' he'd say, throwing whatever money he had down on the dressing-room table and adding, 'That's all I've got. Share it out among you.' Or perhaps he'd say, 'I'll make it up to you next week. I'm on a good guarantee.' In all fairness, there were occasions when the receipts did cover expenses.

All performers are Micawbers at heart, believing that something will turn up. What turned up on many occasions with the Teddy Morris Band was a heap of trouble. We once played a week at Aldershot with the revue, and Teddy asked me to stage-manage in addition to performing. This meant seeing the scenery in on the Monday morning and out on the Saturday night and organizing the carters who would convey it from and to the railway station. By the time we finished on Saturday, the heavens had opened and the rain was pelting down. Teddy handed me an envelope that, I assumed, contained the cash to pay the carter his bill. We got to the loading bay in the goods yard and, in the terrible weather, loaded all the scenery and baskets on to a railway truck. I handed the carter the envelope and had begun to walk away when I was brought up short by a loud shout and some not too refined language. When he had regained the power of coherent speech, the carter protested that all the envelope contained was a note from Mr Morris saying that he wasn't satisfied with the charges for getting in and out, and that the carter should take up the matter with him direct.

None of us – not even me, the stage-manager – had any notion where Teddy was staying, and it was obvious that he was relying on the idea that, once the luggage was safely stowed in the railway truck, it would be a case of the 'soldier's farewell'. As a rule, you see, as soon as a truck had been loaded, an official of the railway company would padlock it and moving heaven and earth wouldn't get it open again until it reached its destination, which in this instance was Chatham, where we were next booked to appear. Unfortunately for Teddy's scheme, the truck had not been padlocked immediately on this occasion, and the carters swiftly transferred several of our baskets back on to their lorry and drove away.

I was in no mood to argue by that stage, and in any case had no intention of roaming round Aldershot in the rain looking for Teddy an hour after midnight. He turned up next morning at Aldershot station ten minutes before our train's departure, and simply couldn't believe what had happened, but it was too late to do anything. When we arrived at Chatham we discovered that the baskets in question had been those containing our evening–dress suits and were not even the property of Mr Teddy Morris. How on earth were we to open our act on the Monday night without costumes of any description? Teddy, himself a Jew, attempted to solve this facer by making a quick dash round all the Jewish tailors, second–hand dealers and pawnbrokers in Chatham. You may be sure that none of us ended up looking like a fashion plate, and the theatre, taking a dim view, cut Teddy's percentage.

154

Fortunately, the Aldershot carters had to return the baskets promptly since they were not the property of the debtor.

There was another occasion when, after a week at the Opera House, Dudley, the ghost failed to walk for the whole band and as a result we could none of us pay our rent for our lodgings. My landlady commandeered my suitcase. I promised to send her the cash, but she wouldn't take my word for it, so I had to leave her a ring as security. We didn't even have our train fares. The comedian with the show, Scott Sanders, who sang the song, 'Rolling Round the World', crammed a number of us like sardines into his car and got us back to London.

Despite my experiences with Teddy Morris, I worked with two more bands, one a cowboy band and the other Paul Zaharoff's International Band. It was my suggestion to call the latter 'International', and very colourful it was, with all its musicians in various traditional and national costumes. Zaharoff was early in his career pianist accompanist to the old-time music-hall star, Gertie Gitana, remembered for her singing of 'Nellie Dean'.

It was during this solo phase of my career that I also worked for a brief while with Fred Karno in a revival of his famous burlesque sketch, *The Football Match*. The thing that made it famous was the fact that Stiffy, the goalkeeper comedy lead, had originally been created by the Lancashire comedian Harry Weldon in 1906, and later taken over by Charlie Chaplin, who had for a while previously been the villain who tries to bribe the goalkeeper. The revival of *The Football Match* formed the nucleus for a touring show, booked by the top agents, Parnell and Zeitlin. The stars of the show were the American musical-comedy actress Marie Bayne, and the comedy musical duo (business with motor horns and violins) Stanelli and Edgar. Stanelli, as a matter of interest, was really a Tessermacher, and therefore one of the genuine gypsies in showbusiness. One of his relatives was composer of the well-known number, 'Where My Caravan Has Rested', and he later had his own band, in which he incorporated motor horns. It was billed as his 'Hornchestra'.

The Football Match commenced with a comic training

routine in a gymnasium and then switched to a football pitch. On the backcloth were little flags apparently being waved by the crowd but in fact worked by electric fans. I was hired for my ability to make up one of a pair for the acrobatic work and knockabout routines, and Mr Karno at that stage still exerted a close control over the details. He was not the most reasonable of men, and when he provided us with real football boots with real studs to perform in, we had to tell him firmly that it would be impossible to wear these without breaking our ankles, or very likely our necks.

At the time when I worked with Karno I did not, to my regret in after years, know of his connections with my family, for you will recall that he was the young acrobat, at that point calling himself Aubrey (though his real name was Frederick Wescott), who worked with my Grandfather Whiteley's short-lived circus in 1884. He, in turn, only knew me by my adopted stage name, Jack Le White. His stage name, of course, has entered the language in the proverbial phrase, 'a right Fred Karno's set-up', used to describe any inefficiently or idiotically run organization that becomes a shambles as a result. Karno's comedy routines, though they included dialogue, had a firm basis in the art of mime and were an immense influence on the early comic cinema, especially through the films of Charlie Chaplin. Stan Laurel too was a Karno discovery. But maybe the Karno legend had lost much of its hold on the public imagination by the 1930s, or maybe his genius had faded. The show featuring the revival of *The Football Match* was booked for a long run, but, after opening at the Empire in Birmingham, it ran for only two weeks before it flopped – a right Fred Karno's set-up. I went home with a month's salary in lieu of notice.

There was one season in the 1930s when I returned to the ring: a small 'in and out' show, just like those in the days of my great-grandfather. It was run by a Mr Bob Gandey. I joined him in Portsmouth and found that, as with all small outfits, it was a matter of 'all hands to the pump'. The whole show consisted of five people beside myself: Mr and Mrs Gandey, their son, their partner and a young contortionist (who would have been billed as a 'posture artiste' in the era of the mountebanks and strolling players). The first thing we had to do was go to the station to pick up the tent. This we did, and immediately discovered that there was no king pole; and we were due to open the next day. We managed to get hold of a redundant telegraph pole and, with much breaking of shoulders, humped it to the showground. Then, the tent being quite a small one, we ended up with yards of pole sticking out at the top, from which there was flown a very large flag. From a distance, the set-up gave the impression of being like a big continental circus, though that illusion was quickly dispelled at closer quarters.

To draw the crowds milling about in the fairground, we had to do a 'Walk up! Walk up!' routine. On Easter Monday we gave some fifteen performances. The effect, amid all the cacophony of the fairground, was nerve-shattering. After that, it was a minimum of ten shows a day. The limbs of the contortionist were like worn-out elastic after three weeks of bending and twisting and putting his legs round his neck. By the end he really was more comfortable with his legs wrapped round his head than in any normal position. It was the kind of show where everyone became more like wound-up robots than human beings. In the last of our seemingly never-ending run of performances, I did a row of flip-flaps in a dream-like manner in my clown costume, went over the canvas ring fence and finished up in an elderly lady's lap. As soon as she'd recovered from her initial shock, she gave me a kiss and I got a big round of applause. The audience took it all as part of the act.

That was to be my last appearance in the ring. The nearest I ever came to it again was in 1935 when I toured in Ireland with Lynton's Colossal Hippodrome. This consisted of a fine tent, a converted lorry for a stage and a small but high-class orchestra. Lynton himself was Jewish, though the audiences would scarcely have been aware of that as they filed past the ever-open door of his van and spotted the picture of the Virgin Mary he'd judiciously hung up inside. As will be clear from the family's earlier adventures in Ireland, you needed to keep in with the priesthood if you hoped

157

to do business across the Irish Sea. It was on this tour under canvas that I played on the same bill as Dr Walford Bodie for the last time. Four years later he was to die, a showman to the last, playing on the Golden Mile at Blackpool. I always remember that he told a story of treating himself to a fine bundle of asparagus ('sparrers' grass' as the profession used to call it), which he left with the landlady to cook for his dinner. When it was served up he found she'd carefully removed the tips.

The England of the 1930s continued to be in the midst of the Great Depression, and I certainly did my share of 'resting', in other words, of being on the dole. During weeks when I was unemployed I received 17s. (85p today), less the contributions for which there were two cards, one for health, the other for unemployment. There had been a period when the actor or music-hall artist was considered self-employed and therefore ineligible for benefit. Equity challenged this ruling, arguing that because all stage artists work under direction, they cannot logically be classified as self-employed. And Equity won the day.

Every unemployed theatrical would each week read the profession's journal, *The Stage*, from cover to cover, especially the 'Artists Wanted' column. It cost you 4d. (just over 1½p) to buy. Alternatively, you could go to the local library and await your turn in the queue and get to read it free. I did the same as all the others, and at last I found an advertisement that said, 'Wanted. Versatile entertainer for fit-ups and summer season.' Up to then I'd played circus and theatre, but fit-ups! This was a return, quite simply, to the strolling players of long ago, also known as 'barn-stormers'. I sent off an answer to the advertisement, emphasizing how versatile I was, and back came a favourable reply with the offer of the princely sum of £2 a week. As a Whiteley, brought up on the adage that half a loaf is better than no bread, I accepted with alacrity. Besides, a performer with nowhere to perform and no one to perform to is like a fish out of water.

So it came about that I travelled to a remote village in Huntingdonshire and asked a local where I might find the village hall. 'Thee must mean the Checkers Barn,' he declared. The Checkers Barn it was indeed, for there I found the man who ran the show, Mr Harry Matto, his wife, Madge, a young lady, Nora McCourt, who was a male impersonator and soubrette, and Chris Mann, the company's pianist. The barn had a stage of sorts, the interior was lit with oil lamps, which made it a very pretty setting, and at least there were running tabs (curtains to the uninitiated). With my arrival, the company was complete! The show in question was a variety presentation titled *Rigmarolles*.

In fact there were a number of people managing fit-ups in those days, and some of them ran both drama and variety. The first half would be given over to a short classic blood-chiller – *Maria Marten, or The Murder in the Red Barn, Sweeney Todd* or *The Monkey's Paw* – and the variety came after the interval. To name but a few of the fit-up actor-managers besides Mr Matto, there was, most famously, Tod Slaughter, who also immortalized his craft for melodrama in various film versions of his stage pieces, including *The Face at the Window*; there was Kit Walters, who later ran a boarding house in Bridlington; there was Bob E. Wray, for whom a bit later I once played a season in beautiful Barmouth (I shall always remember climbing Cader Idris one moonlit night after our performance); and there was Sylvester Stuart, known as 'The Paper King' from his ability to create wonderful stage décors out of nothing but coloured paper. After his death, Sylvester's wife carried on working as May Walden. For some years she played the Duchess in Freddy Frinton's classic 'Drunken Butler' sketch, and later still did a lot of comedy character work on television.

But, to return to *Rigmarolles*, that barnstorming tour was to show me the proof of the truth of the cliché that money isn't everything. I came to love the villages and the village people as we travelled from Huntingdonshire to Shropshire, then north to Cumberland, south to Wales, east to Essex and west to Gloucestershire. Where else except in the remote villages of England could board and lodging be found for rarely more than 17s. (85p) a week? And the board included a cup of tea brought to your bedroom door at 6.30 each morning, home-cured bacon for breakfast and farm butter on your bread. I also developed a taste for partridge and pheasant. Village life has changed a lot since then, and has lost so much of its remoteness. I doubt there is anywhere left today where the Sunday roasts, with the owners' names on labels, are taken to the local bakehouse to be cooked, as I saw it still happening in the 1930s.

We all travelled together in the Mattos' car, which had a trailer for the props and luggage. On the first evening of our arrival at a new location, we would set out to do a pub crawl, the object being to meet the locals and leave our playbills. This was by far the most effective method of advertising and persuading people to want to come and see the show. And it was a show worth seeing. Matto himself was a good comedian while Madge Matto was a fine *chanteuse* and could play the banjo; Nora McCourt was a striking performer, whether she was in her male role in the Vesta Tilley and Hetty King tradition, or being very feminine as a singer and dancer; and Chris Mann excelled on the piano keys. For me, an additional attraction of the village tour was that I began keeping company with Nora McCourt, who came from Wallasey in Cheshire. Her father was chief engineer on the well-known Mersey ferryboat, the *Daffodil*, which some years later played a heroic role in the Dunkirk evacuation.

The *Rigmarolles* would perform at a place for a week at a time, but, because our audiences always contained a lot of the same people, we had to change the show each night. This was obviously where the need for versatility came in. Then, on the Friday, once the show was over, we'd clear the floor, scrape candle grease over the boards and rub it in with our feet, so making everything ready for a Friday-night village hop, or dance. Thereupon, needless to say, we became the band – piano, banjo, violin, with each of us taking a turn on the drums. It was often this event which brought us past our break-even point for the week.

I have particular occasion to remember playing the Women's Institute, Mountnessing, near Brentwood, in Essex, whose hall had large windows on either side of the

160

stage. One of my tricks was to run and dive over four chairs, and it was always difficult to perform on a small stage where the space was tight and I had a job to get a sufficient run-up. As the customary drum-roll sounded, I launched into my run, cleared the chairs and saw one of the large windows coming to meet me. There was an almighty crash. I landed outside in the open air, completely unhurt, and as I shook shards of glass from my clothes became aware of the sound of applause coming from inside. Applause, I had been taught, should always be acknowledged. I made my way round to the front of the hall and took a re-entrance down the centre aisle and back on to the stage. As it dawned on the audience what had really happened – and what the consequences could have been – their reaction may be imagined. Poor Mr Matto had to fork out for a new window, but he was only thankful that all had ended no worse. Now I come to think about it, I was never insured against injury at any point in my stage career. Not even a film stunt-man would reckon on having to dive through a real plate-glass window. Their windows are made of clear toffee.

Our tour continued. In Gloucestershire, I remember, we sometimes played at theatres owned by the miners. At Cinderford business was very poor; our visit coincided with the local cinema's showing of *King Kong*. After that, from July onwards, we were augmented by two more artists and set off to play such seaside venues as the Lounge, Hunstanton, the Pavilions at Filey and Rhyl, and the theatre at Colwyn Bay. In those days no seaside resort, however small, lacked its alfresco or pier pavilion show during the summer. There seems to be a general impression put about today that those shows were amateurish or of poor quality. Nothing could be farther from the truth. Poor shows were the exception. Countless top performers, many of whom became household names – Leslie Sarony, Stanley Holloway and Arthur Askey to name but three – obtained much of their original grounding in such shows. It was a hard school, especially when you played outdoors and had to compete with the sounds of waves, ships' sirens, screeching babies, barking dogs and whatever, and there was no microphone or electri-

161

cal amplification equipment to help you out. It was quite a lesson in projection and timing, I can tell you.

One distinction that I may claim from my fit-up and pierrot days was the introduction of escapology into the pier shows. It delighted me, of course, to be able to emulate one of my boyhood heroes, the great Harry Houdini himself. We would place an announcement in the local press:

Mr Jack Le White accepts the challenge by a local resident to escape from a packing case supplied by the Wholesale Electric Co. The box is to be nailed and fastened with a steel binding machine. He hopes to make the escape within five minutes.

Such an escape was always good for publicity and generally guaranteed us a full house. While we were at Redcar, the local police challenged me to escape from their handcuffs. I went down to the station, where I was duly handcuffed with my hands behind my back. A few seconds later, I walked back into the charge room with my hands free. 'I'm going to send these 'cuffs back,' said the sergeant indignantly, 'and tell them they're no bloody good.'

Another of my escapes was from a steel pillar box secured by a padlock on a staple. A local approached me one morning and said the box was easy to escape from and he would prove it. He had, I noticed, a pair of pliers with him, and I assumed that, since the box was kept on display at all times, he'd observed that the staple was held in position by nuts and bolts, with the nuts on the inside, and thought that all he needed to do was unscrew the nuts and push the pillar-box door open. As this would leave the padlock still on the staple, I could not imagine how he thought he would then get it bolted again. The man was so insistent that in the end I said, 'OK, you have a go. I'm just off to lunch. As soon as you're out, come on round to my digs.' With that he climbed inside and I secured the lock. I went and took a leisurely lunch, from which I returned to find my local friend, despite his pliers, still a prisoner. As it was impossible to stand up inside the box without bending your neck, it took him quite a time to hold his head up straight again after I'd released him.

When you were working alfresco – that is to say, down on the open beach – you needed to be a good 'bottler' as well as a performer. In other words, you needed to be persuasive in getting people to pay up when you went round with the collecting box. Never will I forget the expression, 'Nay, lad, I gave last time!' What a pity that this style of entertainment has all but disappeared from our holiday resorts. It was an institution – a full show put on by just a few artists. The holiday-makers could emerge from their boarding houses in the mornings, go down to the beach for a paddle or swim, work hard at keeping their little ones occupied, and be delighted when, at 11 a.m., the show began and they could relax in deck-chairs for an hour of laughter, music and dancing, and all for 6d. (2.5p). Those who were standing on the promenade could watch for free, giving only when and if they cared to when the bottle came their way. Parents could happily leave their children, knowing that the comedian, always known as 'uncle', would give them all prizes when it came to talent-contest time; and that they wouldn't hear any four-letter words or doubtful innuendoes. What was more, the children gained an early appreciation of good music, since the pianist always had a solo spot and the singers would sing ballads, or maybe arias from Gilbert and Sullivan.

At the end of the summer season, the two extra artists left and Mr Matto's troupe returned to touring the villages. Perhaps, Mr Matto suggested, Nora and I could work up a song-and-dance routine, and so Nora became my tutor and I was able to add dancing to my repertoire. The first dance I did was in clogs to a specially written 'Dutch' number. Its words went something like this:

> Once a little Devonshire gentleman went
> Over to Holland on business intent,
> Married pretty Gretchen and made her a vow
> To say he'd finished with Devonshire now.

(*Chorus:*)
I like my cider down by the old Zuider See,
For cider of Devon
Tastes something like Heaven,
With Gretchen upon my knee.
Upon the sea wall he's fishing
As patient as can be.
He's sitting beside her
Sipping his cider
Besider the Zuider Zee.

Later in my dancing I progressed to the 'Schottische' and 'Buck' and 'Wing', and as time went on was able to introduce acrobatics into the routines. In due course, our spell with the *Rigmarolles* came to an end, and the next year, in 1935, Nora and I were married.

We continued to work together as Le White and McCourt in variety revue and pantomime, and, in April 1936, we played the Argyle Theatre, Birkenhead, a theatre from which some of the earliest live variety broadcasts were made and the scene of my great-uncle Tom Foy's breakthrough to stardom. The Argyle didn't, unfortunately, do for my career what it had done for Tom's, but it did eventually furnish me with an anecdote. With us on the bill were Pat Kirkwood, then aged only fifteen and billed as 'The Schoolgirl Songstress', but later to star with Vic Oliver in the musical revue, *Black Velvet*, and, as I have mentioned earlier, to become one of English pantomime's most famous principal boys. There was also Don Galvan, 'The Mexican Troubador', Bobby Wright and Marion, an American comedy duo, Roy Davey, xylophonist, Rome and Elder, and Ted Ray, comedian. Finally, at the very foot of the bill, came a mysterious act called 'Euston and St Pancras'. It certainly looked good on a bill, but no one had ever heard of them, and most acts in variety knew all the other acts, even if only by name, through the theatrical papers.

I arrived at the theatre on the Monday afternoon to find a rehearsal in progress. The stage was ablaze with light, flash-bulbs were popping and two blacked-up gentlemen were taking up various poses in the manner of the well-known genuinely black cross-talk (straight man and buffoon) act of those days called Scott and Whaley. By the end of the Monday-night performance, the secret was out. Euston and St Pancras were really Bobby Wright and Ted Ray. Some thirty-nine years later, when I was working at the BBC's North Acton Rehearsal Rooms, whom should I spot, standing in front of me in the queue for a cup of tea at the cafeteria's self-service counter, but Ted Ray. On an impulse I tapped him on the shoulder. As he turned to face me I asked, 'Good morning, but am I addressing Mr Euston or Mr St Pancras?' The expression on his face was beyond description, but the moment his initial startlement died down he took it in good part and exclaimed, 'How remarkable! After all these years!' We took our tea together and had a long chat about old times at the Argyle. My sister Leonora had in fact worked with Ted Ray even earlier, when he was appearing as Nedlo, the Gypsy Violinist, and was forbidden to speak on stage on pain of breaking his contract.

In the summer of 1936, Nora and I returned to Redcar to play a season, but half-way through she had to leave. She was expecting a baby. Sad to say, our marriage broke up soon after the birth of our son, Keith. It is always difficult to explain why such things happen, so I won't even try. One thing I can tell you is that Nora and I felt no bitterness for each other in after years, and I shall always be very grateful for the happy, youthful courting days we spent together. Nora never returned to the profession. Keith grew up to become a teacher. The theatrical strain is still strong in him, however, for he has acted, written and produced many school and college shows, ranging from pantomime to classical tragedy. He won an award for his work in theatre in Zambia during the several years he spent overseas, and his wife and two daughters, Claire and Rachel, are all keen theatregoers and proud of the family traditions. His wife says he is also quite a good dancer – though not as good as his mother.

9

Single Again

After the break-up of my marriage I had to start again as a single act in every sense. In 1937 I was on the books of the Ida Lillie Dancing School and Agency. Ida was a charming lady who conducted her agency in the manner of the old school. No matter how many times you wrote to her, there would always be a postcard in reply. 'Keeping you in mind,' it might say, or, as it did on this occasion, 'Come to the office prepared to give an audition.' I then found myself booked through the Tissington & Craig management for the 1937–8 season of the Imperial Players, whose six-handed show, *Serenaders*, was exclusive to the NAAFI (the Navy, Army and Air Force Institute, as many old service hands will remember all too well). Fred and Peggy Payne, a husband-and-wife comedy duo, produced, and May Sansome, a pianist-accordionist, was our accompanist. Besides myself, billed as plain Jack White in this instance, there was also Bob Bent, an all-round entertainer, and Gwen Whitton, a soprano-soubrette very popular with the troops. We played the show wherever they required us to go: in aircraft hangars, aboard ship, in the officers' mess or on table-top stages improvised from lashed-together canteen furniture. It was all very enjoyable, the servicemen were the best of audiences, and the idea of war, even in the midst of all those uniforms, couldn't have been more remote.

Following that engagement, I teamed up again with my sister Leonora for the first time since the car accident at St Albans. We gave an audition – alas, unsuccessful – for the Windmill Theatre, but were booked for the 1938–9 winter season at the Opera House, Dunfermline. The Opera House was a fine small Georgian theatre, intimate to play in and seating five hundred. The manager, an Englishman, believed in equal billing – no top or bottom of the bill. All the acts' names were printed in the centre of a star. If an act wasn't the best in its particular field, he said, then it wouldn't be at the Opera House in the first place. The printed programmes were well thought out, and they flaunted, at head and foot, slogans along the lines of, 'The finest cure for melancholy depression – the Opera House habit' and 'A laugh a day keeps the doctor away'. Variety was still, at the end of the 1930s, following its tradition of giving value for money. The admission prices were, at that time, orchestra stalls, 2s. (10p), dress circle, 1s. 6d. (7.5p), pit, 1s. (5p), and gallery, 6d. (2.5p). When I tell members of a younger generation this, they always say, 'Ah, but people didn't earn anything then.' Ah, but in the 1950s, by which time people were certainly earning more, cinema prices still ranged between only 9d. (3.75p) and 1s. 6d.

At Dunfermline we played revue on a repertory pattern: a new revue each week and two pantomimes for the Christmas and New Year season. Our producer was Billy Malone and our fellow acts on the bill included the comedians Smart and Benson, the soubrette Mamie Riley, a pair of guitar players in what would today be called Country and Western style, Decca and Rex, who were previously in poultry before entering showbusiness as amateurs and winning a popular following, and the Moxon Girl Dancers. One of the revues finished with me singing 'If I Had a Talking Picture of You' and introducing the rest of the cast, who each came on impersonating a Hollywood star of the day. In the revue programmes, Leonora and I did our individual acts, but behind the scenes we found ourselves somewhat cold-

167

shouldered as the only English artists amid a group of rather clannish all-Scottish performers. When it came to the first pantomime, we found ourselves cast in the roles of the Ugly Sisters in *Cinderella*. We knuckled down to making all our own comedy props and, much to the surprise of our colleagues, became a great hit with the public. It was the first of the very few times that I reluctantly played a dame character. Somehow I never was able to see myself in that particular role.

Leonora and I were not such a hit in Ireland, where we briefly and disastrously tried to run our own touring show. It was necessary to rent the town halls in advance, and they, in turn, required a deposit with the booking. I sent the deposits to an agent in Dublin, but we found on arrival that he'd pocketed most of the money. The local fathers were seldom helpful and sometimes openly hostile. Some audiences received us well, but our style of humour seemed to leave others at a loss. It was impossible to find digs. Before long we decided to call it a day. Something went wrong with the van I had invested £10 or £15 in to travel our small company and we crept all the way back to Dublin in first gear. There I sold the vehicle for thirty bob (£1.50) to a farmer who wanted it to cart his beet. The bargain was sealed with the customary slap of the hand over a glass of Guinness. So ended our grand tour.

During the later 1930s, Ben, Harold and Raymond were continuing to work as Tom, Dick and Harry, and Father, approaching his seventies, was virtually living in retirement at his and Mother's Hornchurch home. He did, however, continue to emerge from time to time to work his solo foot-juggling act, Henri Alexander, 'the Antipodean Marvel', the Frenchified spelling of his first Christian name being a well-established touch of class. After Leonora and I had finished our dates at Dunfermline, we had no engagements to follow, but Leonora received an offer through our cousin, Rita Atkins (née Delbosque), to join up with a remarkable show Rita was working with in Germany. *Tropical-Express* was, perhaps, the most extraordinary entertainment of its kind there has ever been – a show on an enormous scale, played

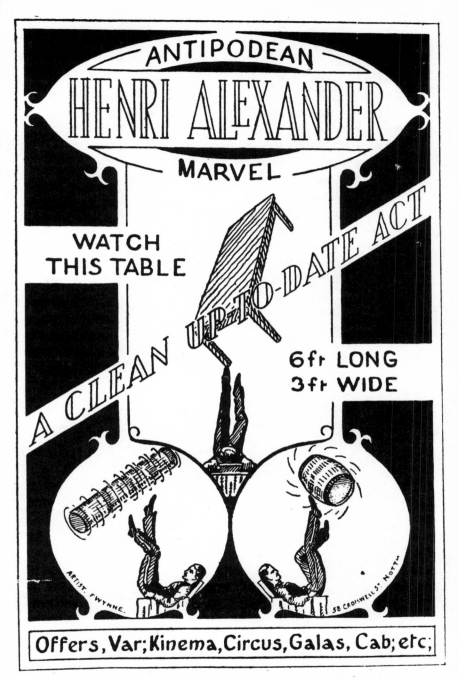

The decoration from Henry Alexander Whiteley's letterhead for the
solo act he still performed at the close of his career

non-stop at breakneck speed, pausing only for the interval. No performer, however famous, was allowed more than three minutes in which to put across his or her act.

In a bill of 101 items played twice nightly, *Tropical-Express* brought together a cast of over a hundred entertainers, supported by seventy animals and four wagon-loads of scenery and costumes. There was an orchestra, in which every performer was expected to take part, and those with no previous knowledge of how to play a musical instrument were obliged to learn from those who could play one, even if it was only a few notes on the accordion for a big spectacle number or something on the sousaphone. There was also a four-tiered pipe organ and a specially made accordion some six feet high that required four men to operate it. Rita was the director in charge of the girls in the show, and her husband, Eddie Atkins, scored all the orchestrations.

The relentless pace of the show often left audiences bemused. The 'Journey Round the World' group of fifteen or so scenes at the end, for instance, was nicknamed 'the stampede', and all the different scenes for this were hung on the same wire. As the opening line-up of a dozen girls finished dancing the first number (say, 'Brazil'), the backcloth would be whipped across and the second line-up would go straight into the succeeding number (say, 'Holland'). Meanwhile the first dozen girls would be doing lightning changes in back-stage cubicles adapted from enormous packing cases, so they would be ready in time for the third number (say, 'Paris 1900').

The 'Svengali' who brought this hybrid extravaganza of revue and circus into being was an extraordinary showman, 'Professor' Curt W. Doorlay. He could be a hard man; he could be ruthless. No mere human consideration was ever allowed to interfere with the show. He had the gift of getting people to do things of which they would never have thought themselves capable. Not even his young wife was exempt, but was expected to turn her hand to anything, from working with tigers to looping the loop on a bicycle. A typical example of Doorlay's method came when he decided that the girls in the chorus line were not smiling enough. He

170

called a rehearsal very early in the day and made it his business to be there in person, so woe betide any late-comers. On stage he had a row of chairs placed side by side, and in front of each chair was a mirror. As soon as the whole chorus was assembled, he announced, 'Good morning, ladies. I have spoken to you on more than one occasion about working with pained expressions on your faces. Be seated, please. Now, look into your mirrors – and SMILE!' And each of them had to smile and go on smiling until they were doing it to Doorlay's satisfaction. The smiles may have become a trifle wooden at times, but they certainly stayed in place.

Tropical-Express began its international tour in the Far East before coming to Europe, and its magazine-format pro-gramme brochure, measuring twelve by nine inches, was decorated with various unexpected and sensational pictures, including a beheading in Manchuria. Leonora joined the show while it was in Munich, and my brothers' act, Tom, Dick and Harry, was with the set-up when it was playing at the Circus Carée in Amsterdam. My brother Harold also became the show's diplomatic manager at about this time and took over all the responsibility for ensuring passports and visas were in order for the vast cast. It was a demanding and rather thankless responsibility, for the foreign tempera-ments involved with the show were many and various. Wherever he travelled, Doorlay had a habit of talent-spotting his performers on roadsides – a snake-charmer begging at a street corner in Calcutta, for example.

As for myself, in that March of 1939 I found myself playing a short season in revue at the Theatre Royal, Bristol – one of Britain's oldest theatres, subsequently to be nationally renowned as the Bristol Old Vic. The man in charge of the show there was Sandy Lauri, a descendant of another famous showbusiness family. Among his forebears was Charles Lauri, who was said to have been the finest animal imperson-ator of his generation and who featured in several of Augus-tus Harris's legendary Drury Lane pantomimes. Sandy's son, Billy Lauri, was also in the show, and so were Harry Gordon, a Lancashire lad, and Connie and Billy Edwards. The two Billies, Harry and I were all in the same age bracket

171

and became like the Four Musketeers, always together in work and leisure. We could get into any cinema free on our 'Wilkie Bard' – theatre slang for professional card – and Sandy, a great one for the horses himself, would treat us all as if we were his sons. Whenever we set off to the pictures, he'd hand his son a few bob and say, 'Share it among you for ice-cream or fags.' Our salaries were very small. After all, about £60 was still the amount of capital needed to provide the guarantee for a revue in those days – enough to cover basic costs and wages for the cast.

The youngest of our little group was red-headed Harry, who came from Ashton-under-Lyme and whom we would frequently ask what his favourite food was, just to hear him reply with a deadpan expression on his face, 'I like pea soup,' in broad Lancastrian tones. It never failed to make us laugh. The show had a strong musical emphasis along with the comedy element, but Harry always maintained a dead-pan demeanour on stage. We closed the first half with a musical ensemble: violin, saxophone, guitar, accordion and drums. To this I added a home-made one-string violin attached to a broom, and used to make my entrance apparently coming on to sweep the stage at the wrong moment. After doing my best to interrupt, I'd lift the broom to my shoulder and start to play next to unsmiling Harry on guitar.

One night I decided it was now or never if I was to raise a laugh from him. As I played, the broom-head of my instrument began to brush Harry's hair, a fact to which I needed to seem oblivious, though the audience caught on at once. As their laughter grew, I watched Harry out of the corner of my eye and, lo and behold, a quiver began to crease his lips. Next there was a smile, and then he began to laugh loudly and to go on laughing till the end of the number. At that point I picked up my real violin and joined in with our closing number, the 'Barcarolle' from *The Tales of Hoffman*. This last item always went down well, bearing out the contention that even people with no pretension to musical knowledge or appreciation can never resist the greatest melodies.

We 'Four Musketeers' were each to see some time in the

172

services during the war, and three of us were to emerge unscathed. Sadly, the exception was Harry, who was reported missing, presumed dead. His parents used to keep a theatrical boarding house, and when I stayed with them some years later, they told that this was all they'd ever learnt of his fate.

Billy and Connie Edwards had met in variety at the oddly named town of Leighton Buzzard. Billy had made an early entrance into showbusiness, having been known, as a child performer, as the Welsh Jackie Coogan. He played piano accordion and guitar, and was noted for his big-boot act, after the style of Little Tich. Eventually he became a top producer with Moss Empires. His and Connie's only son, Glyn, became a producer and director in independent television, one of the many talents working in the modern entertainment media whose lines of descent come out of a long-standing showbusiness tradition.

Connie herself had been all set to become a concert violinist. She had played in the National Youth Orchestra at thirteen and soon been promoted to first violin. She accompanied the great pianist Solomon and was conducted by Sir Henry Wood. She played in the Queen's Hall and the Central Hall, Westminster, and performed for George V's Jubilee in 1935. I discovered that her teacher at the Royal Academy of Music was the very same who tutored my eldest brother, Harry, after the First World War. But Connie's family, especially her mother, Ellie, were great fans of music hall, and Connie decided to put together a 'sister' act with a school friend who was equally gifted musically. There were many such acts then, either of real or stage sisters, all of them talented and able to introduce dance or comedy with music. Back in the 1880s there had been the Richmond Sisters, Josie and Lulu, from America, and from Britain the Sisters Cuthbert, 'received with unbounded applause at the Crystal Palace and the London and provincial halls'. The latter were known as the Hallelujah Sisters from a popular number that was an affectionate dig at the Salvation Army:

They call me happy Eliza and me converted Jane.

We've been so wicked in our time, we'll never do so
   again.
Oh will you come and join us, it's easily understood,
We're Hal-le-lujah sisters and we're bound to do you
   good.

In the 1920s, there were the Houston Sisters, Renée and
Billie, with their comedy back-chat and dance act; in the
1930s, Elsie and Doris Waters rose to immortality as 'Gert
and Daisy'; and in the later 1940s we had the harmonizing
trio of the Beverley Sisters. It was in this line that Connie
began, until she teamed up with Billy Edwards and they
formed their own musical act.

Meanwhile *Tropical-Express* had never yet been seen in
Britain, and Harold had persuaded Doorlay to let him set
negotiations in motion. He arranged for Ralph Marshall, a
senior representative of Moss Empires, to go over to the
Continent and see the show. As a result, an English tour
was arranged and extra British artists were engaged. The
first English date for *Tropical-Express* was for a fortnight at
the Chiswick Empire, and for those two weeks I helped out
in a humble back-stage capacity.

There was a temperamental elephant with the show that
was said to have a wicked sense of humour. It made a point
of picking on any player or dancer who caught its attention
and giving him or her a jostle right in the middle of a
complicated number. Certain performers may therefore have
felt that it got what it deserved when it fell through the stage
at Chiswick, though the bellowing of the unfortunate beast
was pitiful to hear until it was rescued. *Tropical-Express* also
featured a pair of leopards that wore collars and leads and
were taken for walks like dogs. On one occasion I was
backstage as the leopards were returning from their consti-
tutional. One of their handlers asked me to open the cage,
which meant I had to clamber on top of the structure and
raise the barred door. As I turned to go towards the cage,
something caught me a heavy blow on the back. It was one
of the leopards, and I could feel the animal's face close to the
back of my head and its paws on my shoulders. Fortunately I

174

was wearing a thick leather jerkin, and it's surprising how reflex actions come into play at a moment of danger. I managed to grab hold of its collar and pulled it downwards with all my strength. As I flung the leopard on to its back, I heard a tearing sound as my jerkin was ripped asunder. The poor creature had obviously been startled and seized on my back as the nearest target.

While we are still on the subject of animals, I am against their ill-treatment and making them do anything that is unnatural to their natures, but I can never agree with those who would like to see a total ban on performing animals in the world of rings and curtains. To me the animals lie at the very heart of any circus, second only to the clowns. Cruelty can happen anywhere – on the hunting field and race track, for a start – and is more likely to occur in the home than in the ring. In the traditional circus, animals are hardly ever ill-treated. Circus people form a close-knit group and everyone is constantly aware of what is going on around them. The genuine animal-lovers among them will soon put a stop to any acts of cruelty, for the old showmen, like my great-grandfather, W. F. Matthews, knew that cruelty was not a necessary part of training an animal to perform. All that was needed was to channel these creatures' natural skills and intelligences. When an elephant walks over someone lying down, it does so because no elephant will step on an unsteady object. In the same way, sea-lions love to balance and catch fish, all monkeys are gymnasts, and dogs, ever aware of applause, are natural comics and enjoy working. The animals are their keepers' livelihoods, after all. They always come first in terms of feeding, warmth, bedding down and grooming, and are never allowed to go hungry. As that great friend of circus, Lady Eleanor Smith, wrote in her last, posthumously published, book, *British Circus Life* (1948):

My own experience of circus, which – believe me – has been an apprenticeship lasting many years, has made me comprehend exactly how animals are trained for the ring. *They are trained by bribery.* A piece of meat on a pedestal for the lions, a carrot for the liberty-horses, fish for the sea-

175

lions – these, combined with the extraordinary patience of all successful trainers, achieve results which could never be brought about by whips and sticks . . .

I remember words uttered one night at Olympia by the late Sir Frederick Hobday, the famous veterinary surgeon. Said he, 'After looking at sick animals all day long it's a pleasure to see some that are in absolutely first-class condition.'

As the *Tropical-Express* show went on its way to travel the provinces, I joined a concert-party tour to see me through the summer. This one had the fascinating title of *Lavender Follies*, intended to convey that it was a classy, up-market sort of a show. Our manager and director was Edgar Taylor, a fine dancer, and we opened at the City Varieties Theatre, Leeds, from where the music-hall show *The Good Old Days* was televised for so long and so successfully during the post-war years. Meanwhile, in that summer of 1939, the possibility of war still seemed remote and life, following Neville Chamberlain's famous promise of peace in our time, appeared to be stable and promising as the depression years came to an end. Highways were being developed and villages were becoming electrified. Children's playgrounds were being built and public libraries increased in number.

From Leeds, the *Lavender Follies* journeyed across to Bangor in Northern Ireland to play at a small pavilion called the Musical Box. The return trip, to Bideford in Devon, was a nightmare and we didn't arrive until late on a Sunday night. The only one of us who had not been able to fix up accommodation beforehand was our soubrette, a young lady called René. In somewhere like Bideford, to find a spare bed at the height of the holiday season was almost impossible. Finally she contacted a woman who took pity on her and offered to put her up if she didn't mind sleeping in the same room as her daughter. 'My son goes away in the morning,' the woman said, 'and after that you can have his room.' Naturally, René agreed.

It's usual for all artists to arrive early at a theatre on a Monday morning. There is always so much to do to have

176

the show ready by evening. We got down to setting everything up, but of René there was never a sign. At last she
arrived, looking as pale as death. It was some time before
we could get a word of explanation out of her. The landlady
had gone shopping first thing that morning, and shortly
afterwards René went out too, to post a letter, the daughter
remaining in bed. When René returned, she heard screams
coming from upstairs, and ran up to find the daughter still
lying in bed, but dead. Her face and the wall were covered
in blood. The source of the screams was her distraught
mother. René helped the landlady back downstairs and contacted a neighbour to call the police before coming on to the
theatre. By that time she was suffering from delayed shock
herself.

All of René's luggage remained back at the house, upstairs
in the daughter's room, and she knew she would have to
call round and collect it. There was no question of her being
allowed to go back alone, so I volunteered to accompany
her. At the house we found the police, with the local
reporters and photographers, and although the police ques-
tioned René, there was nothing she could add to what they
knew already. As she talked to them I offered to go up and
bring down her cases. The room and the body presented a
ghastly sight. I tried not to look as I grabbed the luggage
and ran. A day or so later we learned from the police that
the killing was done by the daughter's husband, from whom
she was separated. He had arrived at the house and come in;
there had been an argument. He had picked up a flat iron
and beaten her to death. Yes, I'll always remember beautiful
Bideford. 'We don't think we'll need to apprehend the man,'
the police predicted. 'He'll do himself in.' They were right.

As we continued our tour, from Bideford to Guernsey
and on to Leamington Spa, the news built up of Germany's
continuing aggression and threats of invasion. Nevertheless
it came as a great shock when, on 3 September, we heard
that Britain was at war with Germany. Our next venue was
the Alhambra, Devonport, where the manager met us with
the news that all theatres were closed until further notice.
There was nothing for it but to head for home. Poor Edgar

Taylor, our producer. I can see him now, sitting disconsolately on his theatrical basket, surrounded by pieces of scenery and saying, 'I won't see the end of this war.' It seemed a ridiculous remark to be making, for he wasn't an old man, only in his late forties. Yet his prophecy proved correct. He was killed in the blitz on Sheffield.

At the outbreak of war, *Tropical-Express* was playing pell-mell at the Finsbury Park Empire, but came to an abrupt stop like everything else, and had to be disbanded. There was a great fear in the country of so-called 'fifth-columnists' during the early stages of the war. Many German circus and revue artists were in due course interned on the Isle of Man in the round-up of 'aliens' after Churchill gave the order to 'collar the lot', even though many of those affected were Jewish and had no reason to love the Nazis. Most performers were completely apolitical and opposed to war, as artists generally tend to be. In the Doorlay show there was literally only a small minority who were Nazi enthusiasts – a German midget act.

At the outbreak of war I returned to my parents' house in Hornchurch. There I found all the family already gathered, and with them Mother's mother, Grandma Mellors (otherwise Gregory, née Matthews). Preparations for defence were moving space. We dropped by at Hornchurch Town Hall to collect our flimsy gas-masks and carried these home in their small cardboard boxes. We were instructed that we should start digging a large hole, some five feet by four, to take an Anderson shelter. This corrugated-iron contraption needed to be sunk into the ground and to have its rounded roof covered with earth and rubble. Some people, making a virtue of necessity, created miniature rock gardens on the roofs. Under conditions of modern warfare, in the last decade of the twentieth century, an Anderson shelter would be about as much use as a canvas tent, but against the conventional high-explosive bombs of 1940, delivered by aeroplane, they did offer a measure of protection, so long as you weren't in line for a direct hit.

Grandma Gregory, the former Cannon Queen, was by then in her eighties and apt to ramble. She tended to lose track of the time in which she was living as her memories carried her backwards into a world long gone. She would imagine she was back in the ring, or would say, thinking of her husband, the late Chevalier Arthur Gregory, 'Where is he? I bet he's in the bistro.' If she spotted someone in the garden putting up a clothes-line, she would lean out of the window and shout, 'That's not the way to put up a tight-rope!' Nevertheless she could still enjoy a glass of wine and a Woodbine. The one thing she did not enjoy was having to go down into the Anderson shelter each night when, later on, the so-called phoney war ended and the Battle of Britain began to work up to a crescendo during the summer of 1940.

Ben, Harold, Raymond and I had decided in September 1939 that we would troop down together to volunteer for the AFS (the Auxiliary Fire Service). It took four men precisely to manoeuvre one of the trailer pumps, so they made us a crew on our own. The crew itself we soon transformed into an impromptu Four Whiteleys act and outdid the Marx Brothers, I'm sure, as we shinned up and down the ladder and jumped from the tower into the safety net. The only word we came to hate was 'Brasso'.

One of our fire chiefs, a big husky man with a fine physique, decided he'd like to learn acrobatics. We became his collective instructors and before long he could be seen turning back and forward somersaults and performing hand-stands. His brother George, a window-cleaner by trade, made a surprising contrast to the chief. He was, in his spare time, what would nowadays be termed a 'drag artist', though the phrase then still used was the more dignified 'female impersonator'. It was nothing unusual to spot George perched at the top of a ladder as he put on lipstick or varnished his finger-nails. He made quite a hit with his piano playing, and used to sing in a fine falsetto voice in the pubs and clubs.

Our firemen's pay was far from princely, and, while the theatres remained closed, we followed George's example in undertaking engagements in London clubs such as the Mildmay, Newington Gardens. So far we had still only been called out on several false alarms – we'd never yet had to deal with the real thing – and things continued to be quiet. Then, that December, it was decided to reopen the cinemas and theatres. It was acknowledged how important the entertainment industry was for maintaining public morale, a fact already amply borne out by events in 1914. I spotted an advertisement in *The Stage* for a pantomime artist and phoned the name it gave: a Mr C. A. Stephenson, who asked me to drop round and see him.

I arrived at his office, close to Piccadilly Circus, still dressed in my fireman's get-up and with the obligatory axe hanging from my belt. I took to Mr Stephenson at once as he remarked on how well I looked in my 'unicorn'. He had a marvellous sense of humour and was a virtuoso when it came to speaking British dialects. Like me and my family, he came from true theatrical stock: while he was selling programmes in a theatre at about the age of twelve, his father had dropped dead on stage. He then did a stint down the mines before taking to the boards himself. He had one brother who was a scenic artist and another who was simpleminded but who earned his living as a pavement artist outside the Tate Gallery for many years.

Charlie Stephenson obtained his first big break with the famous musical comedy, *The Arcadians*, first produced by Robert Courtneidge in 1909. It featured many of the top names of the day, including – in addition to Alfred Lester, Nelson Keys, Harry Welchman and Phyllis Dare – Florence Smithson and her husband, Dan Rolyat. Dan played the comedy lead of Smith, a cynical businessman who, after stumbling into Arcadia, is magically transformed into Simplicitas, who cannot tell a lie and who accidentally rides the Askwood Cup winner, Deuce. A real live racehorse playing Deuce was then led on stage at the close of the second act, with Simplicitas asleep on his back. On one of the show's later tours, Dan was kicked by the horse and suffered an injury from which he never fully recovered. At this point Charlie Stephenson stepped in to take the role over.

Mention of Florence Smithson reminds me that the Matthewses were once on a bill with her at the Pavilion,

Colwyn Bay, in her home country of Wales. The daughter of a Welsh theatrical manager, she came to be known as the 'Nightingale of Wales' and had a soprano voice with a marvellous range. The song she sang most famously was 'Roses of Picardy', written during the First World War and performed with real roses and real tears.

But to return to Charlie Stephenson, the outcome of my meeting with him was a booking to appear in pantomime at the Palace, Westcliff-on-Sea. I gave in my notice to the Fire Service and received the following testimonial from the chief:

> *To whom it may concern.*
> Mr A. Whiteley has been a whole-time member of the Hornchurch Auxiliary Fire Service since 11 September 1939. He has completed 43 hours training, and has undertaken all his duties in a very satisfactory manner. He leaves the service to take up his former profession, and it is with regret that I am obliged to release him.

At last, on my final day with the service, we attended a real fire. We were in our overalls, polishing away as usual with the Brasso, when the alarm bell rang. Grabbing our tunics, we jumped on to the engine as it moved off, and then hung on for dear life with one hand as we used the other to help us struggle out of overalls and into tunics as we roared and clanged through Hornchurch. The emergency turned out to be a house fire. Someone had gone out, leaving a paraffin heater alight, and this had fallen over and set fire to a horsehair sofa. At last we were able to put all our training into practice. It gave me quite a thrill as I wielded my trusty tomahawk to break a small pane of glass in the front door, insert a hand and free the latch. Taking care to cause as little draught as possible, we crawled inside and kept as close to the floor as we could to avoid being overcome by smoke, which, as you know, always rises. We picked up the sofa and threw it out of the window as the fire-hose was already spraying. I never grudged those weeks I spent in the fire service. The training certainly gave one confidence when facing life's hazards.

The pantomime at Westcliff did fair business despite the blackout. It was a modest show amid the restrictions of wartime, and it only ran for three or four weeks. By the end of January I was back working in revue with Sandy Lauri, this time at the Regal, Southend-on-Sea. It was great to meet old friends and what might be called a fateful date. I was immediately attracted to one of the dancers. At least, that is what she was said to be, but I quickly observed that she didn't know one foot from the other. Nevertheless she had a personality that singled her out at once from the other girls in the chorus. Where female attractions are concerned, I was always a hair and eyes man myself. This young woman was outstanding in both departments, especially in the eyes: brown and as big as saucers. She also knew how to dress.

Our courting began on Southend pier – the longest pier, with a train. Everywhere was covered in snow. We huddled together out of the wind, in one of the numerous shelters, as Pauline Fairchild, for that was her name, started to tell me about herself and how she came to be working with Sandy Lauri despite never having undergone any stage training whatsoever. On the other hand, she was not a complete newcomer to the scene. In her early childhood she had often sat in an orchestra pit, watching as her father conducted a theatre orchestra.

Pauline was born and grew up on Jersey in the Channel Islands. If it had not been for the war she would never have become my wife. She decided to come to England to find work in 1939 and went to stay in Hove with a cousin at an aunt's house. While she was there she spotted an advertisement in the local paper for panto chorus girls. This was how she came into contact with Mr Lauri. The pantomime was due to open on Boxing Day at the Old London Palace, an old theatre at the Elephant and Castle that had been known as the Theatre Royal many years before.

That Christmas of 1939 was to prove unforgettable for Pauline in every sense. Here she was, alone in a big city, cut off from her previous life and having to begin rehearsals with very little money and absolutely no dancing experience. She had to try to pick up the steps and movements from scratch, and could hardly have been the most popular member of the chorus line. Sandy Lauri, however, found that, out of all the girls, such as their numbers were, she had the best voice for delivering a line and realized she could be useful as a comic 'feed' and so on. She soon made friends with one of the other girls and they managed to find a room to share near the theatre. The landlord, though, insisted on rent in advance, which reduced them to their last few pence.

One of the features of Christmas Day in London that year was a real pea-souper of a fog – an unbelievable phenomenon for someone from sunny Jersey. The day passed in intense gloom while the girls' Christmas dinner consisted of a can of tomato soup each. They had no idea where the boss was staying and were too frightened to go out. As they remained trapped in their cold cell, the sounds of celebrations and the aroma of roast turkey came up to them from somewhere downstairs. In the end, they got into bed to stay warm, and remained there till Boxing Morning. Happily the fog had cleared by then, and they made their way to the theatre as early as possible to tell Sandy their tale of woe. He advanced them a sub and said, 'Off you go to the nearest café and get yourselves a good breakfast.'

As we got to know each other, Pauline also told me about her earlier life. Her mother was French, and there had been three daughters, one of whom, Jean, died in infancy. Pauline's surviving sister, Pamela, was seven years her junior. Her early years had been affluent. She was sent to a private school and the family owned a car – a definite status symbol in those days. Her father, Harold James Fairchild, was a musician who, like my brother Harry, had carried the love of his life, his violin, with him when he went off to enlist on Salisbury Plain for the First World War. In his case, he was turned down on medical grounds, and returned to Jersey to take up the post of conductor at the Opera House, then one of the Albany Ward chain of theatres. The Opera House was among the many establishments that changed over to showing silent pictures at about that time, and for a while the orchestra mainly provided film accompaniments and developed a fine library of scores for every mood and occasion. Harold Fairchild also found himself much in demand as a solo violinist. He performed as a concert violinist at the Yacht Club and was an occasional playing guest on Jesse Boot's yacht.

He was a popular figure in island society, often to be seen at the Yacht Club or in the bar of the Opera House after a show, upholding his reputation for being a man who could 'stand his corner'. His home life, however, began to be overshadowed by his French wife's jealous disposition and fiery temper. She had, moreover, been deeply affected by the loss of baby Jean and begun to drink heavily – chiefly brandy, which came very cheap on the island. Quarrels between Pauline's parents grew to be frequent and the good times failed to last. Her mother died when she was just fourteen, and was buried in a grave near that of Miss Lily Langtry, the 'Jersey Lillie'.

Pauline's mother's death left her in charge of her seven-year-old sister at the point where the house was sold over their heads. Their father simply walked out and left them to fend for themselves. It was not that he was a bad man, only a pitifully weak one. From infancy he had been doted on by his mother as an only son, and when his life crashed he could not stand up to the responsibility. Fortunately, Pauline was made of sterner stuff and obtained whatever work she could, serving in shops or, at one time, assisting in a mental home. She was also able to find a family who agreed to look after her sister. It amounted to an adoption in everything except the legalities. When she left Jersey, she could not have known that she was cutting herself off from her family for five years. The armies of the Third Reich were to occupy the Channel Islands during the summer of 1940 and, during all the years of war that followed, she was to receive only one letter from the Red Cross to let her know that her sister and father were 'all right' – which was as good as being told nothing.

While we were with the revue in Southend, I suggested

to Pauline that we could work together in a double act. We began to practise. She was very quick at picking up the tricks of movement and timing, and could already read music, having started on the violin when she was a child in Jersey. Marriage was not yet on the cards. I was still waiting for my divorce to be made absolute. At that time the process took about three years, even when both parties agreed to it, and I still had a year to wait for my freedom.

The usual period of 'resting' followed, with the odd date and one-night stand. Then, to my delight, we received a telegram from a Mr Ernest Knapp, offering a booking for a double act that summer at the Pavilion, Burnham-on-Sea, in Somerset. We arrived to discover that the company consisted of ourselves and two ladies, one a pianist, the other a singer. Of Mr Knapp himself there was never a sign, nor was there a trace anywhere in the town of bills to advertise the show. Mr Knapp, it seemed, had caught us napping. I contacted the town clerk, since the Pavilion was owned by Burnham Council, and found they were as much in the dark as we were. They had indeed agreed with a Mr Knapp that he could put on a show, but subsequently heard nothing more from him and assumed it was all off. Our arrival caught them completely by surprise, but they gave me permission to try to put together a show of some kind. We found ourselves some lodgings, which we discovered we were sharing with an ex-pro, Chris Shendo, who did a one-man-band act. Chris agreed to try and help us out, and I set to work and started to cobble together a show of sorts.

It goes without saying that it was a lost cause in those uncertain times. There was a war on; the summer visitors were few and far between; there was no time to distribute advance billing. The effort was bound to fail, but even so we played out the week and managed to raise enough for the two ladies' train fares home. This left me and Pauline high and dry, and we never did hear any more of Mr Knapp from that day to this. There was nothing for it but the labour exchange. Here I found that the only work available was labouring, and so began my brief career as a labourer with the work gangs who were erecting concrete pill-boxes along

185

the coast against the possibility of a German invasion. The pay I was offered was eightpence (3.3p) an hour, plus one penny so-called 'dirt money'. They started me off with pushing mixed concrete up a plank in a wheelbarrow and tipping it into its allotted place. It was perfectly ridiculous: I could walk along a tightrope or high wire without a tremor or lurch, but as soon as I was pushing a barrow up a plank I began to wobble violently from side to side. By the time I reached the top, I had lost half the barrow load. They demoted me rapidly. I was handed a pair of pliers and shown how to tie the long steel rods used to reinforce the concrete. The one thing I did learn from this episode was respect for the skills of full-time labourers as I compared my puny efforts at digging a hole with the way they expertly wielded shovels.

Pauline also managed to find work: taking money for the deck-chairs on the sea front. Once we saw a German plane shot down and the crew bailing out and descending on their parachutes. One of the airmen broke a leg, but in general they were among the lucky ones. Their war service was over. Mine was about to begin. On 22 November I was attested for the RAF. Actually, I was quite pleased about it. For one thing, it meant wearing a collar and tie, and for another, I could never imagine myself shooting or bayoneting a fellow human being face to face. Firing at an aircraft seemed so much more impersonal (though if anyone were to accuse me of being quite irrational on this topic, I would be the first to agree with them). I therefore volunteered for AG (air gunner), but was informed that this rank had now been designated WO/AG (wireless operator/air gunner). The recruiting officer suggested that, while I was awaiting my official call-up, I ought to go home and study the Morse code.

In fact I had booked to play in pantomime, and they gave me the go-ahead since there was no likelihood of my call-up coming through till after Christmas. With a sigh of relief I abandoned my mud-caked Wellington boots and my labourer's moleskin trousers, and set off to hear once more the welcome sound of 'Overture and Beginners'. On this occasion I was working with Mr Frank Fortescue, who, with Harry Hanson, ran repertory companies throughout the length and breadth of the British Isles.

The bombing in London had meanwhile become very bad. Grandma Gregory, close to the end of her days, went into a home, and Leonora arranged for Mother and Father to be evacuated to Bacup in Lancashire. Here they found accommodation in an establishment that was some sort of working men's hostel. It may not have provided princely quarters, but it must have been like a haven of peace after the din and disruption of the nightly raids. After a while, Father's sister, Madalena, joined them there when her home at 8 Wynne Road, opposite the main GPO sorting office in Brixton, received a direct hit. As good fortune would have it, Auntie was sheltering from the raid in the basement, the windows of which were fitted with heavy wooden shutters. She was sitting on the floor holding a lighted candle as the bomb went off. The next thing she remembered was hearing an ARP warden shout, 'Put that light out!' She discovered that she was sitting outside her house on the pavement, still clutching the candle, which was still alight. The shutters had taken the deluge of bricks from above and the force of the explosion had literally transported her.

10

War Theatres

My call-up date was 6 February 1941. I arranged for Pauline to go to Bacup to meet my parents and then departed for Blackpool, where I was instantly transformed into AC2 Whiteley 1028417. Like my eldest brother, Harry, and Pauline's father, I arrived to begin service life clutching my violin as if it were a talisman. My first date was at the Winter Gardens, where Father had performed many years before, except that I wasn't there to give a performance but to begin my training as a wireless operator. The premises had been taken over by the War Office and furnished with rows of tables, on each one of which were laid out a set of headphones and a Morse key. Morse may be written as dots and dashes, but you have to learn it as *dits* and *dahs*.

There were a good few performing artists in Blackpool at that time. Many units got up their individual entertainments, and Hills, the department stores, took advantage of the available talent and arranged shows. Music for these was provided by the top organist, Sydney Torch, and I remember Max Wall, who became an RAF corporal at Blackpool, being in one of these productions. Max tells us quite a lot in his autobiography, *The Fool on the Hill*, about the strains and stresses of combining service duties with showbusiness, but, despite my violin, I had no chance to become involved on the entertainment side at that stage. All my efforts went into mastering Morse, which I managed to do tolerably well, and I built up to a fair speed. Alas, when it came to procedures, and the mysteries of transmitters and receivers, the mathematics and physics required went somewhat beyond my sketchy education. The general arithmetic I was able to manage, but the rest remained a closed book. Of Faraday's and Lenz's laws I could make neither head nor tail. In the end I was docketed 'CTD', or 'ceased training'.

I was apprehensive over what would become of me after I left the course, especially since I had been observing, as I went to and from my billet – there were no barracks in Blackpool – the presence on the streets of certain airmen in battledress. These were the soldiers of the RAF, known as the RAF Regiment. One day I found myself with a squad being marched down to a rifle range set up in Stanley Park. There was to be a shooting competition, we were told, and the best marksmen would receive prizes. I wasn't a bad shot, having won quite a few prizes on the fairgrounds, but instinct told me that this was not the best time to be showing off any prowess. The sergeant was infinitely patient in his efforts to get me to understand the principle of aiming through the sights, but my bullets kept firing obstinately wide of the target. The authorities decided that the best thing to do with me was move me on as quickly as possible. I was posted to Cranwell, in Lincolnshire.

Here, at least, I was able to get a sleeping-out pass and to find rooms in the small country town of Sleaford, where Pauline could join me. As soon as she arrived she found work in the camp as one of the army of Mrs Mopps. Then one of the officers, with whom she got into conversation, offered her a job in the Pay Accounts office, which she was pleased to accept. She was doing better than I was. At Cranwell, the largest camp for RAF officers and cadets, I was a mere AC2 (aircraftman 2nd class), otherwise defined as an 'AC plonk' or 'erk', the lowest form of camp life. There was a song about an erk, the first two lines of which went:

189

I'm an erk, I'm an erk,
The wallah what does all the work.

In other words, I was on general duties. In the gym on
one occasion I was running through a few tricks from my
tumbling days when the sergeant in charge suggested I ought
to apply for a PTI (physical training instructor) course. I did
so, but before it could come through I found myself posted
to an air station in Northern Ireland.

The small village of Ballyhalbert lay on the coast, near
Newtownards and Londonderry and not far from Belfast.
But while the village may have been small, the camp was
large, the planes stationed there being mainly Spitfires, Beau-
fighters and Lysanders. The latter aircraft, nicknamed 'Lizz-
ies', resembled giant daddy-longlegs. I found myself part of
a support group that had been developed in the RAF under
the heading of 'airfield control'. Our duties were to assist
pilots and air-crews with their take-offs and landings. Sometimes a pilot returning from a mission would forget to put
down his wing flaps to reduce his speed of landing. Or
perhaps the runway being used that day had suddenly been
changed without a pilot's knowledge. In such circumstances,
we needed to make the pilots aware of the hazards by giving
Morse signals with an Aldis lamp, or, if the emergency was
even more urgent, by firing off a Verey pistol. We were
provided with a sort of mobile sentry box that could be
towed by a van to the various runways. It was fitted out
with a field telephone, which we could also use for reporting
to the control tower any sighting of enemy aircraft.

The rainy Northern Ireland climate could be very unkind
to those on airfield control. We became wet through at
times, and often faced long waits before we were free to go
off duty and get back into some dry clothes. We were also
obliged to take part in exercises to combat simulated enemy
attacks, these involving a commando type of drill. Kitted
out in gas-protection capes and hung about with respirators,
rifles, field dressings, water bottles and all the usual arms
and clobber, we had to run, clamber and crawl through
barbed wire and over obstacles. Such exercises were almost

invariably conducted at night in bitterly cold downpours of rain, hail or snow. After such experiences, the little village pub in Ballyhalbert, with its sawdust on the floor, became quite a haven. It was never visited by the officers, who kept to their own mess, and so it preserved a certain lack of sophistication. The first time I ever went into the establishment I ordered a Vermouth. The landlord gave me a quizzical look before starting to rummage about among some bottles on the shelf behind the bar. Finally he took one down, wiped off the dust, blew away the cobwebs and said, 'I've never been asked for this before,' as he poured me a half-tumblerful. 'I'll have to charge you a shilling,' he added apologetically. Every time that I went in thereafter he automatically took down the bottle and poured me a generous measure.

After I had been in Ballyhalbert for several weeks I was able to apply for a sleeping-out pass again and Pauline travelled across to Ireland to join me. We lodged in a cottage with a Mr and Mrs McCullough. It had no electricity, and the only lighting at night was provided by an ordinary paraffin lamp and a hurricane lamp. The floors were of stone and every drop of water for domestic use needed to be carried from the village pump a hundred yards away. The laundry was done in a tub on the open fire. All the cooking, too, was done on the open fire with its antiquated griddle.

Apart from the pub, the village had one shop and a post office. Meat arrived twice a week by butcher's van. From the NAAFI stores on the camp we were able to get the McCulloughs things they'd never seen in their lives, and while Mrs McCullough taught Pauline how to make potato cakes, Pauline reciprocated by teaching Mrs McCullough how to make pancakes. The McCulloughs were good and simple people, profoundly contented with a way of life that struck us as extraordinarily primitive. Mrs McCullough had been sent a sable fur coat by a relative who'd done well in Canada. She used to put it on when she went to feed the chickens, and at night it became a cover for the McCulloughs' bed.

At last my violin came into its own. As soon as it was

191

known that I had been a music-hall artist I was told to make myself known to Corporal Hall of the RAF Police. The corporal, an actor in civvy street, was putting on camp shows and was delighted to find he had a fellow professional on tap. It emerged that the wife of our senior officer, Squadron Leader Puller (of the family of the big dry-cleaning chain of those days, Pullers of Perth), had also been in musical comedy and was another great asset to the shows. The squadron leader himself was a keen supporter of these theatrical efforts. In no time I found myself doing a lot to develop their stage scenery, making wings and backcloths from doped hessian and any other materials I could scrounge. With Pauline having joined me, and my foot half-way back inside the door of rings and curtains, I became quite happy with my lot again, but just at this point my posting to the PTI course caught up with me from Blackpool to summon me back to England. When I asked my warrant officer if I could be released from the course, he said such a thing was impossible, so I went straight to Squadron Leader Puller, who duly pulled the necessary strings and arranged for me to stay where I was for the moment.

The production of the camp shows began to take up a good deal of my time. Once, when I was conducting a rehearsal in Corporal Hall's absence, I heard a voice coming from the back of the darkened hall, saying, 'That's not right.'

The speaker began to approach the stage, and I saw he was an officer. Addressing him in my best BBC English accent, I said, 'Excuse me, sir, don't think me impertinent, but would you mind telling me whether you're full-time or conscripted?'

'Conscripted,' he replied. 'I was a headmaster in civilian life.'

'Well, sir,' I said, 'I know nothing of what is required of a schoolmaster, but when it comes to the stage and producing, that is my full-time occupation.'

The officer took my point without batting an eyelid, and simply said, 'Carry on.'

Later on Flying Officer Harman, for that was his name, became a good friend to Pauline and me. He would get into civvies and take us into Belfast for a meal. He even offered to use his influence to help me towards a commission, but I declined the offer. For one thing, I could not imagine myself as an officer, and for another, I could never have afforded the life-style. Another flying officer with whom we became friendly was Gerald Carnel, who had rented a bungalow locally and lived there with his wife and daughter. We spent many social evenings with them, playing cards, though never for money. At Christmas we put on a show for the local children, and afterwards the Carnels invited us back for a party, at which I found myself the only ordinary airman in a group of pilot officers, squadron leaders and group captains. Off camp, I was on Christian-name terms with some of them, but as soon as you were back within the camp gates, it was all 'sir' and saluting again.

The camp show was worked up until it was proficient enough to tour the area. We once played to the workers on Lord Londonderry's estate at Newtownards in County Down. And then, when I was due for a week's leave, I was able to undertake a professional engagement at the Empire, Belfast. It was as enjoyable as a holiday for me to get back on to a proper stage, and the fact that I was paid for it on top of my service pay made it a lucrative week as well.

Back at camp, my duties on airfield control continued. One day I almost took my final bow. I was standing out in front of the sentry box, watching a Spitfire approach, its flaps down and everything in order, when suddenly there was a burst of firing and a hail of bullets missed the box by inches. The pilot's thumb must have slipped on to the firing button. When I went up to the control tower, shaking like the proverbial leaf, to put in my report, all the officer on duty said was, 'All right, Whiteley? Now go down and check for damage to the runway.'

Our group of ground-crew airmen at Ballyhalbert had been performing airfield control for some time when rumours began to reach us that, somewhere back on the mainland, an airfield-control course had been instituted and that those who passed were automatically promoted to the rank of sergeant. In due course, some of these fresh-minted sergeants arrived in Ballyhalbert and we were instructed to stand by them while they proceeded to take over our duties. Naturally, we resented this greatly, for we felt it would have been fairer to have made us sergeants in the first place. The newcomers needed all the support we could give them. Back at their training school, all their equipment had worked perfectly. Telephones had never failed and vans were always at the ready. The realities were vastly different and they were quite unprepared for them. The towing vehicle might fail to arrive, so that the box had to be moved manually and promptly shed a wheel – and there was little time to spare since aircraft were expected back at any minute. At this point, sod's law applying as usual, the telephone would go on the blink and there'd be no way of contacting the control tower. In such circumstances, the worst thing you could do was panic.

Once the airfield-control sergeants had displaced us at Ballyhalbert, my job there came to an end. I was returned to Blackpool on draft, and Pauline came with me to wait, there was no knowing for how long. They issued me with tropical kit, though by the topsy-turvy logic of service life that could as soon mean I was being posted to Iceland as the tropics. At Blackpool, the drill corporals were still going strong, putting the fresh recruits through their paces. They were on to a good thing – in an advantageous position to negotiate for backhanders from the local photographer for group photographs besides taking commission from cafés when they marched their squads along for a break from square-bashing. Among the drill corporals Max Wall starred prominently and was constantly expected, as he writes in *The Fool on the Hill*, 'to go into a comical drilling routine in the style of Fred Karno'. Nevertheless, he says, he enjoyed it because he 'recognized that it was *acting*: the rising and falling cadences of voice, the timing in giving a word of command, the satisfaction of having a well-turned-out, smart and efficient squad'.

By then Max had for some time been involved, on top of his daytime duties, in putting on two or three shows a week to entertain the streams of RAF personnel who passed through the town on their way to active service all over the globe. It would hardly have been possible for anyone to go on maintaining that sort of stress for ever. One day he was drilling a squad in the town when an officer passed and he gave the order for the customary 'eyes right' – a salute the officer failed to return. Max's temper snapped. He swung about, went after the officer and, rapping him smartly on the shoulder with the back of his hand, said, ''Ere, you, how about a little salute for me, then!' Well, the rumpus may be imagined. The incident was the beginning of the end of Max's service career. The authorities let him down lightly and he was referred to the RAF psychiatric hospital at Matlock with the diagnosis of a nervous breakdown. Eventually he was discharged under the label 'anxiety neurosis'.

As for me, the finalization of my divorce proceedings was pending and likely to require me to go to London. I was therefore taken off draft and sent to Tutbury in Staffordshire. Here I found myself landed in the midst of a group of musicians who played for local dances as well as in camp. I joined them as a fiddler, and also undertook many of the 'vocals'. When we were not playing, however, we became the sanitary squad. Our main camp duty was to keep the ablutions clean – all brasswork shining and every floor swabbed down. The least pleasant side of the job sprang from the fact that lavatories in Tutbury were still 'dry'. That is to say, they were fitted with Elsan buckets that required emptying into a large container which the council dustmen removed when they took away the camp refuse. It was hardly a task to appeal to the artistic temperament. Before long we found a way out of the odious duty. The dustmen already had to clear the dry privies at the homesteads in the village, so we clubbed together to bribe them to deal with those on the camp as well – a task they were happy to take over.

Our double life continued. By day we were sanitary wallahs. By night, in our best blues, we became the Royal Air Force Orchestra. We played in the local village halls and, when required, for ordinary airmen's dances and dances in the officers' mess. At the latter the drink flowed freely and there were always high jinks. On one occasion I remember a well-oiled padré riding all over the dance floor on his bicycle. At the airmen's hops no alcoholic liquor was allowed. Sauce for the gander was definitely not sauce for the goose.

Early in the war, my sister Leonora had married a clever and versatile dancer, Ron Walmer. For the wedding, Ron's dress uniform was borrowed from a props department and Leonora's wedding dress was made from a set of discarded satin tabs. Ron then went off to see war service as a commando. When I went to Tutbury, Leonora made an offer to take Pauline under her wing as her prospective sister-in-law and put together a double musical act. They called themselves Peta and Paula, billed as the 'Two Little Maids from Moscow', the Russians being our staunch allies at that stage of the war. The act was versatile, involving violins, xylophones and bells, and the duo began to get excellent notices wherever it played. Like all the other acts on the bills, they did their share of fire-watching. Once, when they were at Basingstoke, they took part in a show for McIndoe's 'guinea pigs', unfortunate airmen who had been badly burned and who were undergoing plastic surgery when the techniques of skin grafting were still in their pioneering days. Many of the poor brave men in the audience no longer had faces as we know faces. It took a determined act of will on the part of the entertainers to play as if they were in a completely normal situation.

Finally my divorce was through. Pauline had a week out in the bookings for Peta and Paula and I had a few days' leave due to me. We met in London and headed for Caxton Hall, where so many stage and screen folk have been married. We almost didn't reach the hall on time on account of an air raid, but a good old London taxi got us through. Our witnesses were Charlie Stephenson and 'Mademoiselle Veronica', otherwise Veronica Evans, the champion high kicker, who achieved entries in the *Guinness Book of Records* for her high-kicking achievements. There was all too little time to enjoy the idea of being married. I had to return to Tutbury and Pauline had to rejoin the Peta and Paula act.

Back at camp I was browsing through a copy of the RAF magazine *Contact* one day when I spotted an item about Ralph Reader being interested in hearing from airmen with theatrical experience who might like to be considered for his RAF 'Gang Show'. I could hardly get to my writing pad quickly enough. There were few, after all, who could claim theatrical experience more truthfully. Each day became an eternity as I awaited a reply. At last the camp commander summoned me to his office. 'You're to go to London to see Ralph Reader,' he said. 'If you're suitable you'll be released to join one of his shows. Good luck!'

So once again I was off to London, clutching my rail pass and with my fiddle tucked under my arm. I auditioned with my act and, to my great delight, found myself accepted. It was an event which marked the end of normal service life so far as I was concerned.

An orphan from the age of eight, Ralph Reader became one of life's fighters. He began his career acting and producing in New York, and was himself a theatre professional to the finger-tips. He also wrote songs, among them 'Strollin'', made famous by Bud Flanagan. He came to specialize, however, in bringing out amateur talent, and his name will be forever associated with the series of Boy Scout 'Gang Shows' that he produced from the early 1930s onwards. He had a real genius for moulding together large groups of mostly amateur performers to put on rousing entertainments which were capable of filling the Royal Albert Hall. Yet not even the Boy Scout 'Gang Shows' were exactly all that they seemed. Only when it came to his retirement in the 1970s did he reveal that the pre-war shows had provided a cover for counter-intelligence recruitment. With the coming of the war, his talents were much in demand and he adapted his approach to producing entertainments for the forces on a large scale in London as well as putting together smaller groups to tour the camp theatres. The shows, besides giving amateurs their head, were also springboards for showbusiness talent and featured the first appearance in public of

197

various famous entertainers – Tony Hancock and Peter Sellers to name but two.

Service discipline still applied technically, of course, but in practice it very quickly underwent some modifications. Ralph Reader himself was addressed as 'sir' to begin with, but this later became 'chief', even after he was promoted to squadron leader. Our pay-day parades were regularly reduced to confusion by our ventriloquist, Jack Read, who would throw his voice to different parts of the room. We performed in many places, including London, where Anna Neagle and her husband Herbert Wilcox were in our audience one night, and came backstage to meet us after the show. For a time we were based with an American unit at Ashford in Kent. The living conditions there made those in the British camps seem even more Spartan by contrast. The Americans enjoyed luxuries undreamed of by our forces: steaks as thick as your thumb, peaches and cream and unlimited cigars. For some reason, though, the Americans seemed to resent us. Every morning their duty sergeant would burst in on our billet with his bellow of, 'Wakey, wakey, you guys!' Each morning he burst in and bellowed in vain, for we took not a blind bit of notice. In all likelihood we'd have travelled miles to give a show the day before, and miles back again, and we seldom got to bed before 2.30 a.m.

We were due to go on an overseas tour, but I had been finding it increasingly difficult physically to perform my act. For some time I had been suffering from acute rheumatic pains in the shoulders, which I assumed must have been set off by the general dampness in Ireland. The condition reached the point where it was affecting my violin playing and tumbling alike. General fitness was essential for anyone going abroad, and I was sent for a full medical. They found I had a severe form of fibrositis and declared me medically unfit. To await my discharge, I returned to London, which had, since June, been enduring the raids by the V–1 rockets, the so-called 'doodle-bugs' or, as the cockney wits dubbed them, 'Bob Hopes' – 'When you 'ears one, you bobs down and 'opes for the best.'

On 26 September 1944, I reported to Uxbridge and that

was that. I wasn't sorry to be leaving the RAF, for I had never felt myself to be especially cut out for service life, though I was sorry to miss out on the overseas tour. When they discharged you, they let you keep your greatcoat if you wished. They also gave you a suit, a trilby hat, a shirt with detached collar, and even a pair of cuff-links. It was quite an improvement on 1918, when all the discharged other ranks received were a cap and muffler apiece. My only promotion had been from aircraftman second class to aircraftman first class, plus, as the expression had it, a 'Chinese corporal's stripe' for good behaviour. My discharge certificate stated:

Qualifications: none.
Degree of proficiency: none.
Special qualifications: none.
General remarks: a keen worker who has carried out his duties in a satisfactory manner.
Conduct: exemplary.

The last comment did set off a twinge of conscience when I remembered various crafty weekends I had taken without official permission to see Pauline. The service police were ever on duty at the railway stations, waiting to pounce on any travelling airman and ask, 'Where's your pass?' Whenever I saw them coming, I'd always managed to bribe a porter to take me across the rails to another platform. Once I'd even travelled from Blackpool to Bacup covered with bags in a laundry van.

I had entered the services classified as A1 medically speaking, and came out with a small disability pension of 7s. 6d. (37p) a week, though this would be gradually phased out as my health was expected to improve. It was a strange feeling to be a free man again, but now I had to try to pick up my career where it had left off. Leonora and Pauline still had a few 'Little Maids from Moscow' bookings to honour, so I travelled to Bacup to stay with my parents and began to write out for work for our own double act. Before long I was rewarded with a Sunday booking for the new act of

White and Simonne in the beautiful city of York with its wonderful minster and museum. We were to play the Rialto Cinema and also be part of a special show for the Lord Mayor at the Guildhall. On the same bill was Dick Henderson, the Yorkshire character comedian who first popularized the song 'Tiptoe Through the Tulips' and was the father of Dickie Henderson and the Henderson Twins.

We arrived in York on the Saturday without having been able to book ourselves anywhere to spend the night. There was a convention of some kind in progress, and all the hotels were full. We wandered about the town in the blackout, vainly searching for somewhere to stay. At the police station we found a blazing fire and several very contented policemen who showed no inclination to be helpful. Out we went again into the totally darkened city, and were only prevented from walking straight into the River Ouse by someone shouting a warning. In desperation, we took to knocking on doors at random, and at last found a woman who took pity on us. All she could offer was a couch and two armchairs in her front room, which we accepted gratefully. Equally gratefully we managed, after the last show, to catch a train back to Bacup in the very early hours of Monday morning.

At this time ENSA (the Entertainments National Service Association) was still going strong and looking for artists, so I wrote to Mr Bob Lecardo, who was booking acts. Bob was a fellow acrobat whose own act had been called 'Fun in a Bakehouse', but who was now working with ENSA on the production side. The name Whiteley obviously meant something to him and he asked me to call and see him at ENSA headquarters, which happened to be the Theatre Royal, Drury Lane. Its famous stage had been partitioned into sections to provide offices for the various departments, so I can claim that I did once, in a modest way, walk the same boards as Grimaldi and certain of my own ancestors. As a result of the interview, Pauline and I found ourselves booked to join a travelling ENSA unit. The joint pay we were offered was £16 a week, all found except for £2 for board and lodging. It may sound a silly sort of wage in today's terms, but it was then not at all bad, and had we been with ENSA throughout the war, we'd have finished up quite comfortably off.

It was a company of only nine, but it was a good and happy show and everyone was pleased to be doing their bit to keep up morale. We would stay in one base for a couple of weeks at a time, and move out to perform in the camps each day. After a show we would usually be invited to the sergeants' or the officers' mess. This was the only area of conflict within our troupe. The heavy drinkers would always want to stay on and make a night of it, while the more abstemious would be keen to get away as soon as possible. It was never an easy decision for the member of the troupe who was nominally in charge, but we invariably agreed to stay on if a commanding officer asked us to meet aircrews returning from raids over Germany. There were occasions when they'd lost comrades during their mission, but those young men always showed remarkable fortitude. Such hazards as we encountered were merely the results of conviviality, as happened once when our coach driver over-imbibed. As we headed for home, we spotted flashing lights on a control tower and realized we were on an airfield runway and planes were even then coming in to land.

Following our stint with ENSA, we joined a touring revue called *From London to Moscow*. The war was into its closing phase, but the Russians were still our gallant allies and the Cold War was a development no one could yet anticipate. The liberation of the Channel Islands, however, meant that Pauline at last received some news of her family there. Times had been hard for them. During the closing stages of the occupation, her sister's adoptive family had to hide their dog in the cellar. If the Germans had discovered it, they'd have taken it for food. Her father had gone through a tough time immediately after the German invasion, when the only work he could find was in the hospital morgue. Later on he was allowed to resume his profession, playing the violin in Forte's Café. Not even this made things easy for him. As was understandable, the local population tended to frown on the activity, for he was thereby inevitably entertaining German officers and soldiers. They made no allowance for

201

the fact that a musician in those circumstances needed daily practice to keep up standards and protect his fingers against the day when his prayers would be answered and the war would end and allow him to resume his dedicated life. In fact, many of the occupying troops were the equivalent of their British counterparts: conscripts forced to take part in a war they detested. Some of them were music lovers who were prepared to bring back violin strings, sheet music and so on from leave in Germany when such items were not to be had on the island.

From London to Moscow was run by Joe Seymour, whose brother Syd led a well-known band called Syd Seymour's Madhatters. The cast was predominantly female, and I and Frank Lee, whose forebears were a famous circus acrobatic troupe, the Boissets, were the only males. We played a number of theatres taken over by FJB, the F. J. Butterworth circuit, which was one of the first managements to organize a café for its artists – usually under the stage. Among the acts was a rather unruly performing-animals act entitled 'Packham's Pekinese'. It was run by a Miss Packham, who also owned a big house at Kingston-upon-Thames where she rented out rooms, and who was to become a close friend and, in due course, our landlady.

We continued to work for Seymour, but when it came to the pantomime season that Christmas of 1945, Pauline and I had to go our separate ways, she to the Hippodrome, Aldershot, to play Principal Girl in *Aladdin*, I to the Kingston Empire to play Mate in *Dick Whittington*. The Captain in this latter production was Horace Mashford, a brilliant light comedian in Randolph Sutton style, and Cat was played by Leando. By that time Pauline was expecting a baby. As soon as the pantomime season was over, she went to stay with my parents at their house in Hornchurch.

The arrival of peace had set in motion a strong burst of optimism and a general determination to restore life to the way it was on the day before war broke out. Maybe it was over-optimistic to think that life could ever be the same again, but my brother Raymond together with my sister Leonora and her husband Ronnie Walmer (who had returned from the war after having some tough experiences as a commando) and I decided the time was now or never. We put together our army grants to enable us to hire four further artists and began to plan our own summer show for the first year of peace, 1946.

Our line-up eventually consisted of Jack Le White, 'Variety's Newest Comic'; Ron Walmer, eccentric dancer; Leonora, 'The Musicality Girl'; Raymond, 'The Juggling Funster'; Sybil May, 'a smile and a song'; Molicia, contortionist; Madge Lilley, ventriloquist and comedienne; and Bernard Martin, a pianist entertainer. We booked the Pavilion at Silloth, near Carlisle, and settled on our title. It was to be called *Variety Vanities*. While Pauline remained in Hornchurch, waiting to give birth, the rest of us made tracks for the north.

11

The Show Goes On

On the outside the Pavilion at Silloth was in a deplorable
state and showing its scars from having been in the hands
of the army during the years of war. Inside it was pre-
sentable, and the stage and lighting were in sound condition,
though it lacked tabs and curtains. Once again we turned to
Drury Lane, realizing that they would have a lot of stuff left
over from the old ENSA shows. We spotted a heap of
beautiful green silk curtains in a corner, but, when we asked
how much we'd have to pay for them, were told we'd never
want them as they'd been badly burned. We turned them
over and found that the burns only amounted to holes here
and there, and so we obtained them, along with an
unmatching set of tabs, for next to nothing. The tabs we
then dyed in the bath to match the curtains. The burns we
dealt with by covering them with pieces of material cut out
of old beaded dresses and stuck on to circles of cardboard.

Once the curtains were in position at Silloth they created,
along with our rostra, the impression of a truly extravagant
set-up. The council informed us that they could do nothing
about the outside of the Pavilion, but since it was a wooden
building we made them an offer: 'Give us the paint and we'll
finish the job ourselves.' During our rehearsal week, anyone
not needed on stage at any point would carry on wielding a

paintbrush outside. We even painted 'PAVILION' in large letters on the sloping roof, and very effective it looked too. As a troupe, we were just like J. B. Priestley's company of 'Good Companions' in real life: seamstresses, dyers, sign writers, poster artists and interior decorators as well as entertainers. Nothing was beyond us, and everything was ready in time for our opening.

It would now be pleasant to be able to report that our efforts were amply rewarded and *Variety Vanities* was a great success. Not a bit of it, sad to say. The summer of 1946 was one of the few really hot ones of those years, but somehow the weekly holiday-makers did not arrive back in their pre-war numbers. We were playing twice daily seven days week, and the only day on which we had a good house was a Sunday, when the local cinema was closed and our audiences came from all over the district. The rest of each week was a disaster. We were, at times, literally playing to empty seats. To our intense chagrin, one of the Smith gypsy clan, who was running a small fortune-teller's tent close by the Pavilion and charging the same, 2s. 10d. (14.1p), for a ten-minute palm-reading as we were for a full two hours' entertainment, was never without a queue, rain or shine.

Even so we might still have survived, had not the law once again proved itself to be an ass so far as live entertainment on a Sunday was concerned. We were not allowed to open the box office on a Sunday and so the Sunday shows relied entirely on advance bookings for their audiences. The locals soon discovered that they could come along on a Sunday and bump into members of the company outside, who, by happy chance, would have in their pockets tickets for sale for that very night. Just as that aspect, at least, was working well, a letter arrived from the council to say they'd received complaints from a representative of the Lord's Day Observance Society, a body whose voice seemed to be strong in Silloth. We had already met the local vicar, and the only comment he had to make was, 'I hear you have a very good family show. Since you do not start up till after Sunday evening service, I have no objection, and I certainly hope to get along to see a performance one night during the week.'

We therefore knew that the complaint had not originated with the vicar. Finally we traced it back to one old lady of eighty. I went round to see her, but very quickly realized there was no way of reasoning with her that could avoid an argument to cause her much distress. Her interpretation of the Bible did not allow for God's healing gifts of laughter and enjoyment on the Sabbath, and there was no chance of our minds meeting on the topic. She was only obeying the dictates of her conscience, but she brought our season to a premature close. Without a Sunday performance we lost every hope of breaking even, let alone of making a profit. As we packed our bags to depart, the gypsy in her tent was still doing excellent business.

We were at least able to pay off our liabilities in Silloth, and there had been one bright spot for me during the venture: a telegram to tell me Pauline had given birth to a healthy daughter. I was able to see the baby for the first time and to be reunited with Pauline rather sooner than I'd expected. We planned for our daughter to be christened Annette Simonne at Hornchurch, in the small St George's Church in Kenilworth Gardens, built in 1935 and regarded as a good example of 'modern architecture' at the time, but at that stage still lacking a bell. Since its only funds came from the collection plate, we organized a show and donated the profits to the church for the installation of a bell in the little bell-tower. As a leaflet giving the church's history says, 'The need for a bell was met by the generosity of the Whiteley family, a unique acrobatic troupe living near by who specialized in sleigh-bell ringing with their feet!' Annette and the bell were christened together, and the bell is known as the 'Whiteley bell' to this day.

In the wake of the Silloth fiasco, we began to tour the *Variety Vanities* in South Wales for what was left of the summer. We headed for Tenby, which we made our base and where we were the first concert party to play at the pretty little 600-seater theatre, previous holiday shows having been given in the De Valance Gardens. Pauline joined us with baby Annette, though she was still not quite ready to resume working. My father-in-law, Harold Fairchild, also came over from Jersey to work and travel with us. Towards the end of the season, late in September, the weather was growing noticeably colder and travelling was becoming increasingly difficult. Digs suitable to take a baby into had become hard to find. The landladies of former days, who were only too happy to look after a baby while its parents were working, seemed not so much a dying breed as a breed that was dead and gone. At Tenby we tried in vain to find a babysitter and ended up having to take Annette with us into the dressing room. Then the manageress of the theatre suggested, 'I know some nice people who would look after her for you – a Mr and Mrs Griffiths.'

We went and found them at their home, 25 The Maudlins, and the Griffithses were indeed a lovely couple with a family of five. Mr Griffiths was the skipper of a small fishing trawler. One night Mrs Griffiths said to Pauline, 'Mrs Whiteley, why don't you leave the little one with us for a while, till she's a year or so? It's the first year that's so important. We all love her, and you can be sure she'll be well looked after.'

After much heartsearching, we decided that it would be better for Annette to spend a year in a settled home, but it was a sad occasion as we took her up to 25 The Maudlins to leave her with the Griffithses. Early the next morning we had to travel by van to Barnstaple in Devon. It was not a cheerful journey, with Pauline crying all the way as each mile took us farther from the baby. Here was family history repeating itself, of course, but Pauline found it especially hard to accept, and somehow it no longer seemed such a reasonable necessity as it may have done to my parents' or grandparents' generations.

We took one of our friend Miss Packham's rooms on a permanency in Kingston-upon-Thames. This gave us a base, and eventually led to us making our permanent home in Kingston. Miss Packham, besides being our landlady, was an out-and-out circus fan. Pauline's father meanwhile managed to get a job as part of a trio (violin, piano, cello) at the Tudor Café, Grimsby – one of the last of the old 'palm court' ensembles. This engagement eventually ended when the Performing Rights Act raised the cost of performing copyright music and priced them out of the market. The moment the manager dispensed with their services, they became just three old musicians, whose lives had been music, who'd never work again. All the Tudor Cafés up and down the country, with their limelight music, were closing down. The Performing Rights Society gained nothing and the customers, deprived of their harmless nostalgia, drifted away.

I arranged to work in tandem with my brother Raymond for a while. We managed to get ourselves several bookings, including one in pantomime, through the Joe Collins Agency (Joe being the father of Joan and Jackie Collins). By this time, however, television was moving in rapid strides and starting to make inroads into theatre business. Speciality acts were suffering particularly. An act only needed to be shown once on television and there was its novelty – gone! As we had more vacant weeks than were healthy, we decided to fill in the gaps by playing the clubs, or the 'rub-a-dubs', as they were dubbed. For this we took a different name for the act, it being considered *infra dig* for theatre artists to have to fall back on this sort of work. Indeed, if an agent heard you had been working the clubs, he would bar you from working the theatres. Later on, the situation was to change as the closure of theatres and cinemas gathered pace and the agents began to fight each other tooth and nail to get whatever bookings were going. Then, all at once, they became only too keen to submit the acts on their books to the clubs. At the time I am speaking about, all club bookings were still made direct through the club secretaries.

An act for the clubs was expected to provide at least four spots. Raymond and I were able to bring in our comedy and musical acrobatic routine, juggling and fire-eating, and then, believe it or not, we made up our fourth spot by singing. The last we considered a piece of cake after all the hard work of the preceding efforts, and we found it ridiculous whenever a concert secretary or members of the audience liked that part best and said, 'You've got such luvly voices. Go on, give us another song.' Working the clubs was never an easy option. Whatever or whoever else was on the bill, beer always came top. If the local team had lost that afternoon,

208

you knew you were in for a rough night of it. The audiences were completely unpredictable. You could tear 'em up at one club and die on your feet at another only fifty yards along the street.

For our juggling and acrobatics we needed as much room as possible, but the stages of many clubs were so small that we had to ask for the piano to be removed before we could perform, especially if the instrument was a grand. In many places, this was like suggesting an act of sacrilege, and people became quite upset; the piano had never been moved before in its life. It therefore always seemed quite a compliment when they said afterwards that the pushing, heaving and grunting had all been worth while. Another sacrosanct object was often the chairman's chair, placed centre stage, in which the chairman was accustomed to sit throughout the proceedings. Of course we always suggested that it might be as well if he moved it, but on several occasions the personage concerned flatly refused. A change of mind usually came about, and a hasty retreat was beaten, as soon as we'd almost turned a somersault on to his lap, or Raymond had sent off a burst of flame a little too close for comfort during the fire-eating routine.

Raymond was the only one among the wiry Whiteleys to become somewhat stout as he got older. Nevertheless he remained a good tumbler. On one occasion at a club performance he did his usual forward somersault and went straight through the boards. Fortunately it was no more than a shallow stage; on a theatre stage he would have disappeared altogether. As it was, he was instantly transformed into a dwarf. With what I thought was amazing presence of mind I remarked, 'Good gracious – Toulouse-Lautrec!' The audience, I'm sorry to say, showed no sign of being amused.

One group of people who did deserve a special round of applause were the long-suffering club pianists. With only the briefest of instructions from artists, they had to do their best on what were poor and out-of-tune instruments – and in general turned in an excellent job. On one particular occasion, the pianist failed to arrive. The chairman announced to the audience, 'I'm sorry, but our pe-anner player hasn't turned up. We're doing our best to get another, and if we can't, perhaps we could have a volunteer.' Ten minutes went by, by which time the audience was singing, 'Why are we waiting?' as loudly as it could. The chairman re-emerged to face the hostile mob. Spluttering nervously, he cried out, 'Order, order, ladies and gentlemen! We shall start any minute now. You'll be pleased to know that I have secured the services of an excellent prostitute.' He'd meant, of course, to say 'substitute'.

The great thing about the working men's clubs was that, although their responses were such an unknown quantity, if they liked you they asked you back again and again. The side to them we did not care so much for was the fact that they often wanted their humour 'blue' and questionable. This was something our integrity would not allow, but fortunately verbal comedy was never an integral part of our act. Even so, on the whole, we preferred the atmosphere in the clubs of the working men to that in the higher-class equivalents in the West End, such as Murrays or the Embassy, or the Exhibition Club in Kensington. For some reason we never fathomed, the clientele in these more sophisticated establishments always thought it was wildly amusing to tamper with the strings of our violins. They also continued talking throughout the act.

Our separation from Annette was planned to last for no more than a year, but circumstances ordained that it would stretch out into four whole years. Raymond had in the meantime met the lady who became his wife and with whom he formed a double tumbling act, working as 'The Sensational Shermans'. Her stage name was Ann Fay, and she was always billed in revue as 'Ann Fay, the Pride of Broadway'. Her family name was actually Coyne, and one of her uncles, Peter Coyne, was a jockey who later went to the United States and managed the Bing Crosby stables. Another uncle, Joseph Coyne, was a big name in the world of musical comedy and starred in such shows as the London première of *No, No, Nanette*. The Shermans continued to appear in bills up and down the country for quite a few years.

My double act with Pauline took us all over the country

210

to wherever work was offered. Naturally we went down to Tenby whenever we could, and invariably we found Annette the picture of health. Mrs Griffiths spoiled her and certainly spent more on her than we sent for her keep. It was hard for us as we realized how we were missing out on our little daughter's early years, but whenever we suggested the time had come to take her away, Mrs Griffiths would plead, 'Oh, give her a little longer.' Partings were always difficult, because we always knew it would be some time before we could get back to see Annette again.

The months and the years went by, with pantomime seasons succeeding summer seasons, and other dates in between. In the summer of 1950, we joined a touring revue called *Hollywood Way*. It was run by Ronnie Curtis, a film casting agent who'd decided he'd like to run his own theatre show. One of its features was to get members of the audience to act out a scene from *Johnny Belinda*, the popular recent film that had made Jane Wyman a star. Audience participation of that kind has since become a commonplace on television 'family' entertainment programmes, but, like so much else we see on the small screen, it had its origins in the theatre. With *Hollywood Way*, Friday night was always 'pot and pan' night – a set of saucepans being given away as first prize. Despite these attractions, and the fact that it was a beautifully produced, choreographed and costumed show, *Hollywood Way* seemed to be playing at the wrong place at the wrong time. In the end, Ronnie Curtis had to admit defeat and cut his financial losses. Then, two weeks before it closed, a well-known agent, Michael Lyons, happened to be in the audience. Shortly afterwards we received a letter from him to ask if we'd consider joining the supporting team for the Lucan and McShane show.

Lucan and McShane had been a star attraction since the 1920s, both on stage and in the films they made. Arthur Lucan was known as one of the nicest people in the business, but the same could never be said of Kitty McShane, who had a reputation for being difficult, to put it mildly. In fact she was known as an absolute terror. I wrote back to Michael

211

Lyons and said we'd be willing to join the show, but took the precaution of adding this would be only on the condition that McShane herself had first seen our work. A visit was duly arranged. She came to watch us in action one night when we were working the Walthamstow Palace. It was a very poor house. In theatrical terms we were playing to Mr and Mrs Wood and family (the seats). Nevertheless we felt we made a fair impression, and someone who knew McShane said to us, 'You're in. She's put her glasses on.' He was right. Several mornings later we received our contract. We signed it, knowing that, having seen us work before booking us, she'd never be able to say, 'I booked you on my agent's word, but I'm not satisfied.'

Arthur Lucan's creation of Old Mother Riley was one of the great originals in the dame tradition, standing midway between Dan Leno's Mrs Kelly and Barry Humphries's Dame Edna Everidge. Everyone who saw Old Mother Riley naturally took Arthur to be Irish. He was not. His real name was Arthur Towle and he was born in Lincolnshire. He developed an Irish comedian character and was working in Ireland with this when he met Kitty in Dublin, where her mother let rooms and her father was a fireman at the Olympia Theatre. In 1913 he married her. He first tried out a version of an old Irish washerwoman in a dame role in a Dublin pantomime. Lucan and McShane first achieved national fame when they played the London Palladium in 1932 with their sketch, 'The Old Matchseller and Her Balloons'. In 1934 they received the seal of royal approval when they presented 'Old Mother Riley and Her Daughter Kitty' in 'Bridget's Night Out' at the Royal Command Performance of that year. Somehow, whatever the storms that raged backstage, the comedy was perfectly matched in their impersonations of an old back-street harridan and her 'colleen' daughter who was trying to 'improve' her station in life.

The impression on arriving for our first day at rehearsal was unforgettable. We entered the rehearsal room and looked about. At once we spotted Arthur sitting alone in a corner. Before we could greet him, Kitty swept up to us and announced, like a sergeant-major in the barrack room, 'I'm

212

Kitty McShane. All you've heard about me is true, and sometimes I'm even worse.' We were never even introduced to Arthur.

During the show, Arthur had a scene with his supposed 'old flame', Barnacle Bill, a part played on this occasion by Eddie Hart. On the Monday night of our first week, Eddie went down with tonsilitis. The script was thrown at me to cope with until he recovered. You may imagine my state of nerves: almost no rehearsal beyond a talk-through in Arthur's dressing room and, after that, 'Over the top and the best of luck.' In fact, when it came to it, the scene seemed to be going fairly smoothly, with reasonable lines and timing. Then Kitty's voice sounded from the wings in a very audible stage whisper, 'We're running late. Make him cut!' I was concentrating furiously on every line and piece of action, and the laughs from the audience were coming along nicely. No matter how many times she hissed, 'Cut, cut!' I stuck to my guns and played the scene as Arthur had instructed.

There was no doubting that it went down well with the audience, but Kitty was far from pleased. As soon as I came off stage she snapped, 'I'll let it go this time, but remember, in future, when I give an order I expect it to be obeyed.' Then she turned to Pauline, who had been eyeing me apprehensively to judge my reaction, and announced out of the blue, 'I hope you know that you're my understudy, but I don't want to see you hanging about at the side of the stage.'

A press report of the show that week gave me particular delight in the circumstances. It read:

Jack Le White and Pauline Simonne provide an unusual act. Apart from being comedians in a slapstick manner in keeping with the show, they show that violins can be played in more ways than the orthodox. Jack Le White as Barnacle Bill, one of Old Mother Riley's old flames who has just returned after many years at sea, provides an hilarious ten minutes. The dialogue in this scene is especially good.

Pauline's 'opportunity' came when Kitty threw one of her tantrums, chucked a teapot at somebody's head and promptly passed out. Pauline was far slimmer than Kitty and needed to be pinned into her costumes. Arthur simply said to her, 'Don't worry, chuck, you'll be all right'; but it was a tough challenge, for Pauline still had to do all her own work, including our own act, in addition to taking on the role of the 'darlin' daughter'.

One of the bookings for the Lucan and McShane show was at the Empire Theatre, Portsmouth. This was another of the fine Moss Empires. Its dressing rooms, instead of being numbered, bore the names of famous admirals. The star dressing room, needless to say, was called Nelson. To reach Portsmouth we had to catch an early Sunday-morning train from Waterloo, and as soon as we got to the station, we joined up with other members of the troupe and went to enter our reserved compartment. One of the young women in the team had put a massive suitcase on the rack, and I was just asking her take it down, having once seen a nasty accident occur in similar circumstances, when there came a scream from behind me. I turned to see Pauline with her thumb trapped in the jamb of the carriage door. At that moment the guard blew his whistle for departure. I managed to get the door open and to release her just before the train began to move. The poor girl sat and stared at her hand with its squashed thumb. At first she could feel nothing, but then, as the flow of blood was restored, the pain became intense. I opened one of our suitcases, found a shirt and tore it into strips with which we staunched the flow of blood as best we could.

The two-hour journey was a nightmare for her, and must have seemed an eternity. The moment we arrived at Portsmouth I said to one of the others, 'Tell the manager what's happened,' summoned a taxi and took Pauline straight to the hospital casualty department. They gave her a tetanus injection and put her thumb in plaster; after which she insisted we should go round to the theatre at once. When we got there, she said to the show's manager, 'We'll still

214

work. The one thing I can't do is play a xylophone, so we'll put in some extra patter and make up our normal time.'

Kitty McShane never showed her face at a theatre in the mornings. She expected everything to be done for her. When she arrived that evening and the manager told her what had happened, she exploded and demanded, 'Why didn't you phone me? We could have got another act down to replace them.' How she expected to find anyone else to play all the parts we were playing at such short notice was beyond imagining. Meanwhile there were no words of sympathy for Pauline, nor even an inquiry about how she was feeling. Wherever we played thereafter, Pauline had to attend the local hospital, until eventually the plaster was taken off; she was told she was lucky not to have lost the thumb.

The season for Christmas 1950 was fast approaching. Rather to our surprise we were asked to play pantomime with Lucan and McShane – *The Old Woman Who Lived in a Shoe* at the Hippodrome, Boscombe. Prior to our rehearsal week, we had two weeks out, though I was able to fill one of them with an engagement at the Temperance Hall in Merthyr Tydfil. As this was not far from Tenby, we took the snap decision to collect Annette and take her along with us. By now she was between four and five years old, and we felt we could take no more of the emotional wear and tear of our reunions and partings. It was a sad moment for the Griffithses, to whom we would always be grateful for all they had done, but we had made up our minds. For little Annette, it meant a major adjustment from leading a settled life to one that was forever on the move.

We were not looking forward to the pantomime, anticipating ructions from Miss McShane. For one thing she had issued a stern warning: no dogs or children would be tolerated at pantomime rehearsals. Our Boscombe landlady, who was charging us over the odds for our lodgings, then made it clear that she was not prepared to look after Annette as a regular thing, though as a concession she would tell us if she was going to be out so we could take the child with us. With some trepidation, we began to take Annette along to rehearsals. We would say to her beforehand, 'Mummy and

215

Daddy have to go to rehearsal now. You must be a very good girl, and as quiet as a mouse.' We bought her a book and some pencils to keep her amused, as well as some biscuits to eat, and made a point of arriving at the rehearsal room before anyone else and getting her settled in a corner of the big space. All through rehearsals, Annette never moved a muscle. We'd take her home to lunch and bring her back in the afternoon. It all went on like this for several days.

One morning, Kitty asked suddenly, 'Whose child is that?' She knew perfectly well. She'd seen us walking out with her.

Pauline said, 'It's ours.'

'Well,' said Kitty, 'you know my ruling. No dogs, no children. But what can I say? I've never seen anything like it. She's just sitting there!' Then she walked over to Annette and asked, 'What's your name?'

'My name's Annette Whiteley,' said Annette, and offered Kitty an orange.

At this point an extraordinary transformation came over Kitty. It was something we were never able to account for fully. All at once we were allocated our own dressing room, which was something we were most thankful for. It meant we could bed Annette down there when the evening performance was in progress. Many were the occasions when I carried her home afterwards, fast asleep in my arms and never waking even when I popped her into her own bed. She also enjoyed the remarkable privilege of having *carte blanche* to enter Miss McShane's dressing room any time she liked.

There was a big Christmas Day party for the cast. Kitty said, 'No doubt you'll want to spend your Christmas with the child. I'm giving another party later. Come to that and bring Annette.'

We went. Annette was treated like the guest of honour. Kitty commanded the show manager, 'Go and get a doll.'

'But Miss McShane,' he protested, 'the shops are closed.'

'Well then,' she said, 'ask Mr Butterworth' – this was the owner of the theatre and its associated hotel. 'He knows the shop people round here.'

216

Before long the manager was back with a really fine doll.

The Old Woman Who Lived in a Shoe was a big pantomime success for all of us. Pauline and I were the two kids, and I was Dog, and we also did our act. The song preceding the grand finale was 'All I Want for Christmas Is My Two Front Teeth', for which children from the audience were invited up on stage to participate. Annette, who had a fine gap in her teeth at that point, was always included in this during the afternoon show, and would sing a solo. For this she was paid 5s. (25p) a week. On one occasion, after she had sung her solo, Kitty asked her on stage, 'What do you expect to get for that?'

Back came the response, 'Five bob.'

Another time Kitty asked her, 'Who are Jack Le White and Pauline Simonne?'

'My mummy and daddy,' said Annette.

'I don't think much of them,' said Kitty.

'Well, I think they're very clever,' rang out the swift reply.

When the pantomime ended, Kitty summoned us to her suite during the end-of-show party. 'I'd like you for revue again,' she said, and, as soon as she caught the quizzical looks on our faces, quickly added, 'I know you'll want more money.'

We agreed to give it a try, but before long life was back to normal in the Lucan and McShane circus, with Kitty in the wings telling Arthur to drop dead in loud stage whispers. The aggression and abrasiveness were more than we could stand. With our nerves in tatters, we reached the conclusion that the greatest fortune in the world wasn't worth the loss of peace of mind. When we told the show manager we were handing in our notice, he said, 'You can't do that!' I pointed out that the contract Kitty insisted on allowed either party two weeks' notice, and we were sticking to it.

The Lucan and McShane partnership finally split up soon after our departure. Arthur, like so many artists, was no businessman, and became beset by tax troubles. Kitty, who certainly fancied herself as a businesswoman, proved not to be so hot once she was outside the showbusiness arena. The beauty salon she set up in London lost a great deal of money.

Arthur did his best to carry on with the show, but Kitty took to following after him and creating scenes until it became necessary to ban her from going backstage. So many times we had heard her telling Arthur to drop dead in her reverberating stage whisper. In the end, that is what he did. He was in the wings, waiting to make his entrance on a Monday night in 1954 at the Tivoli, Hull, when he collapsed as the music played. They carried him to his dressing room, where he died. In true theatrical tradition, the audience was merely told he had been taken ill, and his understudy – in this case, Frank Seton – went on and played the show through.

Kitty McShane has hardly received the best press in the annals of showbusiness, and it is difficult to think kindly of her. Perhaps it would be most charitable, as we take our leave of Lucan and McShane, to remember the time when, for a brief spell, Kitty showed kindness and generosity to our child – an incident that maybe indicated what tragic wounds must have lain beneath her hardness. Arthur had once confided in us that the early days of their marriage, when they were struggling for recognition, were their happiest time together.

Naturally enough, when we left Lucan and McShane, we were apprehensive over the prospect of being out of work. This was rather more of a worry to Pauline than it was to me. She had never really come to terms with the uncertainties of a showbusiness life. As it happened, the work continued to come along. In August 1951, when we were working for a Leicester agent, Barry Wood, and playing at the Pavilion, South Shields, I received a telegram to say that Father was seriously ill. We were next booked to play the Arboretum, Walsall, so I asked Barry Wood if he'd mind if Pauline filled in with a single act while I went back to Hornchurch. He agreed, and I caught a late train on Saturday night and arrived home on the Sunday morning. I was too late to see Father alive, as were my brothers, who'd travelled from Weymouth, where Tom, Dick and Harry were appearing with the Sanger Circus. Only Mother and Leonora had been with him at the end. He was seventy-nine, had celebrated his golden wedding and lived to see the arrival of seven grandchildren and one great-grandchild. His life was upright and he was never heard to utter a harsh word against another soul. He had also jotted down his own memorial in his hand-written memoirs. How it would have amazed him to know that these would be published in facsimile thirty-one years after his death by the Society for Theatre Research.

As a man of rings and curtains all his life, Father would have been the first to say, 'The show must go on!' Even as he had gone straight back to work after his mother's funeral, so I left the cemetery to catch a train and make my way to Walsall, where Pauline was ably filling in during my absence.

At the end of 1951 we were fixed to do a pantomime season as the Palace Theatre, Camberwell, built in 1896 and formerly known as the Oriental Palace. I had played there in my youth with the Teddy Morris Band. In those days there had been a jam factory facing the dressing-room window, which gave opportunities for long-distance flirtations with the 'jam maidens'. Now there would have been none of that, even if the factory had still been there. I was a respectably married old man. The pantomime was *Mother Goose*, with a script by George Lacy, one of our greatest pantomime dames, who himself played Mother Goose for the first time in 1929 and for the last time in 1985, though he was not in it on this occasion. Pauline played the Duchess and I was Idle Jack.

Our next summer season was at the Esplanade Theatre, Bognor Regis, where the principal comedian was yet another veteran of the Ralph Reader 'Gang Shows' who had also done an apprentice stint at the Windmill. His name was Dick Emery and, of course, he later became one of British television's top comics. The year after that, Jackson Earle asked me to produce the pier show at New Brighton as a complement to his first-class summer show, then an annual event, at the Floral Pavilion. My brief was for a daily change of show for each of the six days a week we played, working with the customary group of seven artists. It is not easy to provide six different programmes with only seven players. The music and choreography had to be arranged, the cameos and sketches written and the practicability of all the costume changes kept track of; and it all had to be put together very rapidly.

The secret was preparation in advance. The traditional pierrot show worked in pierrot costume throughout and used no tabs. I decided to vary the format. I prepared six books, one for each night, marked from one to six. The six scripts were ready, complete with worked-out timing, when we arrived to start rehearsals. I had also seen Jackson Earle and arranged for some of his wardrobe from his *Melody Inn* show at the Floral Pavilion to be added to my *Holiday Time* show at the pier. I told my seven artists that rehearsals would be non-stop until we had everything together, but that they would thereafter be free to enjoy whatever spare time was available. They gave me their total co-operation and after the first fortnight of playing we never needed to rehearse again. One press notice called it a 'revue in miniature'. Another commented that it was

> a perfect aperitif to the parent show at the Floral Hall . . . *Holiday Time* is a bright and breezy offering with more original ideas than one expects to find in a pier show. Records at the turnstile testify to its quality.

There was a sense of swan song about this little triumph, however. The number of seaside pavilion and alfresco shows was dropping off rapidly during the 1950s. The days of the pierrots, until then ever popular since the reign of Queen Victoria, were numbered. Another style of family holiday was rapidly taking over, which had its origin back in 1935 when an enterprising young fellow called Billy Butlin, who had once run his own carnival booth in his uncle's travelling fair, started the first of his holiday camps at bracing Skegness in Lincolnshire. After the war, holiday camps began to open up in various major English seaside resorts, the public being at once attracted by the keyword 'inclusive'.

Accommodation was provided in chalets and there was something going on for all of the family all of the time. To begin with it was all rather over-organized, the Tannoy forever blaring away and an all-pervading spirit of 'enjoy yourselves or else'. As time went on, a little more of a subtle element began to creep into the heartiness. There were plenty of 'uncles' and 'aunties' to keep the kids happy and occupied, and a large proportion of the staff, known as redcoats, was recruited from the world of entertainment. Every camp had its own theatre, and bar-room entertainers were also hired.

We were booked through the Cecil Braham Agency, then being run by his widow Beatrice, to entertain at the biggest Butlin's camp, at Filey in Yorkshire. The deal was to play three days at the camp followed by three days at the Pavilion in the town, alternating with the resident drama company. In this way the campers were provided with three days of variety and three of drama during the course of a week's holiday. We were also contracted to play one Sunday a month at Skegness, but found ourselves having to do this on a weekly basis, travelling down into Lincolnshire to put in two Sunday shows, sleeping there overnight and rising at six the next morning to get back to Filey. The continual packing and unpacking made it a real slog. In the end we started to get difficult over the way they were taking their pound of flesh, and the management agreed to pay us extra for Sunday working.

Playing the camps was very like playing the clubs. You never knew what sort of an audience you would find lying in wait for you. Some weeks there would be a really enthusiastic crowd, but other weeks they could be as hard to crack as granite. As a general rule, it depended on where they came from – the farther north the harder to please. Tynesiders were the hardest to please of all. My family's saying of 'pick and shovel' when it came to the challenge of keeping northerners amused continued to hold good in the post-war era.

The camps in fact became training grounds for live entertainers in much the same way that the variety circuits had been in their prime. Many of today's top performers began their careers as redcoats – Roy Hudd, to cite but one notable example. Mind you, some of the budding comedians who sat in the front row with a notebook, jotting down all your jokes, did give rise to a certain amount of resentment. There was one young fellow who even came backstage and said, 'Excuse me, but I missed the punchline of one your gags. Could you tell it to me now, please?' We've all been guilty of stealing each other's material from time to time, but seldom this blatantly.

During our last Friday-night performance at Filey, we suddenly heard a dreadful continuous moan coming from the prompt side of the stage. I edged towards the wings and slipped off. I found the unfortunate stage manager vainly attempting to pull himself free of the switchboard. I grabbed his jacket, which I knew wouldn't conduct electricity, and pulled him away. He had happened to touch a water heater with one hand while working the switchboard with the other. A second good Samaritan then took over, and I slipped back on stage to finish the act. Happily the man made a rapid recovery.

Father had once worked for the Cecil Braham Agency, so it represented a renewal of an old family association, and Beatrice was, at this time, our sole agent. Braham was a diminutive for Abraham, and the Brahams were Jewish, like so many theatrical agents – and, of course, like a large number of performers. A Braham had been a leading tenor at Sadler's Wells in the 1830s.

When our Butlin season ended, Beatrice booked us to play the Syndicate theatres. In former times, these had spread as far afield as Chelsea, East Ham, Tottenham, Walthamstow and Watford, and included the Metropolitan, Edgware Road, the South London Tivoli and the Euston. By the time we played the Syndicate, its former glory had dwindled to a threesome of theatres: Chelsea, East Ham and the Metropolitan. What a pity we never had the chance to play the Euston. The centenary issue of *The Stage* in January 1980 included a list of what was playing at London theatres during the week of the outbreak of the First World War in 1914. At the Euston were the Five Whiteleys on the same bill as Lily Morris, remembered for her singing of the popular comic song, 'Don't 'Ave Any More, Mrs Moore'.

At the top of our bill was Max Miller, 'The Cheeky

Chappie', famous for asking his audiences whether they wanted the jokes from the White Book or the Blue Book. As John Fisher writes in his wonderful celebratory account of the lives of the great variety comics, *Funny Way To Be a Hero* (1973):

> Somewhere in the latter volume would have come the story of the negress washerwoman's surprise encounter with the elephant's trunk, the one about what didn't happen when an unmarried couple shared the bed with a pillow down the centre to make it all 'religious', and the one about the unsuccessful attempts by a judge to gain a precise definition of what the soldier meant by the 'la-de-da-de-da' that took place when the girl he was escorting home passed out in the middle of some deserted field.

Max was a marvellous performer to see and hear in action, his patter being very fast and timed to perfection. He was a master of the *double entendre* and, like Marie Lloyd, used a mock innocence to put all the sauciness into the minds of his audiences, who'd instantly pick up what he'd left unsaid. He didn't just rely on filth, and it's an interesting question to ask whether he could have been so successful today, when comedians are more or less free to say anything they like. Probably his talent would have been large enough to shine through in any circumstances. 'There'll never be another!' he used to tell his audiences, and there hasn't been anyone to match him since, even with the ending of censorship. It's possible to get the flavour of his work from the recordings of his live routines better than you can for most variety artists, and Roy Hudd includes a very fine imitation of Miller among his acts.

Another panto season came round for us. This time we were at the Garrick Theatre, Southport, for a Sydney Myers production of *The Babes in the Wood*. By now the point had been reached where it was thought necessary to include at least one 'name' from radio or television to draw in the crowds. (Attempts to make sports stars into pantomime artists still lay a long way in the future.) The 'star' for

223

this particular show was Eddie Calvert, 'The Man with the Golden Trumpet'. He didn't actually play a role; he simply played in his own spot before the Palace marchdown. Yet it was a beautiful pantomime, complete with Currie's famous waterfalls, and what better note to finish on than the sweet sound of a man with a golden trumpet?

12

Do You Still Tumble?

There were a number of revues touring in the 1950s, mainly with French-sounding titles to attract audiences with the idea that they were offering something a bit on the daring and saucy side. Of course, those shows would seem tame and innocent affairs in comparison with all we've seen since, which I wouldn't say has necessarily represented an improvement in artistic standards. In the 1950s the writ of the Lord Chamberlain still ran to govern what could and could not be said and seen on the British stage. The demure nude posing that had for so long been a hallmark of the Windmill Theatre remained the strictly applied rule. Pauline and I once played on a bill with the leading stripper, the 'one and only' Phyllis Dixey, and her husband Jack Tracy. Phyllis had helped to keep the troops entertained during the war in the show *Peek-a-Boo*, and was the closest British equivalent to America's famous Gypsy Rose Lee. At the Whitehall Theatre she was promoted as 'the girl the Lord Chamberlain banned'. She was a performer with real talent and her act consisted more of 'tease' than of 'strip'; by the time it was finished, the audience had actually seen very little apart from what their minds suggested. Even so, only essential staff were permitted a view of the stage while she was on.

Two revues of those days were Davy Kaye's *Midnight in*

Montmartre and *French Follies*. We toured with the latter, which was managed by Rosemary Andrée, whose husband was one of the Craggs, another well-known acrobatic and gymnastic family. They had performed a spectacular act together as Gaston and Andrée, and been in the Royal Command Performance of 1933. When they gave up the act they went into the agency and production side of the business.

French Follies was certainly excellently put together and presented. Among a good range of acts it featured the comedian Jimmy Gaye and the beautiful 'poser', Iris Poliakova, who was also a fine classical dancer. After we'd opened at the Manchester Hippodrome, a notice in the *Daily Mirror* called it 'the most talked about revue of the moment . . . For entertainment value two packed houses really had their money's worth . . . It is, in fact, a better than average revue.' The *Mirror* also mentioned that four members of the company had been threatened with death should they be brazen enough to appear nude the following week in Belfast, where we were booked to play the Opera House. As an anonymous letter had sinisterly informed us, 'even a corpse wears a shroud'.

It all made for a nerve-racking week at the Opera House. Certain Irish elements regarded nudity as a greater crime than murder. Fortunately, when it came to it, no one took a pot-shot at the nude tableaux, though there was some trouble with heckling from the gallery on our last night. Towards the end of the evening, Jimmy Gaye had a ten-minute front-cloth solo spot to fill to allow the stage to be set for the final marchdown and finale. When he came on stage, he couldn't get a word in edgeways. Eventually he declared, 'I've been sent on here to stay for ten minutes, and that's what I'm going to do. If you think you know any funnier stories than mine, then carry on among yourselves. I'll just stand here.' He took a watch out of his pocket and added, 'I'll act as time-keeper. When your time's up you can all go home.' The audience in the stalls applauded him and told the hecklers to shut up. Jimmy resumed his patter and, when he came down in the finale, received a standing ovation.

226

We took advantage of what was to be our last visit to Ireland to go back to Ballyhalbert. The old RAF camp had become a ghost town. All that was left of its wartime activity were derelict Nissen huts and the control tower. The local people had, however, gained an electricity supply as a result of the military presence and the nineteenth-century way of life we experienced when we first went there was a thing of the past; though whether outlooks on life had broadened as a consequence was another question.

Another revue that we toured in together was called *Bearskins and Blushes* and starred that clever comedienne Hylda Baker, remembered for her comedy catch-line, 'She knows, yer know'; and also, in a more serious vein, for her role of the back-street abortionist in the film of *Saturday Night and Sunday Morning*. While *Bearskins and Blushes* was playing at the Palace, Attercliffe, near Sheffield, not all the comedy was on stage, however. Our landlady would bring us our meal up and then, as we ate it, would stand by the door, telling us what a dreadful life she'd led and what a terrible man she had for a husband. 'I'd have left him long ago,' she'd say, 'if it hadn't been for me son and daughter. She were a clever lass, and all the pros who stayed here then said she ought to go on t'stage. She'd a lovely voice, very much like Gracie Fields's, but my 'usband would have none of it. All he cares about is his pub and his beer. Of course, it's all too late now. I hate to talk about him – I'm a woman of very few words – but if I once started to open my mouth . . .'

At this point there'd come a voice booming up from downstairs, 'Coom down, Flossie, ye're wanted.'

We'd heave sighs of relief as the door closed, but we were never to be left in peace for long. Up her husband would come with a tray to clear the table and give us his side of things: 'Expect Flossie's been telling yer the same tale she tells all our lodgers, that I'm not up to much. Well, she's never gone short. I started when I were a lad in steel works, and I've been at it ever since. I don't think a bit of baccy and a few pints in t'pub is asking too much. She'll never go with me. As for that son of ours, she treated him as if he were King of England and he's been nowt but trouble. She

227

were a bonny woman once, but I'll tell yer something. She's slipping now. Blood pressure. Don't think she'll last much longer. I've promised myself one thing. If she goes before me, I'll see she's put away nice and tidy, but I'm not coming back to tea.'

Some time later we were engaged for a show on the lovely Isle of Man. By then Annette was eleven and continuing to display an aptitude for the business. We let her enter one of the children's holiday-time talent-spotting contests and were delighted when she ran away with one of the first prizes. Shortly before we left home, we had bought her a hamster, which she called Little Man. From then on, wherever we went, Little Man had to go as well. We thought it might amuse our landlady on the Isle of Man to meet Little Man, but as soon as she saw him she said, very shocked, 'Good gracious! You're not allowed to bring them into the island. When you go back, make sure nobody sees it.' Full of apprehension, we smuggled Little Man successfully back to Kingston.

Several times towards the end of our season on the Isle of Man I jokingly remarked to Pauline, as we came off stage, 'You must be getting old. You're breathing like a broken-down horse.' Little did I know how my joke would soon turn out to be a matter for serious concern. Back at home, work was all the time becoming harder to obtain. With so many theatres closing, a number of London boroughs agreed to the use of town halls for variety performances. We did several town-hall shows before Horace Mashford asked us to help out with entertaining old-age pensioners. It meant a great deal to the old people to be able to see some live entertainment at a time when all the theatres they had known so well since their youth were ceasing to exist. On an expenses-only basis, we also did many shows for mental hospitals, some of which were dismal Victorian institutions, though others had well set-up stages. There was no doubting that the inmates got a good deal of enjoyment out of a live show, even if they did tend to laugh in inappropriate places. More than once the medical staff told us how their patients enjoyed a live show far more than films or television.

228

Our next town-hall show was at Fulham, but as soon as we arrived Pauline began to gasp so much to catch her breath that we had to carry her upstairs. She insisted that the show must go on, and bravely struggled through, but as soon as we got home I summoned our doctor, Dr Hirsch, a Czech whose family had perished in the Nazi death camps. He was one of the rapidly diminishing breed of old-style family doctors. Indeed, his kind seemed to be disappearing as fast as the theatres. He had no bedside manner and could be extremely brusque and direct with anyone he thought was malingering, but in a case of genuine illness or distress, he was undoubtedly your man. He lost no time in diagnosing asthma and giving Pauline an injection. Later on, as her attacks grew to be more frequent, he would often come round at two or three in the morning to attend her or get her into hospital. He also made it his business to see that we had a telephone installed as a priority at our apartment while we were still Miss Packham's tenants.

With work already hard to find, I was now restricted in the amount of travelling I could undertake since I had to look after Annette each time Pauline was in hospital. I decided to look for assignments as a film extra, for which I first needed to join the FAA (Film Artistes' Association). The tactic then was to phone in to their office in Poland Street each evening, and if you were in luck you would be given a call to be at one of the big studios – usually Pinewood or Elstree – by 7.30 the next morning. This meant a 5.30 start for me from Kingston, and you were expected to dress according to the type they needed. An extensive character wardrobe therefore increased your chances of employment.

You were paid on a daily basis. At the end of each day's shooting you then waited around to see if you were needed again for the following day. In this respect, a lot hinged on exactly where you were when shooting finished. There was always a tussle going on among the extras to get themselves in camera for the final take and so ensure themselves a second day's work. It was a good thing, too, to wangle yourself a position close to the leading players. Then you were in what was called a cameo shot and were paid extra.

229

If, say, you got one or two days' filming in a week, you would declare this at the labour exchange and receive four days' unemployment benefit to cover your spell of 'resting'. Overall the film extra's life therefore brought in enough to get by on, though it was not a career for sensitive souls. Even so, you met some extras who'd been at it for years, and there were certain stars' stand-ins who did very well and became close friends of those they represented. Film extras came from many walks of life and included every kind of performer. Besides old actors who could no longer memorize their lines, there were such people as a banker's wife earning some pin money and the spivs or wide boys (cowboys they'd be called today) who were there primarily with the hope of flogging loads of stuff they had in the backs of their cars.

On the disadvantage side, there was the fact that to perform as an extra was to end up type-cast. It excluded you from more prominent roles since no director would hire you if he found out you'd been in a crowd scene. One actress who was called to a casting gave a successful reading but was recognized by an assistant director as having been in a crowd scene previously. That was the end of her chances on that occasion. The agent side of film-extra and stunt-artist work could also be a jungle for the unwary.

Fortunately, the only agent I worked with apart from the FAA was a sympathetic lady who had previously run repertory companies with her husband and realized that many extras were fully capable actors who needed to pay the rent till something better came along. Certain other agents were completely unscrupulous. Where an extra worked for an agent, the agent would receive the money and the extra would have to go along to collect it. At the office he might be told that it hadn't arrived yet; if he then asked to see the agent himself, he'd be told he was out. The objective was to hang on to the artist's money as long as possible to gain the bank interest. Such people would often go into liquidation owing their clients hundreds of pounds, and then start the business up again overnight under another name – the wife's or the secretary's.

230

Because of Pauline's illness, I was booked to go solo in pantomime that year, at the Palace, Reading. The only digs I could find were indescribable. I shared a bedroom with three milkmen who all got up at 5 a.m. and robbed me of my beauty sleep – even supposing that sleep could have been possible on the rock-stuffed mattresses. The landlady was strong on fuel conservation. Her meals arrived thawed out, but could never be described as cooked. I only stayed there till the second morning of rehearsal, when a telegram came to tell me that Pauline was seriously ill in hospital. To the director's consternation, for we had only a week of rehearsals before opening, I returned to Kingston, where the doctors assured me the worst was over and Pauline would improve.

I phoned my anxious director and told him I'd be back but would arrange to commute daily up to Reading. This meant a routine of getting back to Kingston after midnight, calling in at the hospital to check on Pauline's condition and returning to Reading the next morning to be at the theatre in time for the daily matinée. Fortunately it was possible to leave Annette in the trustworthy and generous care of our friend Miss Packham. After a fortnight, Pauline was discharged and I returned to Reading and found new digs – self-catering this time!

By the time the panto finished Pauline was much improved, though we never knew when a fresh attack might strike and there was no question of her working. As chance would have it, I called on an agent I had known in the past, who asked, 'Do you still tumble? If you can find someone to work with and can plot out a routine, I'll fix you up with about a month's film work for good money.' The film was *Further Up the Creek*, the sequel to *Up the Creek*, which had starred David Tomlinson and Peter Sellers. The story concerned the crew of a battleship unofficially taking over the ship and advertising it on the side as a pleasure cruiser. Val Guest directed, as he had the previous film, and David Tomlinson and Lionel Jefferies were among the original cast who carried over into the sequel. They were joined this time by Frankie Howerd, Shirley Eaton and Thora Hird. The parts I and another had to fill were those of a pair of down-at-heel acrobats, the Kentoni Brothers, who were hoping to try their luck overseas. To partner me I found Max Day, who had done an acrobatic act before giving it up to become a welder.

Max and I got down to working on our routines. He hadn't performed any stage work for years and I certainly hadn't done any tumbling lately. We had only three days of practice before shooting began. Talk about stiffness! Our first location was outside Virginia Water railway station, where we emerged with our theatrical baskets and launched straight into an acrobatic display, ending up in the lorry that was to take us on the first leg of our cruise. The rest of the shooting was done at Bray or on board HMS *Aristotle* in Weymouth Harbour. David Tomlinson was in a West End play at the time and could only work on Sundays. The producer laid on an ambulance for him to sleep in on his way to Weymouth after his Saturday-night performance. As for me, it represented a good start to to a new year following one that had been disastrous.

When an offer came through for Pauline and me to do a summer season at Torquay, we didn't know whether she should accept and sought Dr Hirsch's advice. 'My dear,' he told her, 'take the season. The air may do you good. I'll put you on cortisone and get in touch with the doctor at Torquay. Hopefully you'll be able to work through the season.'

So it came about that we spent a hot summer of perfect weather with Annette by the sea. Not long after our return to London in September, Pauline was back in hospital. It was a time of despair again as we wondered whether we would ever be able to make plans for the future. In fact it was to be Pauline's last spell in hospital, and a blessing in disguise was on the way. She was expecting our second child. At first she was in a terrible state about it, knowing that asthma can be hereditary. Once again we turned to Dr Hirsch, who replied quite simply, '*Que sera, sera*, my dear! There's no reason why your baby shouldn't be perfectly healthy, and if it isn't, you'll just have to do the best you can. Many asthmatic children lose it as they grow older, but there's no point in crossing bridges until you come to them.'

232

The baby turned out to be perfect and Pauline's asthma, which was mainly psychosomatic, disappeared for good. We had been going to call the baby Ian if it was a boy, but hadn't settled on a girl's name. Of course, it was another girl. We put an 'a' on the end of Ian, and she became Iana – the only one, to the best of my belief. During Pauline's pregnancy, we had been offered a summer season for the coming year back on the Isle of Man. At last we could look forward to an engagement without going through qualms and anxieties about whether or not we should have taken it.

We were careful not to have a hamster with us when we returned to the Isle of Man in June 1961, but we did have an eight-month-old to look after. Annette was fifteen by this time, so was old enough to do a bit of babysitting. As it happened, we were not to retain her babysitting services for long. She had already appeared under licence as an under-age performer in the popular television series, *Emergency Ward 10*. Most programme serials were then still being shot 'live', which could be nerve-racking for the most hardened professional, but Annette had acquitted herself well in coping when another actor 'dried' just before she made her entrance. Then, a few weeks before we left for the Isle of Man, she had attended an audition for the Eyeline Film Company for a film to be called *Girl on Approval*. A hundred girls in all had read for the part, and since we'd heard nothing more we'd assumed she'd been unsuccessful. Two weeks into our summer season a telegram arrived to say they'd chosen Annette.

We were committed to our holiday audiences, but the film's producer, Harold Orton, very kindly arranged for Annette to stay with the writer of the film, herself a social worker. Still Annette's problems were not quite over. A fortnight before filming began, she upset a kettle of boiling water down her leg, which was still bandaged when she flew to London on 9 July. But she was not going to let anything get in the way of being in the film, whose director was Charles Frend, previously responsible for the wartime classic (starring Tommy Trinder) *The Foreman Went to France* and,

233

after the war, *Scott of the Antarctic* and *The Cruel Sea*. The script for *Girl on Approval* told the story of an institutionalized teenager and the effect she has on the couple who foster her. Annette's co-stars were James Maxwell and that fine Welsh actress Rachel Roberts, hot from her success in *Saturday Night and Sunday Morning*. Miss Roberts was also just in the process of getting a divorce from Alan Dobie and planning to be married to Rex Harrison. A newspaper interview made a comparison between her anxious state of mind and Annette's carefree spirit. Charles Frend was also very complimentary on how easily Annette took his direction.

In the early 1960s we were moving into what became labelled 'the permissive society', along with which went a vogue for 'social conscience' films and television plays. Annette's next assignment was in a film that caused quite a stir, called *The Yellow Teddy Bears*. It was based on fact, a Dr Gibson of Winchester having observed that many schoolgirl mothers who came under his care were wearing gollywog badges. Investigating the phenomenon uncovered the fact that these badges were awarded in classroom 'rites' to any girl who could prove she was no longer a virgin. To save the embarrassment of real people, the gollywogs were changed into teddy bears for the purposes of the film, whose adult leads were Jacqueline Ellis and Raymond Huntley. The director was Robert Hartford-Davis. Annette travelled far and wide to help with the film's promotion, going even as far as Rome. She also appeared on discussion panels with doctors, marriage counsellors and clergymen.

Shortly after this she appeared on stage at the Connaught Theatre, Worthing, in the original version of Philip King's comedy *Big Bad Mouse*, with Mr King himself in the lead. Annette played the rock-'n'-rolling office girl, while the office boy was John Noakes, soon to become well known to a whole generation of children as a presenter of the BBC's *Blue Peter* programme. One night, conspicuous in the audience by his laughter, was the comedian Jimmy Edwards. Eventually the play moved to London, but was largely recast and rewritten to serve as a vehicle for Jimmy Edwards and Eric Sykes. Annette therefore missed out on the pleasure of having a West End transfer, though she was hardly missing chances to demonstrate her versatility as an actress. After playing a problem foster child, a schoolgirl who has an abortion, an office-girl rocker, she now moved into heavy drama with the role of the gypsy girl Ilse in the famous 1965 Royal Court production of Frank Wedekind's *Spring Awakening*. This play was 'a case', wrote the critic Irving Wardle, 'of a European masterpiece that had been withheld from the British stage by half a century of censorship'. Subtitled 'A Children's Tragedy', it represented a powerful attack on sexual hypocrisy through its exploration of the tortured emotions of adolescence.

In the meantime, the world of entertainment was changing more quickly than ever before. The former stability of reputations was gone. Stars were made overnight and equally quickly forgotten as gimmick followed gimmick. The emphasis was all on novelty. Many old pros found themselves doing things they'd never dreamed would be their lot, such as being callers in former cinemas converted into bingo halls. At least they could utilize their vocal projection and ability to extemporize. All-in wrestling, another vogue entertainment, attracted former acrobats who could put on a diverting display of contortions and *oohs* and *aahs*. Those actors who were getting on in years were lucky, perhaps, if they managed to land themselves a spot of seasonal employment as Father Christmas in a department store. That, in itself, could be a pretty demanding role in the new world in which we found ourselves. My old friend Charlie Stephenson once did Father Christmas for Bentalls, Kingston's famous store. When he asked one small boy the traditional question, 'And how old are you, my little man?' he received the distinctly untraditional reply, 'A bleedin' sight younger than you, mate!'

New Year 1965 saw me in pantomime again: *Cinderella* at Sutton in Surrey. It was produced by Horace Mashford. By that stage no show could be considered complete unless it contained its pop group. Ours was Joe Brown and the Bruvvers. I found Joe a nice talented young fellow, and this was only his second pantomime. He wasn't the sort to be content with appealing only to teenagers and was prepared to take advice from more seasoned performers. Like Tommy Steele, he worked hard to become an all-round entertainer and, at the end of that same year, in December, was one of the leads in a hit show at the Adelphi – the première production of the musical comedy *Charlie Girl*, also starring Anna Neagle, Hy Hazell and Derek Nimmo.

Towards the end of our pantomime season, I happened to mention that I had written a song, called 'It's Great to be Young', which I thought might stand a chance of being published. Howard Conder, the drummer with the Bruvvers, said he knew one or two music publishers and would show it around if I could meet him and let him have a copy. We made an appointment that I couldn't keep because I was working, so I sent Annette along instead. This was how the two of them came to meet. Eighteen months later they were married at St Paul's Church, Kingston-upon-Thames, with a reception afterwards at the Assembly Rooms, Surbiton.

It was a wedding with three generations of rings and curtains behind it. People from all branches of the profession were there. To my delight, my mother was able to attend in her ninetieth year, a proud grandmother who stood for each of the many toasts. The bridesmaids were Annette's former film stand-in, Frankie Thomsett, the daughter of a manager of the Wimbledon Theatre, and little sister Iana, still only four but a veteran performer of TV commercials. The best man was Michael Davies, a singer whose latest record was about to be released. True to form, both bride and groom had professional commitments, which meant they had to take a deferred honeymoon.

With all the emphasis on youth and gimmickry, the time had arrived for my own career to undergo a change of direction. I decided to try to concentrate on straight and character acting, where my age might be an advantage rather than a handicap. I was, of course, coming to straight acting relatively late in life, and there were still obstacles to persuading people to take an old variety and circus artist seriously, despite the example of George Robey, who played Falstaff in *Henry IV, Part I* back in 1935. People like Max Wall and

Jimmy Jewel had yet to prove the magical riches their skills could offer in their 'come-back' careers in straight theatre. This all made it difficult to find an agent to act on one's behalf. Either their books were full, or else they specialized only in supplying extras for crowd scenes. I tried my hand at finding work for myself, without the benefit of an agent, and also did some teaching at the Corona Stage School. In my early variety days I had worked with the Corona Babes and Juveniles, and now I was able to use my circus training to teach stage falls, fight effects and tricks and basic acrobatics to a new generation. Among my pupils were Francesca Annis, Richard O'Sullivan and Jeremy Bullock, all of whom I would work with in the years ahead.

After searching in vain for an agent for some time, I was reading *The Stage* one day when I came across a new agency advertising for clients. J. Garrod, Artists Associated, was just setting up in Conduit Street, between Oxford Circus and Piccadilly. I made contact, was invited to call, and established an instant rapport with Jimmy Garrod, for whom I became one of the first clients he took under his wing. Jimmy was a businessman to his finger-tips. He'd joined the Paramount organization as an office boy at the age of sixteen and later worked for Herbert J. Yates as sales manager for Republic Pictures. The great thing about Jimmy was that he never thought it was impossible to mix business and friendship; he was one of the rare and true real gentlemen among agents. He was to be my agent and friend for the rest of my working life, till age and illness made it impossible for me to take on further assignments. It was all done on trust. We never signed a formal sole-agency agreement.

Where circus and theatre might be called businesses, cinema and television are industries. To play in either medium is like being in a factory by comparison. Besides the players themselves, a whole army of craftsmen and technicians is required to create sets and circumstances that come as close to reality as possible. I never ceased to marvel at the results of their skills. At Shepperton in the 1950s, working as one of a vast crowd of extras, I had found myself in the market-

237

place at Rouen where Joan of Arc was burnt at the stake. Realism went to the point where history almost repeated itself.

St Joan, adapted from the play by George Bernard Shaw, was directed by one of the great autocrats of the movies, Otto Preminger, and starred a till then virtually unknown eighteen-year-old actress called Jean Seberg. For the burning scene, in which I was standing only a few feet away from her, Jean's hands were supposedly chained behind the stake. Beneath the faggots were gas jets by which the real flames could in theory be controlled. The flames began gently. A British soldier held up a cross made of twigs before her face. The clamour of the assembled multitude subsided to a mere murmur. At that point there came a flash and the flames leapt up to take hold of the highly inflammable tinder of the faggots. Someone had opened a door and a strong draft of wind did the rest. As Jean pulled her hands free and covered her face, she was plainly heard to cry out, 'Mother!' Still the cameras rolled. It seemed an eternity before Preminger finally shouted, 'Cut!' Two of the executioners, at great risk to themselves, snatched Jean out of the flames. She suffered burns to her knees, hands and stomach, though fortunately none of them were third degree. Despite the shock and pain, she was, in true trouper tradition, back on the set next day. It grieved me, over twenty years later, to hear how this brave young woman had died by her own hand in Paris.

Another miraculous re-creation was the London of Dickens for Carol Reed's film version of the musical *Oliver!*, whose set was so realistic that you were apt to forget it was only made of wood and plaster. The normal practice in the film industry is that they feed you for free on location but you have to buy your own meals in the canteens when you're on studio work. For *Oliver!* the crowds were so vast and time so important that they erected two large marquees and treated the studio as a location.

Oliver! meant eighteen weeks' work for me as an old chair mender. Behind the scenes it was like a reunion of vaudevillians. Among the supporting cast – supporting the stars Ron Moody, Shani Wallis, Hylda Baker, Oliver Reed

238

and Harry Secombe – were Peter Honri, grandson of the famous Percy Honri, the music halls' 'King of the Concertina', and himself a versatile exponent of his family's tradition in musical specialities and later to be the author of *Working the Halls* and *John Wilton's Music Hall*; Claire Ruane, a great revue comedienne in the Nellie Wallace style; Iris Sadler, a splendid lady pantomime dame; the comic, Vic Wise; and that fine old trouper, Frank Cowley, well remembered for the classic music-hall act he performed with his brother as Morris and Cowley. Their most famous sketch was an impersonation of a couple of aged Chelsea pensioners.

Many were the stories told of Morris and Cowley, who were known as irrepressible practical jokers. They had begun their career with the family act, the Birkenheads – mother, two sisters and another brother – before the First World War. After that war was over they worked up a double act as the Vesta Brothers, but soon changed this to Morris and Cowley, as they ever afterwards remained. When they were not playing the halls, they ran and played in their own revues, and made a habit of coming off stage arguing and calling each other nasty names so they could observe the rest of the cast begin to whisper apprehensively among themselves. Then they'd go to their dressing room and laugh their socks off. They'd always give away that the row was part of the act before depression set in too deeply among the rest of the company.

On one occasion, at a time when they were getting to be famous but had a week out, their agent phoned and said, 'I've fixed you a week, but you won't believe this – when I said "Morris and Cowley" to the manager, he said, "Never 'eard of 'em, but time's getting short, so I'll take a chance." '

They arrived at the stage door in caps and mufflers and announced to the stage-door keeper, 'We've coom to do a turn. Which way do we go to get on t'platform?'

'You mean the stage,' said the startled man. 'Down the stairs. Band call's started. You'd better get your books down.'

They looked at each other. 'Books down? What does he mean?'

'Band parts! Music!' the man exclaimed.

'Oh, the band will play music for us now? That's very good of them.'

We may imagine the door keeper frantically trying to ring through to the stage manager to warn him there were two right charlies on the way. Meanwhile the brothers had nobbled the conductor at the front of the stage. 'The fellow on the stage door said you'd play our music now,' they told him.

'It's not your turn,' said the conductor icily. 'You didn't put your books down. Now you'll have to come last.'

They looked at each other as if they couldn't make head or tail of any of this, but when it came to their band call, it was the conductor who was all at sea. The music was perfectly well written with every cue clear, but the idiots on stage seemed to have no idea what they were up to: 'No, Fred, not like that. We said we'd do it the other way, didn't we?' And so on. As soon as all that was over, they went to find the stage manager to ask where they dressed.

'You look on the board,' he told them.

'What board?'

'The board that shows your dressing-room number,' he said impatiently. 'It happens to be No. 5.'

At around lunchtime the stage manager went to their dressing room to find them sitting in their vests and staring at the sticks of make-up as one said to the other, 'Do we have to put this muck on?'

'But gentlemen,' asked the completely bewildered stage manager, 'what are you getting ready for? There's no matinée. I've only come up to get your lighting plots.'

'Oh, yes,' they said. 'We do want some lights. Our friend wrote out these papers. They'll tell you what lights we need. Can we go out of the theatre, then? Where do we clock off?'

The stage manager beat a hasty retreat, presumably to find the general manager to ask who the hell the agent was who'd provided these two and warn him they'd need to find a replacement act by Tuesday. Their act, of course, was a riot when it came to it, and the theatre staff, from the manager down, realized they'd had their legs pulled in no uncertain

240

manner. Morris and Cowley was not an act whose name they'd forget in a hurry.

I shall always remember, too, Frank Cowley's kindness to me during *Oliver!* He used to pick me up in his car each morning on his way to Shepperton and drop me off back home again after each day's shooting. Like many showbusiness people, he was very religious, and always said a brief prayer before starting a journey: 'Please God, grant me a safe journey with my good friends.' The script of *Oliver!* gave me a little scene of my own, complete with a song, 'Chairs to Mend'. Alas, along with hundreds of other feet of film, the scene ended up on the cutting-room floor. I was disappointed, but hardly surprised. The film would have run for a week if they'd used everything they'd shot.

Not all the old friends I met on the set of *Oliver!* were veterans. Jack Wild, who played the Artful Dodger, had, a year earlier, been one of the children – the others were Sally Thomsett and Christopher Cooper – in *Danny and the Dragon*, the film I made with the Children's Film Foundation.

After *Oliver!* I was kept busy in films and television, with the occasional television commercial, right up to the time when my health began to let me down and I could no longer accept commitments to be in a particular place at a particular time. Commercial advertising on television became an important part of many actors' incomes with the payments for repeats. Among the early commercials I did was one for Armour Star Corned Beef, made by Associated Pathé. This brought all my old circus training into play. Dressed as a clown, I dived through a hoop and came up with a tin of corned beef as I sang an appropriate jingle. Another was made at Bray Studios for McEwan's beer, setting off echoes in my mind of the song my father and his family sang to the troops in Cairo at the time of the Mahdi's rebellion. The last commercial I made was for the Prudential. Discovered seated on a wall in the street, I was presented as an example of poverty and neglect until I revealed I was just off on my holidays in a white Rolls-Royce with a bevy of beautiful

241

girls, having had the foresight to take out a Prudential pension policy.

I made television appearances in episodes of *The Troubleshooters*, *The Avengers*, when Honor Blackman was still starring in the series, *Crossroads*, *Dad's Army* and *Dr Finlay's Casebook*. In the latter I, a Sassenach, was the first actor to wear a kilt in the series. When I emerged on to the set for rehearsal, Andrew Cruikshank, who played Dr Cameron and was every inch a Scot and proud of it, took one look at me and said, 'You'd better go back to wardrobe. They've put your kilt on back to front.' Another memorable programme was *Dixon of Dock Green*, with Jack Warner, the brother of Elsie and Doris Waters and himself a veteran light comedian, known for his catch-phrase, 'Mind my bike.' With 'Sergeant Dixon' I enjoyed some interesting natters about the old variety days. My criminal connections continued when I played the sneak thief Alfie Ridyard in *Z-Cars*, and later I had a part in its successor *Softly Softly*.

Among the films I was involved with was *Crooks and Coronets*, which gave Dame Edith Evans a character comedy lead as a dowager who takes command of a gang of crooks who come to rob her mansion. Also starring were Telly Savalas, Warren Oates, Cesar Romero and Harry H. Corbett. At about the same time, I made a return trip to Italy for a part in *Midas Run* (retitled *A Run on Gold* when it was shown in British cinemas) – another yarn about a criminal gang, this one concerning an old secret serviceman who hatches a plan to hijack a consignment of bullion. Cesar Romero was in this one too, and so were Anne Heywood, Ralph Richardson, Roddy McDowell and Maurice Denham. It was mainly a vehicle, however, for Fred Astaire. Since it provided him with a straight role, I could never, to my great regret, say I ever saw him perform the wonderful dancing I had admired for so many years. Our first location was at Siena in Tuscany, where my interest was set alight by the story of this being the place where the last recorded chariot race took place, the winner being a Goth called Tolita. Such spectacles were the ancestors of the circus that had been so important an aspect of my life.

242

In 1969, the year these two films were released, I was up in Leeds playing a reporter in Yorkshire Television's series, *Castle Haven*, when the news reached me that my mother had passed away at the age of ninety-three. The whole family were together for her funeral at Hornchurch, where she was buried next to Father. It was strange to think how she had travelled the world as a performer, relying on steam power to cross land and ocean, but lived to see man leave footprints on the moon.

The year previously, in 1968, the writ of the Lord Chamberlain finally ceased to run in matters theatrical and plays could be presented without prior censorship. This led, among other things, to a spate of plays with a strong social content. After my appearance in *Z-Cars*, I had the opportunity to join the cast of a comedy called *Snap* at the Vaudeville Theatre in the Strand. Its theme was venereal disease – hardly the most cheerful subject, you'd have thought, but it did excellent business, helped on its way by featuring Maggie Smith in the lead. As a hospital porter, I only had to appear in the early part of the play, and then was allowed to go home instead of waiting for the curtain call. For me it therefore had the 'once in a lifetime' advantage of early nights. The play enjoyed a run of three or four months before Maggie Smith had to leave the cast to take up a prior engagement in the United States, and with her departure the audiences fell away.

The closure of *Snap* was a disappointment for all concerned, but another chance came my way when my agent sent me to Liverpool for a small potential part in Carla Lane's popular long-running series *The Liver Birds*. I was there three days, but had still done nothing, when the director, Syd Lotterby, came across to me and said, 'Sorry you've had to hang about, but I think you'll be just right for the Grandad. Would you read a bit from the next episode?'

So I read, and he said, 'Now, forget what you came down for. Go back up to London, and we'll be in touch.'

In this way I landed the role of the Grandad on the Boswell side and was in the series, on and off, for some three years, including the Christmas episodes. It was a happy time with a happy team, the girls being played by Elizabeth Estesson and Nerys Hughes, the mother by Molly Sugden. Molly Sugden kindly drove me home from the studio after each rehearsal. What appealed to me most was that the actual shows were played to an invited audience, and so were the nearest that television ever comes to achieving the magic of live theatre.

Those were the days when BBC television drama was perhaps at its best, and I found many supporting character parts coming my way. I played with Cyril Cusack in an adaptation of Graham Greene's *The Power and the Glory*; with Francesca Annis in *Madame Bovary*. I was in the ambitious production of *War and Peace*, in which Anthony Hopkins played Pierre, and also in an Alan Bennett play, *Rolling Home*. Then I got a small part in Thomas Hardy's *The Mayor of Casterbridge*, starring Alan Bates. This particular role required someone who could play the violin and sustain a convincing Dorset dialect. Thanks to my versatile training and my much-travelled background, I was able to do both. A few weeks after the transmission of the episode in which I appeared, my agent phoned and said there had been an approach from Patrick Garland, a director then well known for having been responsible for producing Claire Bloom in Ibsen's *A Doll's House*, Michael Crawford in *Billy* (the musical version of Keith Waterhouse's *Billy Liar*) and various other productions at the Chichester Festival Theatre.

Mr Garland wanted to meet me, and when he did so said, to my surprise, 'I saw you in *The Mayor of Casterbridge*. I've just been directing my stage version of *Under the Greenwood Tree* at Salisbury, and we're transferring it to the West End. I'd like you for the part of Mr Penny, the shoemaker.'

Naturally, I accepted with delight, and in 1978 found myself back at the Vaudeville. Patrick Garland's script stayed close to Hardy's mellow and beautiful story of the Mellstock Quire, or church band, whose music-making was the great joy of their life until the new parson decided the time had come to bring his church up to date by installing an organ. After Christmas, they are told, their services will no longer be required – a plot that carried some poignant echoes of

244

all I had seen happen during the course of my life in the entertainment business. During their last service, the members of the quire pass a large jar of mead around among themselves in the gallery, fall asleep and begin to snore. When the parson sends someone to rouse them to play the next psalm, they awake bemused and launch into a lively jig – sacrilege of the worst and most entertaining kind to bring the play to a rousing conclusion. We were always applauded warmly and received many curtain calls.

Under the Greenwood Tree was a remarkable piece of theatre and one of the highlights in my varied life. One evening, on entering my dressing room, I found an invitation card: 'Please come for supper on Thursday, 31 December, at 10.30 p.m. The Garrick Club, Garrick Street, WC2.' All the cast were invited, and we were also asked to put together a short programme of Christmas carols. As we made our way to the club on the night in question, I thought how appropriate it was that it should be the Garrick. Before David Garrick no actor would have been considered a gentleman and no club would have allowed him through its portals. Entering the club, we mounted the elaborate staircase leading to the rooms above, aware that all around us were portraits of actors, from Colley Cibber to Sir John Gielgud, from Peg Woffington to Dame Anna Neagle. Even the world of circus had its representative: George Wombwell, proprietor of a zoo that from 1807 travelled the country with its great beast wagons and, later in the nineteenth century, became Bostock & Wombwell's circus and menagerie.

We assembled in the supper room and were tuning up our instruments when Patrick Garland entered, escorting a lady – at which point we realized the reason for all the secrecy. His guest was Princess Margaret, who had been in our audience that night and to whom we were now introduced by name and character. Dearly would I love to have said, 'Your Royal Highness, some 120 years ago the circus of my grandfather, Arthur Gregory, by command of your Great-great-uncle Alfred, Duke of Edinburgh and Admiral of the Mediterranean Fleet, gave a special grand performance in honour of HRH Princess Victoria Melita, and received the sum of

245

twenty guineas, forwarded from Admiralty House, Malta. I am proud to say I possess to this day the envelope in which the money was sent.' Of course, I said no such thing, but we were wined and dined right royally before we took up our instruments and began to process about the candlelit room, playing the evergreen Christmas carols. There was no Scrooge at our feast.

During the course of the run of *Under the Greenwood Tree*, I also celebrated my sixty-sixth birthday and my sixtieth year in showbusiness. The company arranged a party in the large Wardrobe Room and presented me with a tankard inscribed: 'From "The Whiteleys" to "The Greenwood Tree", three score years. Vaudeville Theatre, 4 January 1979.' Unfortunately the run was not to last. Severe winter weather set in, and at one point I had to thumb a lift from Kingston to make a matinée performance. There was also a dustmen's strike, and rubbish piled up in every doorway. Audiences were discouraged and many bookings were cancelled. We played through the treacherous weather, and felt confident of keeping the whole thing going until the tourist season began to pick up again in the spring. We had, after all, signed up to play for a year. The management saw it otherwise and used the one-month 'get-out' clause in the contracts to bring the show to an end.

Among the faces I saw among the portraits of actors at the Garrick Club had been that of Edmund Kean. I could have sworn he tipped me a wink. I returned him a bow, for here too I could claim a distant kinship. My mother's grandfather, John Walter Bowden, in 1846 married Ellen Theresa McCarthy, whose aunt had married into a well-known theatrical family, the Darnleys, one of whose members was the father of Edmund's stepbrother Henry and stepsister Phoebe. Their mother, Ann ('Nance') Carey, was never, I'm sorry to say, married to the fathers of her children, but she took young Edmund on tour with her to exploit his talents as a prodigy in the fit-ups of Richardson and Saunders, performing melodramas and pantomimes in the fairs and markets. Edmund therefore learnt to act, sing, tumble and walk tightropes from a very early age, before maturing into the greatest Shakespearean actor of his day. He shot like a fiery comet across the theatrical sky, and died burnt out at the age of forty-four. Again, it was largely the demon drink, laced with an urge to self-destruction, that brought him low.

One had seen similar tragedies to this repeated again and again in the profession, though, like everything else; the stories it gave rise to could also have their humorous side. An account was brought back from an ENSA tour of Germany concerning a comic who was so partial to a drop of the hard stuff that he had to be locked in a windowless dressing room before the show in an effort to keep him sober enough to perform his act. One night, as he paced up and down, he heard a passer-by and called out, 'I say, old chap, would you mind doing me a favour?' Simultaneously he slipped a ten-bob note under the door. 'Just fetch me a bottle of Scotch and a couple of straws, and be back as fast as you can.'

The unknown messenger complied and awaited his next instruction.

'Now,' said the comic, 'if you'll just put one end of the straw in the bottle and the other through the keyhole . . . ,' and proceeded to drain the bottle to the last drop. 'I don't know who you are,' he said in conclusion, 'but whoever you are, your very good health!'

Another comedian, whose work I admired, was unfortunately also a heavy drinker and, on top of that, suffered badly from indigestion. One Saturday night, after the last performance, I came upon him blind drunk outside the theatre, standing under a lamp-post in the pouring rain. With a solemn expression he extracted a sad-looking pork pie from a sodden brown-paper bag and took a twist of paper from his pocket. He unscrewed the twist and sprinkled a thin layer of white powder all over the pie. I thought at first it might be salt; in fact it was Maclean's Digestive Powder. 'There now,' he said, as glum as ever, before proceeding to eat his supper, 'sort that little lot out among yourselves.'

As I was driven home after our memorable evening at the Garrick Club, I had pondered on the New Year we would soon be entering. Each year brought its changes. There was always a new generation seeking entertainment, and always

247

had been, back to before recorded history. Sometimes that entertainment had appealed to the best, sometimes to the worst in man's nature. The classical world had known its circuses and hippodromes with their chariot races and brutal and sometimes deadly gladitorial combats. The public executions of traitors and criminals had not so very long before been considered a prime spectacle. Personally, I felt that I had seen entertainment at its best during the years before the Second World War, when it truly catered for the family, when theatre, circus and cinema were based on a strong moral code and, as in the Christmas pantomime, good always triumphed over evil. In the course of my own career, I had never made malicious jokes about people's religions or beliefs, about physical or mental handicaps. I hope, and believe, that I never offended a fellow soul by word or deed.

Today, so far as I know, there are no Whiteleys left working in the world of rings and curtains. My eldest brother, Harry, as I told you in the opening chapter, never returned to showbusiness after his war service finished in 1918. A victim of Parkinson's disease, he entered a home for incurables after his wife died. By the end, his head was almost down to his knees, but he still attended church regularly and bore his affliction with fortitude until he passed away in his seventieth year. Whenever my brothers Harold, Ben and Raymond could still work together, the act of 'Tom, Dick and Harry' continued in being; or became 'Tom, Dick and Harry-ette' if Ben's wife Laurel was making up the threesome. They were a well-known name in the world of rings and curtains for more than twenty-five years. After Ben became ill, Laurel continued working with Harold as 'Hal and Laurel, the Tumbling Funsters'.

Raymond and his wife Ann continued to present the Shermans act until she became tragically ill with cancer. He nursed her for a dozen years, and only survived a year himself once the ordeal was over. Leonora and her husband Ronnie went on with their talented duo act for some time after the war, and continued to be in demand. Nevertheless, eventually they decided to opt for a more secure lifestyle for

248

the sake of their young son. Ronnie took a job with Ford's at Dagenham and they retired from showbusiness.

Harold's Clown Rainbow was immortalized in 1981 in a film directed by Stéphane Kleeb for Vitascope, called *Zeit zum Weinen, Zeit sum Lachen: Ein Clown erinnert sich* (*Time to Weep, Time to Laugh: A Clown Remembers*). Clown Rainbow continued to be known for his charity work for some years, but now those of us from that generation who are still in the land of the living find ourselves firmly in retirement. As for the next generation, Annette's stage career, having got off to such a promising start, ended with her marriage. Our other daughter, Iana, was an infant prodigy of the commercials, until we became too appalled by the inconsideration and exploitative pushing attitude of those who made the films as well as the greed and rivalries of certain other parents. Enough was enough, we decided; we withdrew her, and that was that.

The story of the Whiteleys, which began in Yorkshire with Old Crafty and his tumbling mat, has therefore run its course, but they, with the Gregorys and Matthewses, remain indelibly a part of the great wide world of entertainment. And this meanwhile goes on its way, and will continue in ever more varied forms so long as human life survives. It can never afford to lose for long the original rapport it possessed between audience and live performer, whatever technological marvels television may bring us. I am optimistic for the future. In the end, people will again want to be active participating audiences, and to have a good night out, rather than sit passively for ever in front of the dreaded 'box'. I was once in a show of unusual acts called *Well, I Never!* I hope you'll agree the expression seems appropriate in the light of all I have told of my own and my family's history.

Troupers

There once was a company of travellers,
An actor, a tumbler, a clown,
Who entertained audiences far and wide
In every village and town.

The name for these curious people
Was commonly given as pros,
And though many thought them abnormal,
They put on some wonderful shows.

The circus folk lived in caravans,
Shared with monkeys and pigs,
But home for the other performers
Was always referred to as digs.

Some digs were good – others not so.
The story often was told
Of a kipper tacked under the table
In the hey-day of Naughton and Gold.

While the big stars appeared in the cities,
The others toiled on in the sticks,
But no matter how humble the venue,
Live acts were mixed in with the flicks.

Each Monday the reps from the railways –
LMS, SR and the rest –
Came along to solicit your custom,
And assure you their service was best.

A mere ten-bob subscription
Gave you a card for a year.
It entitled travel throughout the land
At two thirds the normal fare.

With compartments reserved every Sunday,
There's no doubt you travelled in style,

Playing cards, reading papers or snoozing
At less than a penny a mile.

If the journey ahead was a short one
An order was sent off in brief:
'The usual Sunday dinner, please –
Roast spuds, Yorkshire pud and some beef.'

One station was never forgotten,
Belov'd of all pros. That was Crewe.
Its refreshment buns were as hard as rocks,
Its tea, it tasted like stew.

Every act had its agent,
Nicknamed 'Old Ten Per Cent'.
His sixpenny telegram winkled you out
Wheresoever you went.

Pros entertained troops during wartime
And came up with many a jest,
And just to hear real hearty laughter
Always pleased them the best.

One comic's last date was in Heaven.
St Peter his name wished to know.
'My name doesn't matter,' he said to St Peter,
'On earth I was known as a pro.'

Appendix

The Whiteley Tapestry:
A Century of Entertainment
by 'Harlequin'

1

Over a hundred years ago people assembled on the cobble-stones of Pomfret Market Place to see a very clever acrobat who came on special occasions like the races, Mayor's Day, the rent audit for the Duchy Estates and the Statutes. Then he would roll out his carpet and do his act.

His name was John Whiteley, and he was born at Slaith-waite in 1812. His nickname was 'Old Crafty' because his sound showmanship caused him to do the apparently impossible.

Exactly when Old Crafty set his face towards London we do not know, but the fans who used to stand upon the steps of the Butter Cross to get a better view of their favourite never guessed when they missed John Whiteley that the man they once applauded was already the founder of a family destined to become one of the greatest in British entertainment. Today no considerable show but has its Whiteleys, wherever it is produced.

The Whiteley Tapestry is an enormous affair. To present it in detail would require at least one volume, maybe more.

Condensed, I bring it to you as told to me by Leonora Whiteley, who was Leonora in a score of acts and is now Peta, of Peta and Paula, Old Crafty's great-grand-daughter.

Probably Old Crafty worked in a number of small shows in London, and devoted all his extra energy to developing his son, John Whiteley II. In this the Market Square player succeeded completely. His son got on at the famous Astley's Circus and elsewhere in London in such style that he was able to marry into the bluest-blooded family in the business. John II's bride was Ellen Delevanti, daughter of one of the first clowns to perform at the famous Theatre Royal, Drury Lane, and 'King' of an amazing team of acrobats called the 'Delevanti Carpet Tumblers'.

In due course John Whiteley II went abroad, and his tours included America. But the Whiteley Tapestry is not just a list of successes. Bad weather and bad trade can ruin the best of shows: particularly tenting shows. Returning to Britain the Whiteleys struck a bad patch with their circus. The end was that everything had to be sold except one horse and one goat. You will remember that the goat is an intrinsic part of every good stable. In case of fire the horses will always follow the goat.

The survivors were taken on to Cleethorpes beach – the goat harnessed into a cart to draw children, the horse saddled for any 'gent' to ride who liked to have a 'go'. Perhaps the goat smelled, as goats sometimes do, and possibly gents were scarce in Cleethorpes about that time, or they feared to risk it. Anyway, there was no gold on those sands, and the Whiteleys were glad to sell out to the celebrated Clown Ohny, who was in Lincolnshire at the time.

But you can't keep good people down and we find the Whiteleys connected with Circo Sociale and later the Gregory World Circus. Circo Sociale was directed by William Hadwin and John Whiteley II.

Over North and South America, Europe, Africa, Australia and parts of Asia the Whiteleys travelled: sometimes playing for a season at one town, sometimes staying one night.

At Modena, in Italy, Henry Whiteley, father of our Leonora II, was born. In the 1880s the family were with

Alegria Circus, which played a season in Barcelona. There Henry made his début and the company included the Gee Family. Belvina Gee's son, George Holloway Jnr, is the entertaining guy we call Jimmy Nervo of Nervo and Knox.

In the Whiteley Circus was a very accomplished trapeze artist billed as Aubrey. The world came to know him as Fred Karno. Fred is probably the only player to have an 'army' named after him. You know how the song goes: 'We are Fred Karno's Army, No earthly good are we.'

The Gregory family, of whom I have spoken, were allied to an even more famous English theatrical and circus family: that of Matthews.

We turn to look at a piece of the Tapestry devoted to Leonora Gregory. Probably this magnificent woman was in her day one of the most versatile and accomplished who ever lived. Born in Buenos Aires, sister of the world famous Clown Gregory, she had every possible talent for the circus.

An amazing equestrienne in every department from trick riding to tumbling, she used to ride over jumps head downwards. Her hair was so long, in pre-bobbing days, that the horses frequently chopped bits from the end of Leonora's locks with their hooves.

Besides riding, Leonora was a fine singer, 'bender', wire walker, trapeze expert and dancer. In any circus she was a 'main prop'. Her very start, at Kimberley, South Africa, was a sensation. She travelled from the crow's nest on the centre pole of the big top to the ring, hanging on to a pulley by her teeth.

The Gregory Circus, with Leonora Gregory, did the Mediterranean tour from Gibraltar to Constantinople: no mean feat in those days of non-de-luxe travel. Corsica and Sardinia were 'dates' and the show crossed to the Riviera and played Italy as a matter of course.

At Malta the Navy were good customers and one of the officers to visit the circus was afterwards HM King George V.

But all these happenings paled before the run along the North African Coast. The Sultan of Morocco was particularly pleased with the performance and this is high praise, as

255

horsemanship is the national sport in the Sultanate and this modern Solomon (yes, near enough to five hundred wives – black, white, and several shades of brown) would look with a critical eye on the attempts of the foreigner.

A neighbouring king went even further. Receiving the company in his fullest costume, which consisted of evening dress, complete with white silk tie, silk top hot, white spats and no boots, this ruler announced that he was arranging for a special gold medal to be struck for presentation to Leonora Gregory. He was as good as his word.

In passing, I can't help thinking that in travelling in an area where even local rulers had a hundred wives, the circus must have been faced with some difficult situations. Charmed with the show, it seems probable that a sultan, used to collecting a few extra wives when he fancied, would go round after the performance and say to the director, 'That blonde about 10 stones (they think weight a virtue over there), how much? Or to take the whole troupe?' Considerable tact would be called into play, for there are no recorded casualties. It says a good deal for the honour of the rulers that there were no captures by force. In the days of Rasuli the Brigand and his kind it would have been quite easy, but it didn't happen.

Henry Whiteley was also a most accomplished performer. At the age of seven he was making a start with Circus Price in Madrid and followed this up with engagements with Rentz, Cory-Althof and Busch combinations. I have seen a photograph of him taken whilst still a boy. He would pass for Grock. In Melbourne he scored one of his outstanding successes and another portrait taken in Australia shows him as a particularly handsome man.

Henry Whiteley met Leonora Gregory whilst they were both playing in Germany with Schumann's Circus. They were married at the English Church at Hamburg. Our Leonora, in proper theatrical tradition, was born in Brixton.

Henry and his Leonora both speak six languages and are now living in retirement in a small Lancashire town, the other inhabitants of which have probably no idea that they

256

entertain two world famous players who have travelled well over a million miles to entertain.

2

Promoting a circus is one of the greatest gambles on earth, and few if any great promoters have also been great performers. The combination of superlative personal entertainment and successful 'big business' seems to be more than human nature can stand.

The Whiteleys were artistes first and foremost and so they built up a series of acts which have continued to this day and retired from management. 'The Five Whiteleys' has gone through many editions and had a notable European tour between the two wars with Circe Amar, a Belgian organizer. Circe Raney also featured the Whiteleys, mainly in France. More than anyone the Whiteleys developed the technique of wire walking. From being 'flat' and uninteresting this turn became a subject for infinite variety.

But tenting shows represent only one portion of the Whiteley Tapestry. Clearly woven into the general picture is stage, and in another corner is winter shows. It is my own opinion that whilst purely stage players do not really relish circus work, circus people revel in stage shows.

It is practically impossible to name a leading variety theatre on the Continent where our Leonora and her generation of Whiteleys have not played, and in nine cases out of ten the youngsters are following their parents. To look at Peta you'd think it was impossible that they should have done all this, but it must be remembered that they start very young.

I spoke of Paris and our Leonora immediately mentioned Bal Tabarin, Kursal and Olympia. Lisbon, The Hague, Brussels, Berlin, Vienna, Rome; wherever the word amusement is spelled in capitals, the people who matter know the Whiteleys.

Coming back to Britain for a moment the Whiteleys have

done some notable work in Bertram Mills's shows, both at Olympia and tenting.

Another interesting tour was undertaken round Ireland with Ted Fossett. To impress the Paddies, Fossett billed his show as the Circus Heckenberg.

Meanwhile the younger Whiteleys were developing their own combinations. With a praiseworthy desire to stand or fall on their own merits they took different names on the bills. The world of performers knew them, of course, but to the public they were fresh folk.

Tom, Dick and Harry were three of Leonora's brothers. Then the act became Tom, Dick and Harryette. Other family concerns were Hal and Laurel and Le White and Paulette.

I know that public memory is very short, but one show that stood out immediately before the war was *Tropical-Express* controlled by that great showman [Curt] William Doorlay, who was also responsible for another great enterprise *Rocket Express* [*sic.* = *Doorlay's Wonder Rocket*].

Tropical-Express started, I think, in China. At least it toured India and came to this country after tremendous success on the Continent. It appears that there is a show motto, 'When in doubt send for the Whiteleys.' Our Leonora was sent for to join the show in Munich.

Mrs Atkins, a director of Doorlays, was a Whiteley and 'Tom, Dick and Harry', three of our Leonora's brothers. Harry was also 'Diplomatic Manager' to the show, undertaking all the complicated business of the visas, passports, etc. There were other Whiteleys in the show!

One criticism of *Tropical-Express* was that too much splendid talent was compressed into the narrow limits of twice nightly. But this is Doorlay's way. He wants to give and give and give to his public. The said public certainly respond.

Tropical-Express ran to 13,000 performances at which over twenty-five million people paid to go in! And as every theatre, however large, played to capacity when *Tropical* came along, Doorlay could afford a lavish salary list.

The speed of the show was terrific. Artists accustomed to play fifteen minutes in 'Big Time' had to do their stuff in three. There was no time for the girls to go to their dressing rooms for some of the changes. Huge packing cases were specially fitted and used as cubicles on the stage.

Turning from the Whiteleys for a moment to the friends, *Tropical* saw two girl artists get their first big chance. These, also close friends, are Delly Kin and Eva May Wong. Both are Chinese girls now doing solo acts in No. 1 Vaudeville, but whilst Eva was born over here, Delly was born in the Imperial City of Peking. Both these clever girls have brought their acts to Yorkshire. Eva was recently one of the two bright spots in a Yorkshire pantomime.

Tropical-Express went through many adventures abroad and one internal disturbance was caused by a temperamental elephant. She, it must have been a she, took a dislike to this or that person and gave him/her the works.

It wasn't a case of retribution. This she-tank just picked a 'mark' and, when opportunity offered, jostled the victim in the course of a concerted number. The elephant took a delight in scaring the life out of nervous girls and men as well: at least they became nervous after a few bumps. One player I know says that the 'humour' of this four-ton clown makes the memory of *Tropical-Express* a nightmare. This girl is passionately fond of all animals, but now she likes her elephants at a distance.

Our Leonora came back to Britain with Doorlay and played with the *Express* at Moss Empires (including Leeds) in 1939. The finish came at Finsbury Park Empire when war broke out and this fine international show had to be disbanded.

A little bit of the Tapestry might be titled 'Houdin Stuff'. Students of magic will remember that Robert Houdin, a famous French magician and author, was the model of one of the greatest showmen of the present century who paid him the compliment of the close study of his works and the adoption of his name with the addition of one letter – Houdini.

Leonora and her brother Jack toured the halls in an escapology act, with considerable success. Leonora has one of those figures which is ideal for concealment in half the space taken by a normal body and can adopt the rigidity essential

259

when one is picked up from a table along with the cover as if the drapery contained nothing at all.

Jack is now in the RAF. Another brother, Raymond, is in the RFA. Leonora's husband is a commando.

With the first flight of ENSA, Leonora went to France and played in Lille, Rennes and other big and small centres, giving well over a hundred shows in ten weeks. When the incidents of army travel, which some of us have experienced, are taken into consideration, this is no mean feat.

Some people are a success in ENSA. Some are not. The troops 'write epistles' to say how they feel, and the controllers soon get to know what is and is not 'bon pour les troops'. Leonora can rate herself first class as she played altogether nearly a year on the 'Lease-Lend' basis existing between the stage and forces amusement.

Meanwhile with circus on the easy list this versatile performer has tackled anything and everything in road shows, revues, single acts, double acts, putting 'pep' into pantomimes or near-pantomimes. She is the good trouper.

At the moment she and her sister-in-law Paula are featuring in Bert Loman's *Blackpool Follies*. In one part they are 'Russians', in another 'Tilda and Sal', two Cockney Donahs in 'Derby Day'. It is all one – they get there. Paula, who comes of a very well-known Channel Islands family, the Fairchilds, is also a musical specialist. It is my opinion that either of these girls could play a recognizable tune on the violin standing on her head in a bath tub, provided there wasn't more than five inches of water!

In passing I may mention that our Leonora, who as you will have gathered is Paula [*sic.* = Peta] pro tem, has one of the finest collections of theatrical autographs I have ever heard of. As almost the baby of the great Whiteley family she, no doubt, has the ear of famous players. Even so, the assembly is a remarkable performance.

A cousin in America – I gather that there are some hundred odd of the Whiteley clan in the United States alone – got Charlie Chaplin to donate a portrait which he autographed. This shows the great Charles in a mood when you would think that his normal part was Hamlet.

Sir Harry Lauder did not give a portrait, but in the precious book he drew a picture of himself. Will Fyffe thought this a good idea, for he did likewise. George Robey's portrait is there in photographic form, and a few of the others are Ivor Novello, Phyllis Dare, Bobbie Howes, Dame Nellie Melba, Jack Buchanan and Evelyn Laye.

Some of the donors have passed on. Amongst these is the one and only Dr Bodie. It is a curious thing, to me, that women players have the greatest affection for 'the Doctor'. In speaking of him they all say, 'The old darling'. Several theatrical men of my acquaintance use terms that could not possibly be construed into 'Good Old Sergeant'.

Sport is represented in the gallery by E. H. Temme, who swam the Channel, and Larry Gains. Every shade of theatrical art appears. Henry Bainton, the Shakespearean actor, ranges; Sophie Tucker and Tod Slaughter are alongside Florence Smithson, now unhappily no more.

Kubelik, Pearl White, Martin-Harvey, Clara Butt, The Two Bobs, Layton and Johnstone and Florrie Forde represent the past, and the signatures and pictures of Matheson Lang, Carl Brisson, Jasper Maskelyn, Tallulah Bankhead, Seymour Hicks, Billy Merson, Greta Nissen, Shaun Glenville and Dorothy Ward conjure up memories of a thousand successes.

Still others in the 'Centre Spot' are Florence Desmond, Binnie Hale, Lucille Benstead and Fay Compton.

I hesitate to put a value on this gallery, for it is not only an assembly of signatures and portraits, but a mass of evidence of 'Whiteley esteem', but it must be considerable.

One more glance at the Tapestry, with special reference to Pomfret. Leonora believes that in the early days of the Alexandra Theatre the then current 'Whiteleys' played this hall at least once. Tom Diacoff, the original Alex manager, had toured extensively abroad with his wife Blanche in the Flying Diacoffs Cycle Act. He would certainly be well acquainted with the Whiteleys.

Today, over a hundred years after their great-grandfather performed in the Market Square, the descendents of Old

Crafty Whiteley visit Pomfret, to witness those exciting contests that take place from time to time in the park.

[Privately printed for the Whiteley family, *c.* 1942]

Index

Canterbury Music Hall, London, 143–4
Canzi, Paul ('Powell'), 57, 95, 98–9; act: Mish-Mash, 99; as Harrods interpreter (P.C. Foy), 99–100
Carey, Ann ('Nance'), 246
Carlile, Florence, 89
Carnel, Flying Officer Gerald, 193
Carrée, Albert, 63–4
Carrée, Circus, 63, 118, 171
Castle Haven, 243
Cecchetti, Enrico, 97, 99
Central Hall, Westminster, 173
Chamberlain, Neville, 176
Chaplin, Charlie, 6, 54, 155, 156, 260
Charley's Aunt, 30
Charlie Girl, 236
Charlot, André, 121
Children's Film Foundation, 139, 241
Chinese Bungalow, The, 118
Christmas Pantomime, 128–9
Churchill, Sir Winston S., 178
Cibber, Colley, 245
Cigalle, Paris theatre, 113
Cinderella, 91, 133, 139, 140, 168, 235
cinema, as threat to live entertainment, 18, 80, 120; and the talking pictures, 124–5; and cinema organs, 149–50
Cinema Palace, Kingston-upon-Thames, 80–81
ciné-variety, 7, 18–19, 83, 120, 124
Cinquevalli, Paul, 102
Circe Madrid, 47–8
circus: horses, 55–6; treatment of animals in, 175–6
Cirque d'Été, Paris, 94
Cirque d'Hiver, Paris, 113
Cirque Medrano, Paris, 113
City Varieties Theatre, Leeds, 123, 176
Clarke, Mr, pantomimist, 45
Clarke, Denis J., 95
Clarke, John; and Clarke's Circus, 29, 30, 31–2, 33
Clevelands, acrobatic troupe, 86

clowns, 75–6, 130–1; and Clown in pantomime, 130
Cochran, C.B., 121
Cody, William F. ('Buffalo Bill'), 92
Coliseum: Cheltenham, 86; London, 78, 88–9
Collins, Jackie, 208
Collins, Joan, 208
Collins, Joe; and agency, 208
commedia del'arte, 129
Compton, Fay, 121, 261
Conder, Howard, 236
Connaught Theatre, Worthing, 234
Contact, 197
Cooper, Christopher, 241
Cope, Mr and Mrs, foster parents, 53
Corbett, Harry H., 242
Corona Babes and Juveniles, 237
Corona Stage School, 237
Corradini, Signor (Blondin Horse trainer), 88
Cory-Althof Circus, 256
Cotton, Billy, 151
County Theatre: Bedford, 146; Kingston-upon-Thames, 80
Coup & Barnum Circus, 51
Courtneidge, Robert, 180
Courville, Albert de, 121
Covent Garden Theatre, 129, 131
Cowley, Frank, 239, 241; *see also* Morris and Cowley
Coyne, Joseph, 210
Coyne, Peter, 210
Cragg family, acrobats, 226
Crawford, Michael, 244
Crippen, George, 70
Crockett, Mr, lion tamer, 41, 42
Cromer, Lord, 75
Crooks and Coronets, 242
Crosby, Bing, 210; and the Rhythm Boys, 151
Crossroads, 242
Cruel Sea, The, 234
Cruikshank, Andrew, 242
Curtis, Ronnie, 211
Cusak, Cyril, 244

Dad's Army, 242

89, 90, 97–101, 104; act:
'Mademoiselle La Foy', 97–8
Matthews, Leontine, 88, 89, 93–4
Matthews, Madeline (Maddie), 88,
89, 90, 92–3
Matthews, Ted, 101
Matthews, Theodore, 46, 48, 49,
88, 91
Matthews Jun., Theodore, 91
Matthews, Will, 81, 83, 91
Matthews, William Frederick,
great-grandfather, 13, 28–49, 50,
51, 81, 87, 88, 101–3, 104, 130,
156, 175
Matthews, Willie, 48, 49, 88, 91
Matto, Harry, 159, 160, 161, 163
Matto, Madge, 159, 160
Maxwell, James, 234
May, Sybil, 203
Mayor of Casterbridge, The, 244
Mazeppa, 13, 31
Meadows, Lonnen, 89–91
Melba, Dame Nellie, 261
Mellor, Buddy, 152
Mellors, Arthur, *see* Gregory,
Arthur
Mellors Jun., Arthur, 52–3, 56
Mellors, Charlotte, 51
Mellors, John, 51
Mellors, Melita, 52
Mellors, Laurina, 52
Melody Inn, 220
*Memoirs of Circus, Variety, etc., As
I Knew It*, 8, 72, 73–4, 75
Menken, Adah Isaacs, 13
Merrick, Joseph ('The Elephant
Man'), 88, 103
Merson, Billy, 261
Metropolitan Theatre, Edgware
Road, 222
Mickey Mouse, 152
Midas Run, see Run on Gold
Midnight in Montmartre, 226
Mildmay Club, 179
Miller, Max, 222–3
Mills's Circus, Bertram, 258
Miracle, The, 122
Mires, Jim, 42, 102
Mistletoe Bough, The, 38–9
Mix, Tom, 6
Mohawk Minstrels, 72

Molica, contortionist, 203
Monkey's Paw, The, 159
Montague, Bertram, agency, 135
Moody, Ron, 238
More, Kenneth, 87
Morocco, Sultan of, 255–6
Morris and Cowley, 239–41
Morris, Lily, 222
Morris, Teddy; and the Teddy
Morris Band, 151–5, 219
Morton, Charles ('The Father of
the Halls'), 143
Moss Empires circuit, 1, 173, 174,
214, 259
Mother Goose, 219
Mother Hubbard, 138
Moulin Rouge, Paris, 113
Moxon Girl Dancers, 167
Mumming Birds, 54, 86
Music Hall Artistes' Railway
Association (MHARA), 20
Musical Box, Bangor, Co. Down,
176
Musicians' Union, 151
My Man, 125
Myers, Sydney, 223

National Youth Orchestra, 173
Neagle, Dame Anna, 198, 236, 245
Nervo, Jimmy; and Nervo and
Knox, 86, 255
Nijinsky, Vaslav, 98
Nimmo, Derek, 236
Nissen, Greta, 261
No, No, Nanette, 210
Noakes, John, 234
Norman, Tom ('The Silver
King'), 103
Novello, Ivor, 261

Oakley, Annie, 92
Oates, Warren, 242
Ohny, Clown, 254
Old Curiosity Shop, 30
Old London Palace Theatre, 182
*Old Woman Who Lived in a Shoe,
The*, 215–16, 217
Oliver!, 238–9, 241
Oliver, Vic, 164
Olvas Brothers, 134
Olympia, Paris theatre, 113, 257

271

Opera House: Belfast, 226;
  Dudley, 155; Dunfermline, 167;
  Jersey, 183–4; Kingsway, 96;
  Melbourne, 79–80
Oriental Palace, *see* Palace Theatre,
  Camberwell
Orton, Harold, 233
O'Sullivan, Richard, 237

Packham, Miss ('Packham's
  Pekinese'), 202, 207, 229, 231
Palace Theatre: Accrington, 149;
  Attercliffe, 227; Bradford, 145;
  Britton Ferry, 93; Camberwell,
  219; Leicester, 66;
  Northampton, 14; Reading, 231;
  Walthamstow, 212; Westcliff-
  on-Sea, 181
Palladium, London, 78, 212
pantomime, 41, 45, 46, 48, 96,
  123, 126–7, 128–40, 168, 171,
  223–4, 248; and the
  Harlequinade, 45, 70, 89,
  129–30, 131, 134; and trap work,
  133, 134–5
Parnell and Zeitlin, agency, 155
Passing Show, The, 121
Pavilion: Blackpool, 3; Burnham-
  on-Sea, 185; Colwyn Bay,
  180–81; Filey, 161, 221; Rhyl,
  161; Silloth, 203, 204–6; South
  Shields, 218
Pavlova, Anna, 98
Paxton, Sir Joseph, 31
Payne, Fred and Peggy, 166
Peek-a-Boo, 225
Peel, Sir Robert, 101
Pélissier, Harry Gabriel, 121
Pélissier's Follies, 121–2
Performing Rights Act, 207
Performing Rights Society, 207
Perils of Pauline, The, 20
Petit Casino, Paris, 113
Philadelphia Sunday Transport, 48
Pier, New Brighton, 219, 220
pierrot shows, 121–2, 220
Pledge, Monsieur, acrobat, 33
Plunket, Mr, acrobat, 32
Poliakova, Iris, 226
Pollard, Snub, 6
Polo, Eddie, 5, 19–20

Pope's Hall, Shadwell, 29
Pot-Pourri, 121
Power and the Glory, The, 244
Preminger, Otto, 238
Price Circus, 256
Priestley, J.B., 205
Primavera, Ada, 115
Prince of Wales Theatre, *see*
  Kennington Theatre
Pringles Cinema, Edinburgh, 119
Puller, Squadron Leader, 192
Puss in Boots, 88

Queen's Hall, London, 173

Radiance Toffee Company, 123
Rainbow (comic), 131
Rambert, Dame Marie, 98
Raneleagh Cinema, Barnes, 146
Raney, Circe, 257
Rastelli, Signor, juggler, 102
Ray, Ted, 164–5
Read, Jack, 198
Reader, Ralph, 197–8, 219
Reed, Carol, 238
Reed, Oliver, 238
Reeves, Alf, 54
Reeves, Billy, 54
Regal Theatre, Southend-on-Sea,
  182
Relph, Harry, *see* Little Tich
René, soubrette, 176–7
Rentz, Mr; and Rentz Circus, 70,
  130, 256
Revudeville, 86
Rialto Cinema, York, 200
Rich, John ('Lun'), 129, 130, 133
Richard, Charlie, 35–6
Richardson, fit-up proprietor, 246
Richardson, Sir Ralph, 242
Richmond Sisters, 173
Ridgeway, Mr, animal parodist,
  88
Rigmarolles, 159–64
Riley, Mamie, 167
Roberts, Rachel, 234
Robey, Sir George, 236, 261
Robinson, Mr ('The Flying
  Bluebottle'), 45–6
Robinson, Kendal, 80–81
Robinson, Charlotte, 133

273

stage bands, phenomenon of, 151
Stahl, Stella, *see* Lorimer, Stella
Stanelli; and Stanelli and Edgar;
    and his 'Hornchestra', 155
Stanley Park, Blackpool, 189
Steele, Tommy, 236
Stephenson, Charlie A., 180, 181,
    196, 235
Sterling, Ford, 6
Stoll theatre circuit, 1
Strange, Mr, chaplain, 58
Stuart, Sylvester ('The Paper
    King'), 159
Stubbs, Mr, cinema manager, 5–6
Sugden, John, 68–9
Sugden, Molly, 244
Surrey Comet, 80–81
Surrey Music Hall, London, 45
Surrey Theatre, London, 125
Sutton, Randolph, 202
Sweeney Todd, 159
Sykes, Eric, 234
Syndicate theatre chain, 222

Tanner, Mr, portable theatre
    proprietor, 30
Tanner, Lauretta, *see* Matthews,
    Caroline Lauretta
Tate, Harry, 14; and sketch
    'Motoring', 124
Tate Jun., Harry, 89
Taylor, Edgar, 176, 178
Tchaikovsky, Peter Ilich, 98
Temme, E.H., 261
Temperance Hall, Merthyr
    Tydfyl, 21, 215
Ten Loonies Comedy Band, 151
Tewfik Pasha, the Khedive
    Mohammed, 58
Theatre Royal: Bolton, 89–90, 91;
    Bristol, 171; Castleford, 148;
    Coventry, 100; Drury Lane, 70,
    131, 132–3, 171, 200, 204, 254;
    Elephant and Castle, *see* Old
    London Palace; Hepburn-on-
    Tyne, 117; Huddersfield, 134;
    Leicester, 53
Thomsett, Frankie, 236
Thomsett, Sally, 241
Tilley, Vesta, 53, 160

Tissington & Craig, theatrical
    management, 166
Tivoli: Birmingham, 77; Hull,
    218; Sydney, 79
Tom Katz Saxophone Six, 151
Tomlinson, David, 231, 232
Torch, Sydney, 188
Toulouse-Lautrec, Henri de, 114
Towle, Arthur, *see* Lucan, Arthur
Tracy, Jack, 225
Trinder, Tommy, 233
Troise and His Mandoliers, 151
Tropical Express, 168–71, 174–5,
    176, 178, 258–9
Troubleshooters, The, 242
Try This One, 123–4
Tucker, Sophie, 261
Tudor Café, Grimsby, 207
Turpin, Ben, 6
Twelfth Night, 130

Uncle Tom's Cabin, 80
Under the Greenwood Tree, 149,
    244–6
Union Square Theatre, New
    York, 48
Up the Creek, 231

Valois, Dame Ninette de, 98
Van Damm theatre management,
    86
Van Lutin, Mr, yodeller, 81
variety, 1, 18; and backstage view,
    24–7; *see also* ciné-variety
Variety Vanities, 203, 205–6
Vaudeville Theatre, London, 243,
    244, 246
Venuti, Joe, 151
Vesta Brothers, *see* Morris and
    Cowley
Victoria, Queen, 92, 220
Victoria Hall, Cowes, 81
Victoria Melita, Princess, 58, 245
Virello, Tom, 72

Walden, May, 159
Walker, Mr, acrobat, 32
Wall, Max, 12, 188, 194–5, 236
Wallace, Nellie, 239
Wallis, Shani, 238

274

275

276

277